**DISCARDED**

# REVOLUTION'S OTHER WORLD

*Also by Ken Post*

ARISE YE STARVELINGS: The Jamaica Labour Rebellion of 1938 and its Aftermath

* COMMUNISTS AND NATIONAL SOCIALISTS: The Foundations of a Century, 1914–39

* REGAINING MARXISM

REVOLUTION, SOCIALISM AND NATIONALISM IN VIET NAM
    Volume I    Viet Nam: An Interrupted Revolution
    Volume II   Viet Nam Divided
    Volume III  Socialism in Half a Country
    Volume IV  The Failure of Counter-Insurgency in the South
    Volume V   Winning the War and Losing the Peace

SOCIALISM AND UNDERDEVELOPMENT (*with Phil Wright*)

STRIKE THE IRON: A Colony at War, Jamaica, 1939–45

STRUCTURE AND CONFLICT IN NIGERIA, 1960–66 (*with Michael Vickers*)

THE NEW STATES OF WEST AFRICA

THE NIGERIAN FEDERAL ELECTION OF 1959

THE PRICE OF LIBERTY: Personality and Politics in Colonial Nigeria (*with George D. Jenkins*)

* *From the same publishers*

# Revolution's Other World

## Communism and the Periphery, 1917–39

Ken Post
*Emeritus Professor*
*Institute of Social Studies*
*The Hague*

in association with
INSTITUTE OF SOCIAL STUDIES

First published in Great Britain 1997 by
**MACMILLAN PRESS LTD**
Houndmills, Basingstoke, Hampshire RG21 6XS and London
Companies and representatives throughout the world

A catalogue record for this book is available from the British Library.

ISBN 0–333–71766–X

---

 First published in the United States of America 1997 by
**ST. MARTIN'S PRESS, INC.,**
Scholarly and Reference Division,
175 Fifth Avenue, New York, N.Y. 10010

ISBN 0–312–17631–7

Library of Congress Cataloging-in-Publication Data
Post, Ken, 1935–
Revolution's other world : communism and the periphery, 1917–39 /
Ken Post.
  p. cm.
Includes bibliographical references and index.
ISBN 0–312–17631–7
1. Communism—History—20th century.  2. Communism—Developing
countries—History—20th century.  3. World politics—1919–1932.
4. World politics—1933–1945.  I. Title.
HX40.P69 1997
335.43—dc21                                                97–18514
                                                              CIP

---

© Ken Post 1997

All rights reserved. No reproduction, copy or transmission of this publication may be made without written permission.

No paragraph of this publication may be reproduced, copied or transmitted save with written permission or in accordance with the provisions of the Copyright, Designs and Patents Act 1988, or under the terms of any licence permitting limited copying issued by the Copyright Licensing Agency, 90 Tottenham Court Road, London W1P 9HE.

Any person who does any unauthorised act in relation to this publication may be liable to criminal prosecution and civil claims for damages.

The author has asserted his right to be identified as the author of this work in accordance with the Copyright, Designs and Patents Act 1988.

This book is printed on paper suitable for recycling and made from fully managed and sustained forest sources.

10  9  8  7  6  5  4  3  2  1
06  05  04  03  02  01  00  99  98  97

Printed and bound in Great Britain by
Antony Rowe Ltd, Chippenham, Wiltshire

For
Mir-Said Sultan Galiyev,
pioneer of Third-Worldism, who died in Stalinist
captivity;
Bhagat Singh,
revolutionary Marxist and atheist,
hanged by the British in March 1931;
and Olga Benario,
murdered by the Nazis in February 1942

# Contents

| | |
|---|---|
| *Preface and Acknowledgements* | ix |
| *List of Abbreviations* | xi |

**1 The Problematic**     **1**
Some Basics     2
Subjects and Struggle     4
Revolution in History     8
Theorizing the Revolution     13

**2 Expanding to the East**     **21**
The Problems of World Revolution     22
The Bolsheviks and National Self-Determination     25
The New Emphasis     35

**3 Comintern and Other Perspectives**     **46**
Foundations for a Discourse     47
Changing the Line     57
Possible Alternatives     66

**4 Semi-Colonial Complications**     **74**
The Chinese Revolution: Relying on the Workers or the Peasants?     74
Brazil: Workers and Soldiers     97

**5 Confronting Colonialism: Revolution and the Raj**     **114**
The Foundations     114
Getting a Foothold     118
The Comintern's Long Arm     121
The Competitors     130
From Disarray to Infiltration     139

**6 Leninism/Stalinism as Theory and Discourse**     **151**
Basic Problems     151
Strategy and the Complexities of Class     154
The Issue of the Revolutionary Subject     163
Pragmatism and Universalism     165

| | |
|---|---|
| Vanguardism as a Solution | 170 |
| The Stalinist Shift | 174 |
| Leninism/Stalinism as Discourse | 178 |
| General Conclusions | 181 |
| *Notes* | 188 |
| *Bibliography* | 202 |
| *Index* | 212 |

# Preface and Acknowledgements

In these last years of the twentieth century, when the global triumph of capitalism is being celebrated and it is said that socialist revolution and its main historical doctrine, Marxism, have been relegated to the shelves of the great historical archive, why write a book with this title and orientation? Hopefully, those who have any feeling for history will quickly agree with one answer: like the need to climb mountains, because it was *there*. Indeed, not only did Marxist-inspired revolutions happen, but, for better or worse, they shaped the whole history of the world.

In retrospect, I would suggest that the key revolutionary shift in this century, hence of Marxist thinking, took place when, beginning in November 1917, the main communist activity increasingly shifted out of the developed capitalist centre and into the 'colonial and semi-colonial' periphery. This was not what was predicted, yet, given later successes in China, Viet Nam and Cuba (to mention only the most prominent cases) and longer-term failures, it is clear that this was a major, even epochal, development. This study, therefore, seeks to begin a re-examination of the first stage of the revolutionary shift, between 1917 and 1939.

Hopefully, there are more people concerned with history, those who wish to have some understanding of why things have happened as they did, than there are mountaineering buffs. Another small group, perhaps destined to fall behind mountaineers in numbers, at least in the developed capitalist countries, is Marxists, and I must confess to a deep concern with them. We must not become a dying species, like rhinoceroses. They are being slaughtered because of the reputed aphrodisiac powers of their ground-up horns, we must fight to retain the power of our *ideas* to excite. My re-examination is therefore also intended to contribute to a retention of potency in a future world where the issue of socialist revolution will not die out.

As for acknowledgements and thanks, basically these should go to the students from Asia, the Middle East, Africa, Latin America and the Caribbean whom I tried to teach over a span of 31 years. It is a pity I didn't learn more from them. Specifically, Marcel van der Linden gave me very sage advice, namely that it was probably unwise to attempt re-evaluating the Comintern's experience until its archives are fully open. Two counter-considerations in the end swayed me. Firstly, this study is basically an evaluation of Leninism and Stalinism, about which we *can* make judgements, not of the Comintern as such. Secondly, given that Russian political and bureaucratic mills still grind slowly, it cannot be known when – or if – archives will be fully available, and it seems to me that an interim reassessment of the Comintern from a Marxist perspective as a secondary theme is worthwhile. No doubt less friendly people than Marcel will point out that I was wrong, hopefully with reasons.

Major contributors to this project were library staff at the Institute of Social Studies in The Hague, the International Institute for Social History in Amsterdam and the Centre for the Documentation and Study of Latin America (CEDLA), also in Amsterdam, who cannot be blamed for what I did with the sources they helped me find.

# List of Abbreviations

| | |
|---|---|
| AITUC | All-India Trades Union Congress |
| CCP | Chinese Communist Party |
| CPGB | Communist Party of Great Britain |
| CPI | Communist Party of India |
| CSP | Congress Socialist Party (India) |
| ECCI | Executive Committee of the Communist International |
| KMT | Kuomintang (National People's Party, China) |
| LAI | League Against Imperialism |
| NLA | National Liberation Alliance (Brazil) |
| PCB | Partido Comunista do Brasil (Communist Party of Brazil) |
| RSDLP | Russian Social Democratic Labour Party |

# 1 The Problematic

In the period 1989–91 a tidal shift in global power structures occurred, which removed the Soviet Union, and hence one of the two 'superpowers', from the scene. Clearly, human history has recently taken a new turn; the march of capital is once again unrestricted, and no-one knows where it will ultimately lead us.[1] The fact above all that most of the world's people – including those in the former state socialist countries – remain bogged down in the most backward forms of capitalism is of especial importance, because it leaves the possibility of revolution, long the trademark of communists, on the agenda.

With this perspective, the Second World War becomes a watershed, since after it, with the Soviet Union elevated to 'superpower' status, the global setting for communist revolutions became quite different. The key revolutionary successes, in China, Viet Nam and Cuba, were all shaped by the Soviet Union's position, although China less than the others, for reasons which we shall see. Since 1991 we need to re-evaluate the communists' record in launching revolutions with a central question in mind: might they, or, more widely, those inspired by Marxism in some way, play a part in future attempts?

This study focuses on the first period of attempts to further world revolution, between 1917 and 1939, when the Soviet Union was isolated in a capitalist world and laying the flawed foundations of its future power.[2] If lessons are to be learned for tomorrow's new world, above all in terms of liberation in the capitalist periphery, it seems more likely that they will be derived from that first set of experiences, when superpower nuclear confrontation did not govern all else.

Although the sovereign status of what the pre-1939 communists termed the 'colonial and semicolonial' periphery, and much else there, has changed, it still remains the soft underbelly of an otherwise triumphalist capitalism. This is because for the most part its societies have failed to attain 'developed' capitalist status, so the concomitant constant is that the periphery remains the part of the globe which Marx and Engels, the founders, had *not* seen as the true nursery of world socialist revolution. That makes the period 1917–39 all the more significant, in that it witnessed the decisive turn by communists to a major revolutionary effort there. To learn lessons, therefore, we need to look at their strategy and tactics during the first period in which they attempted to extend the removal of part of the world from capital's control beyond the new Soviet Union. We also need to examine the theoretical underpinnings of that struggle. That double reassessment is the objective of this study.

SOME BASICS

Only a very few years present themselves as chronological points – conjunctures – in history when it can really be said that human destiny took a new turn. 1917 is one of those. In that year ethnic Russians and associated peoples in large numbers suddenly ceased to be merely latent agents and subjects of history and became clearly manifest ones. The tsarist empire late in the First World War suddenly became the key arena of world history, and certain political parties and trade unions, and more generally social groups which had become conscious in class and other terms, became agents and subjects whose actions had a global impact which reverberated for the next 70 years.

Moreover, Vladimir Ilyich Lenin and the other leaders of the new Soviet state which consolidated by 1921 did not mean to stop there. They intended to use it as a base for a series of earthquake shocks which would lead to the global overthrow of capitalism, the universal revolution predicted by Marx and Engels.

However, the 'world revolution' took on a quite different form from that envisaged by Marx, Engels and Lenin. In William Shakespeare's *Coriolanus*, when the hero is banished from Rome he declares his lack of concern, for 'there is a world elsewhere'. The new, real world communist movement based on the Soviet Union, at least after it became clear in 1923 that revolution was not imminent in Germany, was forced to emulate the fictional character and seek a new arena for action. Global transformation had not begun in the central capitalist countries where the founders had expected it, but in tsarist Russia, and Marxist initiatives from 1917 began to be undertaken in the elsewhere of the capitalist periphery.[3]

I would argue that, although the post-1917 ideas came organically out of Marxism as it developed at the capitalist centre from the early 1840s, there was an absolutely crucial historical shift after 1917, more particularly after 1924 under the heavy aegis of Iosif Stalin, into a 'Leninism' or 'Marxism-Leninism' which found some eventual success on the capitalist periphery.[4] The point is that *the latter development was not how the original theory had said history would work itself out.* Capitalism was supposed to develop until it reached its limits, in the process creating its own potential destroyer, the proletariat, into whose ranks it would reduce peasants, artisans and small capitalists who could not compete. Working class consciousness would then develop out of the contradictions of capitalist exploitation, leading to inevitable revolution and the building of new socialist societies on the basis of capitalism's technical and productive achievements.

An immediate problem with the original theory is that it had been based on an assumption of a more or less identical capitalist development in individual 'national' social formations. In so far as it predicated global crisis – as it did – communist-led revolutions were still seen as separate events, and not on an international scale. Thus, and especially pertinent to this study, Engels had written to the young Karl Kautsky in November 1882 that any future revolution in countries like India, Algeria and Egypt would be dependent on the proletariat first seizing state power in the metropolitan countries.[5]

Moreover, it was assumed by Western Marxists like Kautsky that the seizure of power by working-class parties would be based upon a prior successful establishment of bourgeois democracy as part of capitalism's full maturation. In Engels's last major pronouncement, his 1895 introduction to a new edition of Marx's *The Class Struggles in France*, he spoke of the end of the 'time of surprise attacks, of revolutions carried through by small conscious minorities at the head of unconscious masses'. The struggle was now a question of 'utilizing the suffrage', '[s]low propaganda work and parliamentary suffrage'. Two years before, Kautsky had written that 'today it is beginning to become clear that a genuine parliamentary regime can be as much an instrument of the dictatorship of the proletariat as an instrument of the dictatorship of the bourgeoisie', and in another work suggested that 'economic, legislative, and political pressure' was more likely to be the method of struggle in Germany than 'armed violence' (Henderson (ed.) 1967, pp. 294–5; quoted, Salvadori 1979, pp. 37 and 40).

The economic and political logic of this orthodoxy was that communist revolutions could only come, and socialism be built, in capital's heartland, not in its 'colonial and semi-colonial' periphery, which, except in parts of Latin America, knew no sort of bourgeois democracy. Beginning in Russia in 1917, the original Marxist logic was defied, flouted, overturned. The other world which capital had created beyond its own imperial centre was complex, corroded, damaged, downtrodden. The periphery was capitalism's sphere of untrammeled activity, where, in the language of the *Communist Manifesto*, all that was solid in indigenous cultures was melted into air and the new consolidations were often brutalizing.

Yet Marxism, like the bourgeois social and political theories which became the ideological basis for capitalism, was the intellectual child of the European Enlightenment. The rival doctrinal stances were both committed to expanding knowledge and to social progress, both convinced that mankind (with the gender implications of that word) was fated to become master of the natural and social environments. A key point for this study is that on the periphery created by capital's imperial expansion these ideas gave intellectual licence to the brutalities and inequalities. Conversely, Marxism subscribed in its own way to the Enlightenment's political concept of popular sovereignty and to its radical statement in the French Revolution, the goal of Liberty, Equality, Fraternity.

It is in the spirit of the Enlightenment's – and therefore Marxism's – desire for general understanding that this study is being written as an assessment of the latter's history made, as it were, from within itself. Although many readers may wonder about the continuing relevance of Marxism, and even in these postmodernist days tend to fight shy of theory in general, part of our problematic must be to look at that level.

## SUBJECTS AND STRUGGLE

My approach is ultimately rooted in the 'philosophical anthropology' of the early Marx and leads me first of all strongly to affirm that human history has an overall meaning.[6] In this perspective, history has 'subjects', human beings who have the double status implicit in the English word, those who are subjected to alienation and estrangement and those who can be the active movers of a historical predicate towards an object. It is the dialectical interaction between these two moments in contradiction which gives a shape and at least a direction, if not a teleological drive, to history. However, in order for active subjects to assert themselves, or for established regimes to reproduce themselves as distributions of power in a given social formation, some of the subjects have in fact to be more active *agents*, on one side or the other. In the present context, this means basically servitors of dominant class elements or leaders of some sort of resistance.

'Class' is the central Marxist concept and basic to this study both theoretically and historiographically. From the beginning it has been related to control over means of production, extraction of surplus labour power, and, hence, exploitation of some classes by others. In my opinion, this view of the structural location of individuals in classes – their assignment to one or the other, as it were – is crucial in moving to the social nature of our human subjects, but needs refining if we are to move from class member to class agent or subject.

A key point here is that the basic structural aspects of class positions necessarily imply consciousness. Clearly, for example, even in identical structural positions and at the same conjuncture – Russia, say, in November 1917 – all class members have not chosen the option of becoming a revolutionary subject. This role in fact might or might not be consciously chosen, but even in the case of those subjects participating in revolutionary action without a full sense of their own exploitation and general structural oppression, they would need to be heavily estranged from the system.

Heretical though the statement may be, one of Marxism's basic flaws has been an inadequate postulation of the revolutionary subject. From the theory's early days this has been seen as the developed working class, with a tendency to treat this further as male and, given the factor of a developed industrial economy which initially characterized only the capitalist centre, as white. Moreover, an automatic link between objective class membership and the development of a 'true' consciousness has been assumed. This study postulates that a necessary distinction must be made between class member and class subject, and much of its discussion will be centred on the major issue of how action-oriented consciousness is created in subjects, leading to potentially liberatory confrontations.

However, crucially, this study proposes that, in class terms, *the pattern of capitalist development on the periphery was incapable of following the full 'proletarianizing' logic of that at the centre.* In other words, most peasants, artisans and petty traders were not 'freed' from the means of production and turned into full 'proletarians' (apart from the few who might be promoted to the rank of capitalist). This had a very important effect upon the nature and timing of such revolutions as did occur on the periphery. These came, in fact, at conjunctures which made them analogues – although not replications – of the crisis situations which beset the central formations in the *early* stages of industrialization or even, as in the case of most of Germany in 1848, *slightly before it and only partially because of it.* In those earlier cases, significantly, the crises worked through without lasting revolutionary consequences.

We shall explore the implications of this conjunctural factor. Immediately, another central proposition of this study must be raised, namely that *liberation struggle may actually be on class, race, gender or national bases.*

Such a reference to alternative bases for liberatory action, other than class, raises a key issue in considering the displacement of revolutionary action – from the classical Marxist point of view – to the periphery's elsewhere. The necessary approach for coming to grips with that historical phenomenon requires laying the foundation for a concept of the 'polyvalent' subject. Part of postulating a 'philosophical anthropology' of human liberation requires recognizing that every individual carries around a bundle of identities, each of which may be more relevant to their situation and actions than the others at different times. It is very important, moreover, that such identities imply membership of some collective body.

To put it in another way, different concrete situations, ranging from daily life to societal crises, will invoke different shared identities, gender, generational, racial, national, religious, class. Sometimes, of course, these come in complex combination; throughout South African history, for example, being a white male worker has been very different from being a black male worker, and even more so a black female worker. Classes are thus not merely internally stratified economically, but divided into genders and racial and national segments or by religious affiliation (of course, within common limits).

It is therefore crucial to any critique of Marxism's presentation of the revolutionary subject to take into account both the interplay of the structural elements in class membership and the possibility of an individual selecting an identity other than that of class as more relevant in a given situation. It is central to the argumentation of this study that both interplay and identity are *shaped*; in other words, *the polyvalent subjects do not objectively, often not even consciously, select which identity to bring into play, but have this done for them, by agents.*

This, for example, lies behind the concept of the 'vanguard' party of the working class, one of Leninism's/Stalinism's most dubious formulations as we shall see, but also behind the dominant class's control of subordinated subjects. Consideration of this shaping requires theorizing the place of ideological discourses in constituting the political, more specifically revolutionary, subject.

Discourses in the perspective of this study are structured presentations of ideas about political power, and therefore are ideological.[7] They are structured around a central idea, or group of related ideas, like Marxism's production–class–exploitation cluster. They must have the epistomological capacity to assimilate new data and reformulate ideas; this whole study is in one sense an examination of this in the case of Marxism. As they become more complex, they acquire extended cosmological and ontological references; Marxism includes a whole view of human nature and life, if only in a rather submerged way. They analyse existing situations and prescribe suitable actions, as Marxism does revolution. Discourses often also contain organizational models, like the party prescribed by Marxism.

The shaping – better, perhaps, constituting – of the subject by discourses implies that agents consciously interpellate them, that is, 'call out' to potential subjects and at the same time insert the discourse into existing cognitive and political spaces. Moreover, the latter are largely under the control of the dominant class or classes and their agents, although that control may be slipping and thus giving an opening to the interpellation of an opposition discourse. One of the basic focuses of this study will be upon the difficulties of doing this in the conditions of the 'colonial and semi-colonial' periphery.

Clearly, it must try the reader's patience to continue at this level of abstraction. More specifically, the patience of believers in Marxism as a materialist theory must already be tested. Let me assure them that, in trying to set up an appropriate theoretical base for looking at Leninism/Stalinism, as Marxism became with the shift to the periphery after 1917, as an ideological discourse, I shall always keep in mind the material foundation.

This study is therefore above all concerned with the way in which Marxists tried to conceptualize the formation of conscious revolutionary subjects in peripheral formations in the crucial period of a shift in major activity following the Bolshevik Revolution, the deviant event from the orthodox Marxist point of view which is the pivotal assumption of this analysis (an assumption because space precludes looking at it in detail). In particular, it is postulated that the problem of the polyvalent subject was first put squarely on the agenda by that second revolution in Russia in 1917 and its subsequent reverberations on the capitalist periphery.

Nineteenth-century industrialization and urbanization in the capitalist centre had given plausibility to the view that the overriding experience, and hence identity, was that of proletarianization and the formation of counter-poised capitalist and working classes. Gender, which should always have been an unavoidable issue in considering liberation struggle, was subordinated to this class reading, as were race and nationality, which in the context of imperial arrogance – to which male white Marxists were not totally immune – were also submerged. Anticipating conclusions, it may already be said that Leninism/Stalinism also incorporated such identities into its discourse by subordinating them to class, thus making no real break with the original problem of Marxism's undervaluing of them.

One last broad generalization is in order, and a materialist one. It proved to be the case that 'socialist' revolution could come on the periphery without the full capitalist development of the revolutionary class subject which Marx and Engels expected. As already stressed, it was the Russian Revolution led by the Bolsheviks which was the first major breach in the world capitalist system by actual historical agents and subjects. On that basis, Bolshevik agents tried to create a new discourse for revolutionary struggle on the periphery and in so doing transformed Marxism as the twentieth century's prime emancipatory doctrine, which then contradicted itself by its own practice. The central issue which holds together the theory and the historiographical practice in this study is that contradictory role of Marxist-inspired revolutions in the story of human liberation. The centrality of this concept of 'revolution' to both Marxism and this study requires some examination of it as part of establishing our problematic.

## REVOLUTION IN HISTORY

Beginning classically with the German Social Democratic Party at the end of the 1890s, the rival aims of Marxist-inspired movements have been described as either 'reformist', that is to say realizable within the existing political structures, or 'revolutionary', that is, requiring their overthrow, most likely by violent means and including a seizure of state power. The most important thing is to grasp the meaning of 'revolution', which, despite the initial reformist efforts of Eduard Bernstein and those of many successors, has remained a key term in Marxist discourse and the pivot for Marxist political action. The basic proposition is that Marxism provided the vehicle for the emergence of the first real conceptualization of revolution as a seizure of state power by new class subjects with an intention of totally transforming existing society. The crucial historical development, of course, is that this doctrine, both in theory and practice, became tied to the capitalist periphery.

The French Revolution of 1789, viewed as the political expression of a sea-change in European thought beginning about 70 years earlier, marked the emergence in what became capital's central terrain of a new secular concept of an abrupt changing of the world. The events of 1789–95 made concrete a new way of thinking about social change. The vital point for the Marxism which was to grow out of the Enlightenment and French Revolution was precisely that 'revolution' now came to carry the meaning of a *future* event which was first imagined and then planned and organized by *conscious* agents. It now became the most radical way in which historical subjects could act to change their conditions of life, by destroying the old order and building a new one.

In this context, we must remember that the original English and French Revolutions which inspired Marx and Engels were shifts which opened the way for the bourgeoisie to turn themselves into a capitalist class and begin the first stage of capital's deployment. On the other hand, and very relevant for Marxism as a radical class doctrine, a major result of the French Revolution was the introduction of a form of radical ideology opposed to big capital and based on mass political action which was to enjoy an uneasy and even antithetical relationship with Marxism.

Particularly problematic for Marxists in competition with what we might term later 'Jacobins' in countries like Egypt and Indonesia is the point made by Antonio Gramsci on the historical role of the originals, that they 'awakened and organised the national-popular collective will, and founded the modern States' (Gramsci 1971, p. 131). Later 'Jacobin' ideologies were strongly nationalist in content, competing with Marxism's narrower concerns with class. The nature of Jacobinism as it emerged from the French experience of 1789–95 thus gives us a clue to one weakness of its Marxist successor. This follows from a point already made in the context of theory, the latter's reduction of social struggle to the direct impact of class alone, and the historical privileging of one particular class, without recognizing that a very complex web of mediations is in fact always involved in creating revolutionary subjects.

The failed European revolutions of 1848–49 were further developments of the attempted consolidations of bourgeoisies through 'Jacobin' appeals in order to win a broad base. After this the revolutionary momentum associated, in a very complex way, with capitalist development at the centre faded away and the predicted next stage of working-class revolutions there did not occur. In effect, we can now see that, with the very partial exception of a brief spasm in Paris in 1871, the dynamics of a possible communist revolution began to shift to the periphery which, not coincidentally, capital began to shape from roughly that point onwards.

Marxism's shift to a world elsewhere beyond its birthplace has, of course, to be located in that structuring of a division between capitalist centre and periphery, a crucial distinction for this study's argument. Clearly, space does not permit an examination of the development of the capitalist world system which consolidated in the period roughly 1880–1914.[8] What must be noted here is that Marx's revolutionary perspective had of course always been global, in the sense that he had a clear view of the expansion of capital from the centre, even if he could of necessity not fully grasp processes of transformation which it completed after his death.

Already in August 1853 Marx had noted that

> [t]he bourgeois period of history has to create the material basis of the new world – on the one hand the universal intercourse founded upon the mutual dependency of mankind and the means of that intercourse; on the other hand the development of the productive powers of man and the transformation of material production into a scientific domination of natural agencies.[9]

Marx linked this immediately to world revolution.

> When a great social revolution shall have mastered the results of the bourgeois epoch, the market of the world and the modern powers of production, and subjected them to the common control of the most advanced peoples, then only will human progress cease to resemble that hideous pagan idol, who would not drink the nectar but from the skulls of the slain.

In mid-1853, although the founder cast his comments within the framework of a concept of progress and 'civilization' derived from the European Enlightenment, he clearly perceived its contradictory dialectics. 'Has the bourgeoisie', he asked, 'ever effected a progress without dragging individuals and peoples through blood and dirt, through misery and degradation?' From this he drew a concept of resistance, not only the class struggle among what he had called 'the most advanced peoples' but on the periphery also. Thus,

> [t]he Indians will not reap the fruits of the new elements of society scattered among them by the British bourgeoisie, till in Great Britain itself the now ruling classes shall have been supplanted by the industrial proletariat, or till the Hindoos themselves shall have grown strong enough to throw off the English yoke altogether.

Moreover, he saw the latter, indigenous, nationalist resistance as justified. In September 1857, in discussing the atrocities inflicted by British forces on Indian rebels, he wrote that 'dispassionate and thoughtful men may perhaps be led to ask whether a people are not justified in attempting to expel the foreign conquerors who have so abused their subjects'.

Marx and Engels of course never came up with a full theory of the global system (the above citations are actually from newspaper articles), and passed on to their followers the emphasis on capital's heartland. Nevertheless, there was one significant exception, which the founders studied but on which their findings did not pass into the Marxist orthodoxy. During the 1870s they became much concerned with the place of Russia in the global capitalist system and the chances for revolution there. Their tentative conclusions are important for us because of their more general relevance to the periphery. These were:

- the idea that an anti-capitalist revolution needed to be grounded in the peasantry as well as in the proletariat;
- the idea that such a revolution could come before capitalism was fully developed;
- the idea that revolution in a peripheral formation might precede socialist revolution at the centre and even help to accelerate it.[10]

By the eve of the First World War (1914–18), the failed revolution in Russia of 1905–6, then the first two great twentieth-century revolutions, significantly both in peripheral formations, Mexico and China, had telegraphed a new historical message. Both of those may be seen as poised between old and new revolutionary forms. Thus, they were based on pre-capitalist class elements, above all peasants, now being severely squeezed by capital's penetration and with strong 'Jacobin' elements, but were led by bourgeois and middle-strata elements interested in fostering capitalist development. However, although analogous to the European uprisings in the late 1840s in the latter sense at least, they took place in a world changed drastically enough to ensure their success.

The Mexican Revolution was in fact not planned to be a radical mass movement by its initiators in late 1910, who wanted rather to overthrow a particular dictator and his controls on their enterprise. The problem for them was that their call to rise brought into action autonomous peasant and rural worker movements which had their own agendas, including preservation of pre-colonial land rights.[11] In China, the October 1911 action was in fact a military revolt, given a mass base by

Sun Yat-sen's United League, which had strong contacts with the old Triad societies, but also with a Western-influenced 'Jacobin' ideological programme of democracy, national liberation and 'people's livelihood'.[12]

Although there were socialist, syndicalist and anarchist influences in Mexico and Sun had acquaintance with, for example, the writings of the American agrarian socialist Henry George, these major events were not social revolutions in the most radical sense. The Mexican Revolution moved further towards benefiting workers and peasants, but also consolidating national capital, capped by the programme of President Lazaro Cardenas in the late 1930s. The Chinese Revolution, as we shall see, led only to worsened conditions for the oppressed, although, again, it did open up possibilities for Chinese capitalists.

As we shall also see, it did the same for Chinese communists, who, like all Marxists, posited a revolution led by the working class as the universalization of all exploited elements, planned for it as such, consciously set out to create a class base for action by creating active subjects, and put a premium on organization.[13] Discussion in Chapter 4 will show that concrete conditions in China were to lead to a very distinct execution of the new ideas established by Marx and Engels on French Revolution foundations, with scant preparation by the penetration of bourgeois-democratic and 'Jacobin' ideas from Western Europe during the nineteenth and early twentieth centuries.

It was of course Russia which was destined for the historical honour of becoming in 1917 (after the unsuccessful 'dress rehearsal' in 1905–6) the first true 'weak link' – in a communist perspective – to appear in the capitalist world system. The circumstances behind this momentous event and the course it followed must be taken as read in the present argument. It suffices to say that it was a new form from a Marxist perspective, a working-class revolution led by a vanguard party in a newly industrializing formation of the periphery, but strongly supported by autonomous peasant action.[14]

Whatever hints of grasping the revolutionary potentials in peripheral formations there may have been in scattered writings of Marx and Engels, there can be no doubt that their mainstream predictions on the nature and timing of revolution were focused on the central ones and therefore an ambiguous legacy to their successors in both centre and periphery. The main ideas which affected Lenin and other revolutionary theorists in the periphery were the related ones of 'stages' of the revolution and of making it 'permanent'.

## THEORIZING THE REVOLUTION

As Michael Löwy has argued, it was the reaction of Marx and Engels to the attempted revolutions throughout Europe in 1848–49 which introduced the ideas of a revolution proceeding through stages and also launched the key concept of 'permanent revolution' on an irregular and ultimately indecisive trajectory of its use and development.[15]

The key here was Marx's and Engels's idea, already put forward in 1848, that history had developed/would develop through a series of modes of production – primitive communist–slave–feudal–capitalist–socialist–communist – with all but the first and last marked by relations between classes with unequal power. In this sense, each of the other historical stages had a dominant class which during it carried out its assigned historical task; that of the bourgeoisie, of course, was to establish capitalist production and the political form of representative democracy. At least by this stage, the transition was postulated as a revolution.

The basic factor is that those bourgeois necessities were not yet working-class drives for socialism, but attempts to open autocratic political systems by introducing limited democracy or, at their most radical, by 'Jacobin' movements by petty-bourgeois and middle-strata elements. We must remember that the initial Marxist 'model' for social revolution was France in 1789–95, which the founders saw as a bourgeois thrust made more radical by alliance with the peasantry against feudalism, and with a petty-bourgeois radical Jacobin element which the bourgeoisie in time repressed. Out of this 'reading' grew (although never fully formulated by the founders) certain ideas which profoundly affected the future strategy and tactics of Marxist revolutionaries.

First of all, Marx and Engels reacted to the next major revolutionary wave in Europe, that of 1848–49, by pushing the strategic idea of a revolution in stages, which transposed those on historical development in general into a concept of a phased revolutionary process with different tasks at different conjunctures, that is, a 'bourgeois' revolution to replace feudalism and then a 'proletarian' revolution to overthrow capitalism. This was to create major problems in application because it shifted analysis of the rhythm of development of events from the long range to the short. It was much easier to predicate broad historical changes tied only loosely to specific events than to predict and even create the latter as part of a revolution.

The relationship between the two, historical and revolutionary, concepts of stages also raised the profound issue of whether, as Marx wrote in 1859 in his *Preface to a Critique of Political Economy*, capital must fully complete its historical role before socialist revolutions could be possible. If so, the bourgeois revolutionary stage would have to ensure the completion of the historical one in order to create conditions for the proletarian revolution, in particular by creating a developed working class, with the inference of a protracted period of time.

The second profound strategic innovation of the period 1848–50, in fact opposing that reading of the stages concept, was the idea that, even in the absence of a fully-developed working class, revolutionary manoeuvring could be pushed by a communist organization into a continuous or 'permanent' movement from a 'bourgeois' to a 'proletarian' stage, without allowing the former to consolidate in terms of state power. Already in their 'Communist Manifesto', before defeat, the founders had claimed that 'the bourgeois revolution in Germany will be but the prelude to an immediately following proletarian revolution' (Marx and Engels 1973, p. 98).

This raised two issues for the embryo communist organizations: what attitude to take to other movements, and how to push them as far as possible in promoting change. To put it in another way, both the idea of revolutionary stages and that of a 'permanent' revolutionary process raise the issue of a 'war of position' as the necessary building of a bloc of classes, having it in common that they oppose the existing regime. This bloc must be strong enough to provide a terrain firm enough to bear the full interpellational and organizational effort necessary for a 'war of manoeuvre' leading to the actual revolutionary seizure of state power, which may take decades.[16]

In this connection, in the aftermath of the revolutionary failures throughout Europe in 1848–49, Marx devoted a number of pieces written during 1850 to the tactical issue of class alliances. Thus, in March 1850 he postulated the need for an alliance between the working-class organizations and the 'petty-bourgeois democratic party', but did not see their interests as common.

> While the democratic petty bourgeois want to bring the revolution to an end as quickly as possible ... it is our interest and our task to make the revolution permanent until all the more or less propertied classes have been driven from their ruling positions, until the proletariat has conquered state power and until the association of the proletarians has progressed sufficiently far – not only in one country but in all the leading countries of the world – that competition be-

tween the proletarians of these countries ceases and at least the decisive forces of production are concentrated in the hands of the workers (Marx 1973, pp. 323–4).

In 1850 Germany and ever since, a major problem for Marxists has therefore been the relationship with 'Jacobin' organizations during the manoeuvring for power. In March 1850 Marx laid an apparently clear line:

> The relationship of the revolutionary workers' party to the petty-bourgeois democrats is this: it cooperates with them against the party which they wish to overthrow; it opposes them wherever they wish to secure their own position (ibid., p. 322).

In a later passage his analysis had resonances which we shall find echoing in China, India and indeed throughout the periphery:

> At the moment, while the democratic petty bourgeoisie are everywhere oppressed, they preach to the proletariat general unity and reconciliation; they extend the hand of friendship, and seek to found a great opposition party which will embrace all shades of democratic opinion; that is, they seek to ensnare the workers in a party organization in which general social-democratic phrases prevail, while their particular interests are kept hidden behind, and in which, for the sake of preserving the peace, the specific demands of the proletariat may not be presented. Such a unity would be to their advantage alone and to the complete disadvantage of the proletariat. The proletariat would lose all its hard-won independent position and be reduced once more to a mere appendage of official bourgeois democracy. This unity must therefore be resisted in the most decisive manner (ibid., p. 324).

As we shall see, had later communists studied this passage carefully, they might have avoided some grievous errors.

Nevertheless, our judgement must be tempered by the recognition of an inadequacy in Marx himself. As Ernesto Laclau noted, the 'essence of Jacobinism' is 'the conviction that the struggle against the dominant bloc can be carried out as an exclusively democratic struggle, apart from classes' (Laclau 1977, p. 116). Marx and his successors failed to recognize clearly that a radical, even in certain circumstances revolutionary, struggle could be conducted on the basis of a discourse and programme not based solely on class. In other words they on the whole failed to recognize the force of the identities of race, nationality and religion, except as reactionary elements in a situation.[17] That inheritance was bequeathed to their successors.

Nationalism in particular was a key absence there. The scattered references to national movements by Marx and Engels could not have helped their disciples very much after 1917, since the views of the founders were almost always based on conjunctural assessments of the relations between national struggle and 'reaction' in Europe. In May 1851 the Poles for Engels were 'a doomed nation, to be used as a means until Russia itself is swept by the agrarian revolution. From that moment on, Poland has no raison d'être any more' (Avineri (ed.) 1969, p. 449). When the Poles rose in rebellion against the tsar in 1863, however, the two German communists supported them.

One important basic position, however, had already been taken in the *Communist Manifesto*, where the founders had said that the proletariat 'must first of all acquire political supremacy, must rise to be the leading class of the nation, must constitute itself as the nation'. This could be taken as implying a proletarian nationalism (leading 'the nation') as a first post-revolutionary phase, with implications for taking the lead in a nationalist struggle before winning power. Moreover, by the early 1860s Marx was prepared to entertain the view that, at least in the British case, Irish national struggle would be a key to the revolution. He and Engels in fact expected national differences and rivalries to begin to disappear once the workers had taken power in at least 'the leading civilized countries', since not only class exploitation but 'the exploitation of one nation by another' would come to an end.[18]

The Russian Marxists like Lenin took over the founders' more overt views on the class nature of nationalism, namely that it was historically linked to the bourgeoisie. That was bound to affect their views on its ideological place in the stages of revolution, a further concept they adopted without any recognition of latent weaknesses. At the time of the crucial Second Congress of the Russian Social Democratic Labour Party (RSDLP) in 1903, the idea dominated that the historically chosen class – the 'proletariat' – would be crucial even at the stage of bourgeois supersession of 'feudalism' (a concept which remained loose). As this Marxist position was to take further shape, largely via Lenin, it postulated that the task of the privileged class would be to cajole or force the bourgeoisie to carry out its historical mandate if the latter were too weak or cowardly to take the initiative.

Indeed, if necessary, the working class and its peasant and pettybourgeois allies might themselves even assume the bourgeoisie's tasks, basically the destruction of 'feudal' land tenure and establishment of

## The Problematic 17

democracy. We shall find that the political consequence of this line of reasoning in peripheral conditions was the seeking of alliances through the concept of the 'united front' of classes. This led communist parties during the 1920s and 1930s, as we shall see, into a maze of short-circuited concepts of historical stages, class tasks and consequent political positions which, combined with the difficulties of grasping the nature of the revolutionary subject in peripheral conditions, made Leninism/Stalinism an inadequate revolutionary doctrine for the 'colonies and semi-colonies'.[19]

All the above remarks have been cast in terms of the working class, since that was the one privileged by Marx, but in fact must be seen in the context of other subordinated classes, given that it has already been suggested that peasant action, at least, was important in the Russian case and we shall find it to have been decisive when we come later to look at China and India. We are thus brought specifically to the question of revolutionary blocs.

In terms of propensity to class actions, we may posit that peasants and petty-bourgeois artisans and traders would be more bound to their immediate class economic structures, primarily because they possess/ have access to small property, which would shape their structural class position. This would in turn shape any political action by them within systems controlled by capitalists and landlords. However, as we shall see in the Chinese case, if those power structures began to disintegrate, the peasants at least could be broken loose from the system by a determined organization which found an appropriate strategy and interpellated a new discourse.

There is another key class element to consider, the so-called middle class of professionals and white-collar workers. In post-1917 communist class analysis, following Lenin himself, these were in fact assigned to the petty bourgeoisie, as a 'new' stratum added by capitalism. However, this seems unacceptable, since the more recent group are sellers of labour power, not holders of small property. Their locations in class structures, therefore, have enough similarity with those of the workers to place them in the same contradiction of contributing surplus labour, although differences of consciousness and perceptions of class relations would tend to hold them back from direct revolutionary action except in very exceptional circumstances.[20] Nevertheless, *individual* dissidents from this social level were very important, beginning with Marx and Engels themselves, in providing the revolutionary leadership.

We shall see how difficult it would prove for communists in the periphery to build revolutionary blocs based on class elements with different consciousnesses, and that in general the conscientization of revolutionary class subjects was a far more complex matter than almost all Marxists allowed before Russian events of 1905–6 – and, indeed, after. In this respect, it is important to note that the whole range of issues raised above was not necessarily fully explored in the course of the prototype breakthrough on the periphery in 1917.

In fact, we may postulate that, in terms of theory and of revolutionary discourse, directly out of the first Russian experience came five issues which were matters for consideration in the next 20 years (and remain so today), although very uneven attention was given to them in the circles of the Communist International (Comintern), set up in 1919, where what became the orthodox model was basically formed. The five issues were:

- the relations between workers' economic and political struggles;
- the conditions for changing class consciousness;
- the necessary organization for revolution;
- the role of intellectuals in workers' struggle;
- the appropriate strategy for revolution in peripheral formations.

It follows from the way I have raised issues myself that my general propositions on revolution, and therefore my approach to analysing Leninism/Stalinism, are not in line with either these or the basic Marxist predictions as they became doctrinally formalized. My basic propositions are meant to provide an analytical approach to both the issues that emerged after 1917 and to the whole question of the Marxist concept of revolution. *They thus remain valid in the coming epoch, beyond the year 2000.* The key difference will be that the situation will not be overdetermined by the existence of a 'socialist' power supposedly dedicated to furthering the revolutionary cause, which we shall see became crucial already before 1939.

The propositions are as follows:

- Revolutions are not single-class affairs, but carried out by complex blocs of class and other social forces, which provide the social – and therefore political – terrain upon which the revolutionaries manoeuvre to power.
- The key political element in a revolution, as established already in 1789–95, is therefore always the way in which different dissident groups are constituted as subjects, joined together and brought into action. This effects the class content of the ideological discourse involved in creating such a bloc.

- The creation of a space for autonomous action by dissidents is a necessary precondition for any revolution.
- The creation of revolutionary terrains, with spaces which potential revolutionaries fill ideologically and politically, necessarily involves a 'rupture' between the dominant classes and the dominated classes and groups.
- The existence of such an expanding space presupposes a condition of regime crisis.[21]
- Any revolutionary 'vanguard' has to undertake two basic tasks: building an organization and interpellating the ideological discourse, which together mobilize people for revolutionary action. This may begin before the rupture and regime crisis.

The last point requires adding to the previous discussion. Above all with the 1903 RSDLP Congress Lenin began to postulate the party as the key 'vanguard' element. Leninist theory – which of course became orthodoxy after 1917 – postulated an 'iron' discipline in its ranks, and in May 1920 Lenin himself stated that the factors maintaining, testing and reinforcing party discipline were: the class consciousness, devotion, self-sacrifice and heroism of 'the proletarian vanguard'; the party's ability to link with 'the broadest masses of the toilers – primarily with the proletariat, *but also with the nonproletarian toiling masses*'; and correct political leadership, strategy and tactics, 'provided that the broadest masses have been convinced *by their own experience* that they are correct' (Lenin 1953(f), p. 345, original emphasis). We shall find these to be key factors in communist efforts in the capitalist periphery from 1917 onwards.

The foregoing pages have in fact raised many issues which will appear and reappear in our following analyses. The problems of shifting class consciousness, of combining different kinds of struggle and pointing them in a revolutionary direction, and of building the vanguard party, will constantly recur. As for strategy, the 'stages' concept in particular, with its issues of class content and necessary alliances for socialist revolutionaries, will be a recurrent theme. So will the 'permanent revolution', which did not replace the idea of alliances but profoundly modified it because, above all, it implied that one class could take over the historical tasks of another. These will also appear again in decades to come, although in a situation of a fully globalized capitalism which is new.

We have now opened up our basic problematic, that the key issues of Marxist revolutionary theory began to work themselves out from

1917 on the periphery, not, as was stressed at the beginning of this study, at the predicted centre, and with political success already achieved in Russia. From November 1917 onwards, there was an actual base for further efforts in one of the world's largest geographical formations and states. We shall see how, in facing the new post-1917 situation, this circumstance shaped the transmutation of Marxism into Leninism, the doctrinal basis of Marxism's shift to the peripheral other world. The Mr Hyde to Leninism's Dr Jekyll was Stalinism, and the implications of this duality cannot – and should not – be avoided by any contemporary Marxist. The rest of this study is intended to explore these phenomena, with possible developments beyond 2000 held always at the back of our minds.

# 2 Expanding to the East

Within two years of the October Revolution the issue of its continuation on a global scale became acute for the Bolshevik leaders. Above all, the failure of the Spartacist rising in Germany (January 1919) and the brief soviet republic in Hungary (March–August 1919) showed that the revolutions in the West believed necessary to support Russia's were not to be readily forthcoming. In April 1920, with the failure of direct imperialist armed intervention in the post-revolution civil war, Lenin nevertheless noted that

> it was easy for Russia, in the specific, historically very unique situation of 1917, to *start* the socialist revolution, but it will be more difficult for Russia than for the European countries to *continue* the revolution and bring it to its consummation.

Making a point which clearly remains relevant 80 years later, he warned that

> [a]fter the first socialist revolution of the proletariat, after the overthrow of the bourgeoisie in one country, the proletariat of that country *for a long time* remains *weaker* than the bourgeoisie, simply because of the latter's extensive international connections, and also because of the spontaneous and continuous restoration and regeneration of capitalism and the bourgeoisie by the small commodity producers of the country which has overthrown the bourgeoisie (Lenin 1953(f), pp. 389 and 396, original emphasis).

Although Stalin, true to the theme of 'world revolution', had noted in November 1918 that the October Revolution had created 'a new revolutionary front, which runs from the proletarians of the west through the Russian revolution to the oppressed peoples of the east, *against* world imperialism', he doubtless agreed with Lenin in still hoping for support from a revolutionary socialist regime in a developed industrial country of the centre (quoted, Carr 1966, p. 237, original emphasis). Conversely, in August 1919 Stalin's future enemy Trotsky, always an internationalist, wrote that 'the road to Paris and London lies via the towns of Afghanistan, the Punjab and Bengal' (quoted, Datta Gupta 1980, pp. 38–9). By mid-1920, therefore, a basic process of reassessment of the world revolution was under way. As a first task in this chapter, we must establish the basic parameters of that effort.

## THE PROBLEMS OF WORLD REVOLUTION

Already in the context of tsarist Russia, Lenin had been faced before the October Revolution with elaborating a view of world capitalism beyond anything Marx and Engels had ever attempted. His main analysis of what he saw as a more advanced stage of capitalism was presented in *Imperialism, the Highest Stage of Capitalism*, published in April 1917. In this he argued that imperial expansion was a product of concentration of capital and the dominance of its finance sector. Having in fact disguised his conclusion in what was an openly published work, in the July 1920 preface to the French and German editions he made it explicit: '[i]mperialism is the eve of the social revolution of the proletariat. This has been confirmed since 1917 on a world-wide scale' (Lenin 1953(d), p. 441).

However, three points must be noted about Lenin's much-cited work. Firstly, it did not in fact present a full theorization of the nature of global capitalism, and was conjunctural in nature, tied above all to Russian revolutionary needs at a particular conjunction. Secondly, Lenin assumed that imperialism, the 'monopoly' stage of capitalism, must necessarily be its last, which has proved to be quite untrue. Thirdly, Lenin was still fixed in the pattern of attempting a Marxist analysis of revolution country by country, not with a fully global perspective.[1] Simply adding comments in later editions, in a postwar situation of capital's international reassertion, did not lift theory to new heights, and we have already seen that Lenin's reaction to the new Soviet regime's international isolation was expressed in orthodox terms: to back the Russian revolution, there must be a German revolution, a French revolution, and so on. There was no conceptualization of a global *system* now radically affected by the presence of the new socialist state.

We shall find this issue, of the global role of the new Soviet regime as such, to be central in the doctrinal formation of Leninism/Stalinism and this will be documented in the next chapter in terms of debate between Stalin and Trotsky. Here it must immediately be recognized that there *was* a concrete reality behind the orientation to separate 'national' revolutions. The global capitalist system was structured, above all politically, as a series of sovereign states and the colonial possessions of some of them. In the end, the seizure of state power as the culmination of revolutionary wars of manoeuvre would have to be done at that level and socialist systems built on that basis. We shall see that the actual relationship between the historical phenomena of globally active capital and 'national' states and revolutions was to prove theoretically and practically complex.

Analyses by Rudolf Hilferding, Rosa Luxemburg and Nikolai Bukharin had in fact preceded Lenin's, permutating capital's need for markets, locations for new investment and maintenance of a high rate of profit in explanations of varying degrees of importance. All of them also associated this new expansion with ultimate crisis and collapse.[2] In terms of the more complex approach to revolutions postulated in Chapter 1, none of them effectively moved beyond the economic level into questions of state forms and political struggle, treating the latter as an automatic question of a rise in working-class combativity (as did Lenin). Two of their points only need be noted here: firstly, Hilferding's view that the global expansion of capital was a sign of economic strength, so that collapse would be long-term and involve intense political struggle, and secondly, Luxemburg's specific association of imperialism with capital's penetration of non-capitalist modes and its collapse with their final supplanting. Both views were of course very relevant to revolution in the periphery after 1917.

In fact, in the full period covered by this study, 1917–39, following the First World War and the Russian Revolution, Marxist theory had to come to grips with four new developments which changed the shape of the global system which had emerged by 1914. First, the structure of the centre had changed, with the capitalist powers confronting one another in a situation in which Germany, France and Britain had been exhausted economically and morally by war and the USA conversely strengthened. Second, the old hybrid absolutist formations which had spanned the centre and its immediate periphery (Austria-Hungary) or formed part of the latter (Russia, the Ottoman Empire) had disintegrated. Third, the October Revolution had in fact brought Marxists to power in one of those old formations, contrary to the basic propositions of their original theory, and at the very latest after an abortive rising in Germany in October 1923 it was clear that this revolutionary phase was not going to extend directly to the centre.

This meant in effect a shift of revolutionary terrains, a fourth, absolutely crucial, new development. Marxist theorists and practitioners (in principle, the same people) were faced with extending the revolution on a global scale, but now with the realization that the periphery might present more immediate opportunities than the centre, and in that sense might be Marxism's world elsewhere.

This shift after 1920 opened up the long-range strategical questions which dominated the life of Marxism as capital's enemy from then on and remain in reshaped forms today, which we may state as follows:

- Most broadly, what would be the nature of the 'world revolution' in a basically capitalist world with one major socialist state?
- Could revolutions be carried out in the 'colonial and semi-colonial' formations, and if so, could they result in the creation of socialist systems?
- What would be the class content of such revolutions, given the underdevelopment of the working class? How would the class content relate to nationalism?
- More specifically, given the assumption of a leading role for local communist parties, how would they take and hold that position?

Analytical complexities will not permit these issues to be treated separately and in any sequence, and in any case they were completely intertwined in the sense of shifting causes and effects concretely among themselves. The implication in the coming pages is that these should be read with the above questions constantly in mind.

Put in another way, therefore, the key analytical themes being presented here will be, first of all, the compounding of the difficulties of applying the basic Marxist tenets developed since Marx's death, already raised in the Russian case, in the conditions of even more peripheral formations. Secondly, we shall see the problems caused by an 'internationalism' which was in fact a monopoly on authoritative decision-making of the Executive Committee of the Communist International (ECCI), and increasingly after 1924 of the Stalinist leadership in the Soviet Union. In this respect, we have always to remember that discussion of global theory and strategy must also necessarily be related to the actual disputes among the Soviet leaders, since for the first time Marxism was being directly tested by the demands of its use as the basis for specific state policies and the legitimation of a particular regime. The removal of this factor is the major single change since 1991.

Thirdly, we shall see how difficult it was to establish a communist party as a viable political force with at any rate ultimate revolutionary intentions in a situation where other, 'Jacobin' nationalist forces were strongly established. That was a problem of building a revolutionary terrain as a basis for manoeuvring up to the seizure of state power, as, fourthly, was the issue of forms of class politics, involving alliances and the relationship of class identity with others in constituting revolutionary subjects.

All these issues will be brought together above all in examining the real significance of Leninism/Stalinism, the form which Marxism assumed on the periphery, as a discourse. In terms of concepts introduced in the previous chapter, I shall also in effect analyse a series of ideological interpellations made between the two world wars in an attempt to create revolutionary subjects. The most crucial case proved to be China, which was seen by Comintern theorists as central to the whole issue of continuing revolution on the periphery. In order to explore the full concreteness of the interpellatory process, however, I shall not only look at what happened in that 'semi-colonial' formation, but also at the cases of India as a colonial possession and Brazil as a 'dependent state'.

On the other hand, the new world revolution was perforce having to be launched from one specific base, what in January 1923 was given final constitutional form as the Union of Soviet Socialist Republics. A basic proposition in this study, therefore, is that the approaches to revolutionary terrain-building and interpellation emanated more directly than has usually been supposed from developments in Russia itself and that relevant new ideas emerged not merely from the Bolshevik leaders but from members of that country's own minority nationalities.

Moreover, contrary to what came to be claimed especially under Stalin, the latter were not simply a 'national communist' deviationist group but interpenetrated and overlapped in ideas with those of Lenin and others. Basically, the issue revolved around what came to be seen in the Soviet Union as the 'nationalities' question. Given that this ultimately played such a key role in the collapse of the Soviet Union, its continuing importance seems clear; the 'national communists' were not a marginal deviation but central to the 70-year period of Marxism's special association with the peripheral formations.

More immediately from the point of view of this study, the early 'national communism' debate in the new Soviet Russia raised two issues that were to prove central for revolutionary prospects in 'the East' and still are in so-called 'less-developed countries'. These are: the issue of the general linkages among various regional and 'national' revolutionary movements; and relations, in specific cases, among class, racial, national and religious struggles (gender, as usual, was relegated to the background).

## THE BOLSHEVIKS AND NATIONAL SELF-DETERMINATION

A key factor in the Russian Revolution which tends to be forgotten because of its initial concentration in Petrograd and Moscow is that tsarist Russia was an empire in which actual Russians were a minority;

they totalled 43 per cent of the population, with Ukrainians 17 per cent, Poles 6 per cent and White Russians 4.5 per cent (Trotsky 1967, vol. III, p. 40). Most of the remainder were racially not caucasian and were Muslim in religion, and although some were still at a tribal level, others, like the Turkomans and Uzbeks, were nationalities which had once had independent states of their own. For their peasant majorities, cities had served as 'centres of Russification and colonisation' (ibid., p. 47), around which were formed such local elites as the Russian power bloc permitted, while Russian peasants settled in their rural hinterlands.

However, a local working class also emerged in some centres. By 1917 there were some 56 000 Muslim workers in and around the Baku oilfields (largely controlled by the Swedish Nobel family), basically Azeris, Daghestanis, Persians and Azerbaijanis, and more than 50 000 Christian Russians and Armenians, and an estimated 100 000 Tatars in the coal mines of the Krivoi Rog-Donetz region.[3] In fact, '[a]t the beginning of the twentieth century Baku was probably the only place in the entire Muslim world, from Morocco to Indonesia, which could claim an authentic industrial proletariat'.[4]

In addition to workers, potentially revolutionary intellectuals were being formed, although related to the peasantry rather than the proletarianized.

> Alongside the Russian or Russianised intelligentsia, composed of the more respectable and well-provided elements, there was formed in the borderland cities another layer, a younger layer, closely bound up with its village origins and lacking access to the banquet of capital, and this layer naturally took upon itself the task of representing politically the national and in part also the social interests of the basic peasant mass (Trotsky 1967, vol. III, p. 50).

Speaking of his own people, the man who was to become chief spokesperson for 'national communism' described the intellectual ferment among the Azerbaijanis following the 1905 revolution, which was spurred on by the unsuccessful democratic movement in Persia in 1905-9 and the Young Turk coup in 1908 which attempted a modernization of the Ottoman Empire. The first theatrical production in the 'Tatar' language in 1906 sparked off conflict between Islamic traditionalists and reformers, with mob attacks on modern schools and teachers. Reforming scholars like Musa Bigev (Bigi) attacked the conservatives; he argued, for example, that meritorious infidels could also enter paradise. New Muslim schools were founded combining Western sciences with Islamic teaching, and women gained admittance to schools and public life, although naturally 'within the restricted limits authorized by the czarist regime' (Sultan Galiyev 1921(a), pp. 138–9, 1921(b), pp. 152–3). The basic issue which this particular uneven and combined class formation among the minority nationalities raised was that of the place of each class in the revolutionary process, what we have already seen conceptualized by Marxist theoreticians in terms of 'stages'. In applying the ideas of Marx and Engels to Russia, Lenin had basically put his revolutionary eggs in one proletarian basket, but did see as a result of the 1905 failure that the working class would have to form an alliance with the peasants and would itself shift politically during the war of position.

As things worked out in tsarist Russia, in 1917 revolution was above all the work of conscious worker-subjects, who moved in both March and November. The wars of position and manoeuvre were made possible by the existence since 1905 of this potential class terrain into which various agents of revolutionary discourse, mainly, but by no means exclusively, drawn from the dissident middle strata, were able to move, with the Bolsheviks gradually taking the political initiative. At the time, this subordinated the potentially rival 'Jacobin' stream based on a non-class conceptualization, above all one based on national feelings. However, this was certainly present, and a strong contributory factor in Poland, the Ukraine, Finland and the Baltic areas, the Caucasus region and Central Asia.

For Lenin and the other Bolsheviks, both basic theory and the way the revolutionary process in fact seemed to work indicated that a strategy of stages had become irrelevant; in so far as the 'national' bourgeoisie had some place in the power bloc after March 1917, it was thanks to workers' political action, and this situation was brought to an end as soon as those class subjects moved autonomously again in November. On the basis of this experience, in late 1918 Lenin polemicized against Kautsky, who did not believe directly socialist revolutions to be possible on the periphery. Lenin distinguished between the first, 'bourgeois-democratic' revolution, and the second, socialist one, based on different class blocs. 'The attempt to raise an artificial Chinese Wall between the first and second', he wrote,

> ... to separate them by anything else than the degree of preparedness of the proletariat and the degree of its unity with the poor peasants, means monstrously to distort Marxism, to vulgarize it, to substitute liberalism in its place (Lenin 1953(e), p. 114).

Nevertheless, the issue was not so clear in the non-Russian regions. In Central Asia, what revolutionary feeling there was involved middle-strata intellectuals from the different nationalities hoping to mobilize workers and above all peasants on a patriotic and religious basis. There were even some local capitalists who felt suppressed under the Russian-biased tsarist regime. Thus, the two parties which allied with the Marxists before 1917, Uralchylar and Hümmet ('Endeavour'), both formed even working-class adherents as subjects more in terms of Muslim and national identities than through class consciousness. Others, especially the Kazan Tatar party, Tangchylar, had contacts with the rival Socialist Revolutionary Party, which looked to peasants rather than workers (Bennigsen and Wimbush 1979, pp. 11–12 and 21).

After the March 1917 revolution, various groups of radical Muslim intelligentsia formed support committees for the socialist movement, most notably the Muslim Socialist Committee in Kazan, which drew on all varieties of the left, including anarchists (ibid., p. 22). Its most notable member was Mir-Said Sultan Galiyev. Born in 1880, son of a teacher and himself trained as one, although he in fact became a journalist, he joined the Bolshevik Party just after the October Revolution and, as an accomplished organizer, became head of the Central Muslim Commissariat of the Commissariat of Nationality Affairs and editor of *Nationalities' Life*, its organ.

Clearly, this complex constellation of class and other issues would seem to imply an approach based on a conceptualization of stages by those seeking orthodoxy, postulating first a 'bourgeois-democratic' move against 'feudalism'. Formally, this was the position taken, in the sense that three categories of constituent members of the new socialist federation were recognised between 1918 and 1923, namely 'socialist soviet republics', 'people's soviet republics', and simply 'people's republics'. In Central Asia, only Azerbaijan belonged to the most advanced category.[5]

On the other hand, in practice the Commissariat of Nationality Affairs, headed by Iosif Stalin, himself a Georgian who spoke heavily accented Russian, found no difficulty in carrying out the policy wherein 'Bolshevism insisted upon a rigid centralism, implacably warring against every taint of nationalism which might set the workers one against another or disunite them'. The writer of these words, Stalin's later opponent who did not oppose centralization, noted that urban soviets dominated by Russian workers '[u]nder a false banner of internationalism . . . would frequently wage a struggle against the defensive nationalism of the Ukrainians or Mussulmans [sic], supplying a screen for the oppressive Russifying movement of the cities' (Trotsky 1967, vol. III, pp. 41 and 48). In Tashkent, for example, Muslims were excluded from high positions in the Bolshevik Party 'because they do not possess any proletarian organization' (Bennigsen and Wimbush 1979, p. 23). Naturally the conservative Muslim leaders in any case bitterly opposed the Bolshevik government, with its open campaigns against religion. The saying of Uzun Haji, leader of the Chechens' Naqshebandi brotherhood, 'often put into practice', was 'I am braiding a rope with which to hang the students, the engineers, the intellectuals, and ... all those who write from left to right' (i.e. like Russians).[6] From 1918 until as late as 1936 a series of uprisings known collectively as the Basmachi movement (Uzbek for 'brigands') resisted soviet control over that nationality and others. Even socialist Muslims turned against the Bolsheviks; one former leader of 'Endeavour', for example, became head of the anti-Bolshevik independent Azerbaijan Republic in 1918–20 (Bennigsen and Wimbush 1979, p. 21).

On the other hand, during the civil war which followed the revolution and lasted until November 1920, many Muslims came to realize that the Russian anti-communist Whites were no less prejudiced against them, and many switched back to the Red side; Muslim troops formed almost half the Red forces on the most important front, in Siberia, and 'Endeavour' became the nucleus of the Azerbaijani Communist Party (Bennigsen and Wimbush 1979, pp. 25 and 29). In an unpublished but widely circulated book, Hanafi Muzaffar, an associate of Sultan Galiyev regarded as the chief ideologue of 'national communism', argued in 1922 that

> [t]he essential point for us is the survival of our nation and even more broadly, the survival of all Muslim peoples and all colonial peoples who are oppressed and threatened by European imperialism. . . . It would be a great mistake for us peoples oppressed by Europe to fail to recognize that Marxism is fighting imperialism. As the Communist Party is fighting the same imperialism in Russia and abroad, we must accept Soviet power. We must not fear the antireligious character of the dictatorship of the proletariat because the alliance between the Russian proletariat and the Muslims could deal a death blow to Europe.

Indeed, he put these views into a pan-Islamic context, holding that '[l]ike communism, Islam rejects narrow nationalism. Islam is international and recognizes only the brotherhood and the unity of all nations under the banner of Islam' (quoted, ibid., pp. 29 and 30).

Muzaffar's linking of all Muslims in a general anti-imperialist struggle opens a wider perspective still with us in the late 1990s, which we must now adopt. From mid-1919 the Bolshevik leaders were faced with the problem of the exact form in which their revolutionary state was going to get what they regarded as indispensable support. They had first to face this issue during the civil war, in terms of the non-Russian minorities within the old tsarist empire which they had basically inherited, a factor which actually led them, in the name of defending the Russian Revolution, into reannexing the breakaway Ukraine, Georgia and other areas by force.

Issues of national struggle and independence were thus overridden in the context of the composition of the new Soviet state in the name of international working-class revolution, of which that state was held to be the centre and sponsor. The broadening of this focus to the global 'colonial and semi-colonial' periphery, and the content which Marxism-Leninism consequently derived, revolved around three issues: the attitude socialists should take to national self-determination; the class content of nationalism; and how national and class issues were to be built together into revolutionary strategy. All of these were problems in whatever 'national' variant.

In terms of the tsarist state, the principle of self-determination had actually been written into the RSDLP programme at its Second Congress in August 1903 and accepted by both Bolsheviks and Mensheviks. However, this merely put the issue on the agenda without solving it, and debate continued in Russian revolutionary circles and among various Marxist pundits internationally, featuring such comrades as Kautsky and Luxemburg. In an analysis published not long before the outbreak of war in 1914, which was largely a critique of Rosa Luxemburg's rejection of national liberation as an inherently bourgeois issue and therefore not a revolutionary socialist concern, Lenin agreed with Kautsky that 'the national state is the rule and the "norm" of capitalism'. However, he saw the demand for self-determination as progressive from the revolutionaries' point of view because it implied economic development, the necessary basis for socialism. Moreover, the events in Persia, Turkey, China and Russia itself since 1905, which Lenin saw as 'a *whole series* of bourgeois-democratic national movements, striving to create nationally independent and nationally uniform states', led him to emphasize the importance of a stance on national self-determination.[7]

Lenin's view of these bourgeois-led movements clearly throws light on the issue of revolutionary stages. Commenting on the Chinese uprising in October 1911, which overthrew the imperial regime, he represented the Western capitalist class as 'decayed' and 'already confronted by its gravedigger, the proletariat'. In Asia, however, 'there is *still* a bourgeoisie capable of championing sincere, militant, consistent democracy, a worthy comrade of France's great men of the Enlightenment and great leaders of the close of the eighteenth century'. On the other hand, support for such a national movement was also seen by the Bolshevik leader in 1914 as tactical or expedient: working-class support for the bourgeoisie on the national issue was only meant 'to secure equal rights and to create the best conditions for the class struggle' and could not be an unconditional support if 'the bourgeoisie of the oppressed nation stands for *its own* bourgeois nationalism'. Moreover, Lenin still only attached real importance to European revolutions; the failed Easter 1916 rising by nationalists in Ireland was, he said shortly after, 'a hundred times more significant politically than a blow of the same force struck in Asia or Africa' (quoted, Claudin 1975, pp. 50–1, original emphasis; Lenin 1953(c), pp. 333 and 336, original emphasis; Carrère d'Encausse and Schram 1969, p. 147).

In November 1917 Lenin and his comrades came to power in Russia, although their grip was to remain incomplete for the next three years. Possession of state power inevitably brought about the modification of theory by practice. Thus, in terms of self-determination, in his major pronouncement in 1914 Lenin had already said that 'the given state', marked by 'the privilege of the Great-Russian nation', was the starting-point of struggle, but that 'we cannot vouch for any particular path of national development'. Significantly, as an example he distinguished between the undoubted *right* of the Ukrainians to an independent state and the *possibility* of their achieving one, 'a matter that will be determined by a thousand factors' (Lenin 1953(c), p. 338). The key factor actually proved to be the determination to keep the Ukraine under communist control and the key instrument in 1921 was the Red Army.

As for the role of nationalism in extending the revolution, Sultan Galiyev may claim the credit for anticipating the major swing of Lenin and the others towards the 'colonies and semi-colonies'. The Azerbaijani socialist already in 1919 saw the current civil war itself in a global way, as bound to draw more and more peoples and countries into conflict until it became 'the last world-wide butchery of humanity', which was 'inevitable and unavoidable' if 'renewal, an entirely new harmony' was to come. In that perspective, the October Revolution was only a 'moment' in an international struggle, with the 'international bourgeoisie' coordinating its forces through the new League of Nations.[8]

This made the 'Eastern Question' the key to future victory, in two respects. First, Sultan Galiyev argued, the failures in Germany and

Hungary already indicated that 'without the participation of the East, it is impossible for us to achieve the international socialist revolution'. This was 'one of the inevitable and unavoidable phases in the natural development of the world socialist revolution'. On the other hand, in their first two years of power the Bolshevik leaders had displayed 'onesidedness'.

The task of transforming the October Revolution into an international socialist one was understood as the transmission of the mechanical energy of the Russian Revolution to the West, that is, to that part of the world where the contradiction of the class interests of the proletariat and the bourgeoisie appeared most sharply and openly and where, for this reason, there seemed to exist a relatively solid basis for the success of the class revolution.

However, 'in no way can we confidently say that there is enough strength in the Western proletariat to overthrow the Western bourgeoisie'. The latter was in fact international in scope, and 'its overthrow demands a concentration of all the revolutionary will and all the revolutionary energy of the entire international proletariat, including the proletariat of the East'.

Sultan Galiyev, in a way particularly relevant to today, was thus pushing the world revolutionary struggle onto a scale which Lenin and the others did not themselves yet envisage, in the sense that they saw the decisive struggle as to be fought in the West, with even their own ultimate success in Russia dependent on this. Moreover, the East was the key for Sultan Galiyev in a second sense. In a remarkable twist, he saw the European capitalists (ignoring the USA) as using the Asian periphery (in my terminology) as a base for counter-attacking workers' regimes at the centre, if revolutions there *should* be successful, just as the ousted classes in Russia were currently using the non-Russian regions as bases for counter-revolutionary civil war. The European bourgeoisie would thus employ against embryo socialist regimes at the centre 'the ancient national and class hatred of the East toward the West, which is always alive in the breast of the East toward Western Europe as the bearer of the imperialist yoke, and it would launch a campaign of blacks [sic] against Europe'. Again, this made it imperative to take up the struggle in Asia as a full part of the world revolution.

For Sultan Galiyev, therefore, the East (in which he in effect included Africa) was 'the chief source of nourishment of international capitalism' and '[d]eprived of the East, and cut off from India, Afghanistan, Persia, and its other Asian and African colonies, Western

European imperialism will wither and die a natural death'.[9] By implication, although he did not explicitly draw that conclusion, the founder of 'national communism' therefore attached the decisive weight to the struggle in the periphery.

From what we see here, Sultan Galiyev can also be viewed as the founder of the 'third worldism' which remains a controversial issue at the end of the century. He also pioneered the concept of 'proletarian nations' and thus may be considered as the (unacknowledged) ideological father of the 'non-aligned nations' movement which arose with decolonization after the Second World War. His position already in March 1918 was that

> [a]ll Muslim colonized peoples are proletarian peoples and as almost all classes in Muslim society have been oppressed by the colonialists, all classes have the right to be called 'proletarians'.... Therefore, it is legitimate to say that the national liberation movement in Muslim countries has the character of a Socialist revolution.

It followed from this identity of class, national and religious struggle that Muslim socialists from the minority nationalities in Russia had a special duty to spread the word across Asia and the Middle East, lest it be taken as coming from 'simple successors to former Russian imperialism'. By mid-1926 another 'Tatar' communist was actually claiming that his compatriots 'objectively are more revolutionary than the Russians, because they have been more heavily oppressed by czarism than the Russians' (quoted, Bennigsen and Wimbush 1979, pp. 42, 43 and 55).

The overall tendency of the 'national communists' who gathered around Sultan Galiyev was to emphasize the low level of class formation, and therefore consciousness, among the non-Russian peoples, making the key issue for them national liberation. On the other hand, Sultan Galiyev himself did not ignore the class struggle. Like Lenin in 1905, he saw the revolution as taking place in two stages. For him these were, first, 'the overthrow of the power of Western imperialism'. In this the 'national bourgeoisie' and even the 'clerical-feudal bourgeoisie which pretends to be liberal' could be involved on the revolutionary side. In a comment which carries us to the heart of the issue of radical Islamic fundamentalism today, he pointed out, however, that the former was just as exploitative towards the labouring masses as the imperialists, and the latter was 'brutally despotic and ... capable, for the sake of its own selfish interests, to instantly change its stance toward its former foreign adversaries'.

There is no guarantee against the possibility that the feudal lords of China, India, Persia or Turkey, having liberated themselves with our help, will not unite with imperialist Japan and even with some other European imperialism, and will not organize a campaign against their 'liberators' in order to save themselves by this means from the contagion of 'bolshevism' (Sultan Galiyev 1919, pp. 136 and 137).

A second stage of the revolution, it followed, would have to be carried through against the 'feudal lords', although interestingly the national bourgeoisie at this point fell out of the picture.

Other groups based on the minority nationalities in Russian Central Asia also took a class stance. The largely Bashkir leadership of the Socialist Party of Turkestan ('Will'), who sought affiliation to the new Comintern separately from the Communist Party (the renamed Bolsheviks), saw a potential base in April 1921 in an alliance of the workers and cotton-growing peasants. Taking a more radical stance than Lenin and his lieutenants, they spoke in April 1921 of the need for a separate party of the workers, youth and intelligentsia in face of 'the small bourgeois democratic groups' in Azerbaijan, Turkestan and 'certain other Asian countries', who had started 'to organize themselves as a class' and argue in favour of 'national capitalism'.

The 'Will' group, however, also had a special reason for opposing a united front with the national bourgeoisie. They accused contemporary 'socialists of the metropolis' of 'hiding their suspicions of the native proletarians and socialists under slogans such as "a single front against world imperialism"'. Worker–peasant struggle was to be directed against 'Russian imperialism', spoken of in the present tense and even contrasted unfavourably with British rule in India. The real fear of extensive Russian settlement was expressed, along with cultural pride; the people of Turkestan were not 'savage natives similar to the [American] redskins' but 'representatives of a much older and incomparably higher rural culture than the Russians' [sic]. The unifying culture (basically Islam, although this was not specified) which had been at work for centuries was still threatened as under the tsars by deliberate fostering of 'a nonviable tribal tradition', 'antiquated feudalism' and 'the old familial and patriarchal system'. Only 'the political independence of the country' could allow it to use its own cotton and other raw materials 'to become again what it has been in the past, a producer of textiles and metal products'.[10]

We have now seen that very important issues of class formation and alliances, political organization, relations among forms of struggle and the place of the new Soviet state in a broader anti-capitalist movement had been raised in what was in effect the Soviet internal periphery by 1921. We shall find all of these replicated with the new revolutionary emphasis on the global capitalist periphery.

THE NEW EMPHASIS

Lenin and the other Bolsheviks in fact began to catch up with Sultan Galiyev in mid-1920.[11] Already in March 1919 they had founded the Third – Communist – International (Comintern) as a federation of parties dedicated to international socialist revolution. (Indeed, Sultan Galiyev's 1919 article should doubtless be seen as a reaction to this First Congress.) In April–May 1920 Lenin wrote of the need for a new centre 'that would be capable of directing the international tactics of the revolutionary proletariat in its struggle for a world Soviet republic'. In a way which foreshadowed a shift to 'the East', he also wrote that '[w]e must clearly realize that such a leading centre cannot under any circumstances be built up on stereotyped, mechanically equalized and identical tactical rules of struggle' (Lenin 1953(f), p. 420). At its Second Congress in July 1920 the Comintern shifted its focus decisively from 'West' to 'East'. The Comintern's Second Congress was thus a pivotal event in the whole development of revolution on the periphery.

Lenin himself acted as rapporteur to the Congress Commission on the National and Colonial Question and prepared draft theses, but the most interesting point in retrospect is that a supplementary set was presented by the young Indian communist Manabendra Nath Roy, who came directly from Mexico, where he had just helped found the Communist Party. The final version was therefore the Commission's compromise.

In his review of the international revolutionary situation in April–May 1920 Lenin had seen the climactic struggle as definitely based on the working class. In organizing for 'the final and decisive battle', he wrote,

> we must not only ask ourselves whether we have convinced the vanguard of the revolutionary class, but also whether the historically effective forces of *all* classes – positively of all the classes of the given society without exception – are aligned in such a way that everything is fully ripe for the decisive battle...[12]

This alignment, the taking of positions for the showdown, he thought, would involve three conditions which would polarize the struggle and give the initiative to the workers' party. First, the class forces hostile to the revolution would be 'sufficiently at loggerheads with each other' and already weakened by the struggle. Second, the 'wavering, unstable ... petty-bourgeois democrats' should have 'sufficiently disgraced themselves through their practical bankruptcy' – in other words, there would be no apparently viable alternative to the revolutionaries. The third condition was that 'among the proletariat a mass sentiment in favour of supporting the most determined, supremely bold, revolutionary action against the bourgeoisie has arisen and begun vigorously to grow'. If all these were present, 'revolution is indeed ripe' and 'if we have correctly gauged all the conditions indicated ... and if we have chosen the moment rightly, our victory is assured'.

Lenin's draft on the national and colonial question a few months later had rather different emphases, doubtless because he now had 'the East' more in mind. It called for the 'cornerstone' of the Comintern's line on the national and colonial questions to be a closer linking of 'the proletarians and the working masses of all nations'.[13] However, the fact that the 'bourgeois-democratic movements in the colonies' were now recognizing that 'their only salvation lies in the triumph of Soviet power over world imperialism' made 'the closest alliance of all national and colonial liberation movements' with Soviet Russia essential, with its form determined by 'the degree of development attained by the communist movement among the proletariat of each country, or by the bourgeois-democratic liberation movement in backward countries or among backward nationalities'. It followed from this that in the 'more backward states and nations, where feudal or patriarchal and patriarchal-peasant relations predominate', communist parties, especially those of the relevant colonial power, must assist 'bourgeois-democratic liberation movements'. This meant a strategy of 'temporary alliance' but not merger, with 'the independence of the proletarian movement even in its most embryonic form' preserved 'at all costs', and formation of 'Soviets of toilers'. A special priority must be the peasant movement against landlordism and 'all manifestations or survivals of feudalism', without the support of which communist activity would be 'utopian', and a further task to be inculcated was 'struggle against the bourgeois-democratic movements within their own nations'.

Looking to the more distant future (and to what was actually to happen after 1945), it was necessary, Lenin said, 'to explain constantly and expose to the broadest working masses' that the colonial powers might use the trick of establishing politically sovereign states which were in fact 'completely dependent upon them economically, financially and militarily'. Moreover, in backward countries 'petty bourgeois prejudices . . . of national egoism and national narrowness' were 'particularly strong and tenacious' in proportion to the strength of 'small agricultural production, patriarchalism and ignorance'. This meant 'particular caution and attention' on the part of communists and 'certain concessions' to national feeling and that of especially oppressed nationalities within colonies during the period while 'distrust and national prejudices' were being eradicated, which would require radical change of the whole economic basis of society.

In his original formulations, Lenin was therefore rather ambivalent about nationalism, apparently wavering between 'bourgeois' and 'petty-bourgeois' forms and finding the former potentially progressive in the sense that 'liberation movements' headed by it (like the Indian National Congress) could be supported by communists even while the latter organized separately. (And assuming that the simultaneous struggle against the bourgeois-democratic movements would not alienate them.) Further, it is clear that he stuck to the general Marxist view of nationalism as historically an expression of the bourgeoisie, but saw it as potentially progressive in the anti-imperialist sense. Lastly, he in effect took a modest view of the possibilities of organization by communists in the colonies and of the level of class awareness there.

The Soviet leader was not putting forward a strategy of the working class and 'its' party taking over the historical tasks of other classes, as he had for Russia, but one based on alliances of classes through their separate parties. Roy's 'supplementary' theses placed different emphases. He distinguished between bourgeois-democratic nationalist movements and 'the mass action of the poor and ignorant peasants and workers for their liberation from all forms of exploitation' and, rather than speaking of allying with the former, stressed instead the need to block their control of the peasants and workers and 'help to develop class-consciousness in the working masses of the colonies'. In this respect, however, he had already made the key reference, in terms of actual future developments, to the fact that, by keeping the masses ignorant, imperialism had limited the emergence of the 'spirit of revolt' to 'the small educated middle class'.

Apparently not recognizing any possible problem of 'vanguardist' elitism here, Roy felt that the priority task was to advance the development of communist parties, which would 'organize the peasants and workers and lead them to the revolution and to the establishment of

Soviet Republics'; revolutionary parties or groups already existed in most colonies as the 'vanguard of the working class' and, although not yet very large, 'reflect the aspirations of the masses', which would 'follow them to the revolution'. The masses would have to go through 'the successive periods of development of revolutionary experience', but with the help of the working classes of the advanced capitalist countries would be able to avoid 'capitalist development'.

The colonial revolution, according to Roy's draft, would not immediately be socialist, nor would its key agrarian programme, but with a communist vanguard 'the revolutionary masses will not be led astray'. In what was in effect a 'permanent revolution' perspective, although elements in the agrarian programme might 'include many petty bourgeois reforms, such as division of land', this would not be implemented under the leadership of bourgeois democrats but through 'proletarian parties' and 'peasants' and workers' Soviets'. Moreover, those soviets would work with socialist republics set up in the advanced countries to complete world revolution.

Soviets had only been an afterthought for Lenin, added to his draft at proof stage, and the link with the peasants was taken over for the final version of the theses by the Commission on the National and Colonial Question. From Lenin's presentation of this to the full Congress, it emerged that Roy and other colonial delegates had strongly supported the idea, which the Russian leader felt was not borne out by much experience in his country, although the peasant issue had arisen in areas like Turkestan. However, peasant soviets seemed a 'useful weapon', and, as a 'simple idea', the principle of soviet organization 'can be applied, not only to proletarian, but also to peasant, feudal and semi-feudal relations'. The seventh final thesis preserved the class purity of the revolutionary party, however, by calling for 'the formation of a non-party [sic] organization of peasants and workers'.[14]

This reformulation was a crucial turning-point, since it led, as we shall see in the Indian and Brazilian cases, to a policy of forming 'workers' and peasants' parties' as stepping stones for (or ancilliaries to) communist parties and eventually opened the way for communist organization in China, Viet Nam and indeed all the countries where Marxist-Leninist revolutionary movements became strong and in some cases successful in gaining state power. Moreover, a further point on which the Commission overruled Lenin (an enormous contrast with later 'democratic' practices in 'vanguard' organizations) was his use of the formula 'bourgeois-democratic' to describe potential allies, substituting 'revolutionary liberation'. Lenin reported that members had felt that, while every nationalist movement must be regarded as bourgeois-democratic, since even with peasant support it remained within the framework of capitalist relations, a distinction must be made between reformist and revolutionary bourgeois movements. The latter were those which were 'really revolutionary', meaning that they did not fight simultaneously against the imperialists and 'all revolutionary movements and revolutionary classes' and further that they did not prevent communist organization of the peasants and 'broad masses of the exploited'.

As for Roy's proposed supplementary theses, the Commission brought these into line with Lenin's by inserting a reference to 'the cooperation of the bourgeois nationalist revolutionary elements' as being 'useful', but it was clear that Roy's general thrust was towards pushing for separate communist organizations which would act alone and more radically. Further, the young Indian had taken a different perspective on the whole global situation and struggle, giving much more weight to the periphery. He had declared, for example, like Sultan Galiyev, that 'European capitalism draws its chief strength less from the industrial countries of Europe than from its colonial possessions', which in turn meant that '[t]he European working-class will not succeed in overthrowing the capitalist order until this source has been definitively cut off'. Imperialist activity in the peripheral countries 'has unquestionably handicapped their social and economic development and prevented them from reaching the level of Europe and America', so that the 'first step towards revolution in the colonies must be the overthrow of foreign capitalism'. These comments were modified to reduce emphasis on profits from the periphery as the mainstay of capitalism and chief block to working-class revolutions at the centre. Significantly also, the idea of peripheral working people reaching the level of those at the centre was changed to one of developing 'side by side' rather than equally.

From the way Lenin introduced it, another point of absolutely vital future significance seems to have followed from the discussion on Roy's draft. Someone, perhaps Roy, raised the issue of whether 'backward nations which are now liberating themselves' must inevitably pass through 'the capitalist stage of national economy'. The Commission's answer was 'no': '[i]f the revolutionary, victorious proletariat carries on systematic propaganda among them', with help from 'the Soviet governments' and 'the proletariat of the most advanced countries', and with the 'theoretical grounds' laid down by the Comintern, the 'backward countries' could move to the 'Soviet system'. Then, 'passing through a definite stage of development' they could attain communism 'without passing through the capitalist stage of development'. Once again, this laid the basis in principle upon which all subsequent attempts to build socialism (except for Czechoslovakia and East Germany) were to be founded.[15]

The Second Comintern Congress in July–August 1920, therefore, marks a key conjunction in the history of Marxism as a theory of socialist revolution, because from then on its main interpellation came to be in the periphery. In no way did this mean that debate ended, at least not in the relatively open atmosphere which prevailed until 1925. In the early 1920s both the progressive nature of nationalism and the best forms of class alliance remained controversial.

With regard to the role of nationalism in the revolutionary struggle, doubts had always been expressed. In August 1908 Rosa Luxemburg had written in an article addressed to Polish socialists that

> [i]n a society based on classes, the nation as a uniform social-political whole simply does not exist. Instead there exists within each nation classes with antagonistic interests and 'rights'. There is literally no social arena – from the strongest material relationship to the most subtle moral one – in which the possessing classes and a self-conscious proletariat could take one and the same position and figure as one undifferentiated national whole (quoted, Nettl 1966, p. 849).

Given its stress on class differences in approach to national questions, this remained a timely warning in 1920, and Lenin's attempt at a definitive statement in April of that year, not long before the Second Comintern Congress, was in line with it.

> As long as national and state differences exist among peoples and countries – and these differences will continue to exist for a very long time even after the dictatorship of the proletariat has been established on a world scale – the unity of international tactics of the communist working-class movement of all countries demands, not the abolition of national differences (that is a foolish dream at the present moment), but such an application of the *fundamental* principles of Communism (Soviet power and the dictatorship of the proletariat) as will *correctly modify* these principles in certain *particulars*, correctly adapt and apply them to national and national-state differences (Lenin 1953(f), p. 420, original emphasis).

In the context of 'colonial' and 'semi-colonial' formations, it was relatively easy for communist strategists to agree that nationalism could be a progressive force, but, as we have already seen in the case of the

Lenin–Roy debate, the class alliance issue was more contentious and complex. In January 1922, in answering Luxemburg's criticism of the Bolsheviks' conduct since taking power, made just before her murder three years earlier, the Hungarian Georg Lukács actually felt she had underestimated 'the importance of the non-proletarian elements in the revolution', both within the working class and external to it. This led in turn to 'the decisive point of her misinterpretation' – 'the *underplaying of the role of the party* in the revolution and of its conscious political action, as opposed to the necessity of being driven along by the elemental forces of economic development'.[16]

In thus stressing the party's leadership of a multi-class bloc, the Hungarian communist doubtless had the failure in his own country in mind. This would also have been the case when, in a later passage, he drew attention to Luxemburg's writings on imperialism, in which she had postulated the progressive destruction of 'those strata which are neither capitalist nor proletarian' by capital, which 'must take more and more violent forms'. The effect of this, the critic argued, must be that

> [b]roader and broader strata separate out from the – seemingly – solid edifice of bourgeois society; they then bring confusion into the ranks of the bourgeoisie, they unleash movements which do not themselves proceed in the direction of socialism but which through the violence of the impact they make do hasten the realisation of the preconditions of socialism: namely, the collapse of the bourgeoisie.

Of course, he noted eight months later, only the class-conscious proletariat can lead the revolution 'along the right road' and there were dangers in a multi-class movement.

> If, however, other strata of the population become decisively involved in the revolution they may advance it under certain circumstances. But it is just as easy for them to deflect it in a counter-revolutionary direction. For in the class situation of these strata (petty bourgeoisie, peasants, oppressed nationalities, etc.) there is nothing, nor can there be anything to make their actions lead inevitably towards the proletarian revolution.

In this context, Lukács admitted that even a revolutionary party could not ultimately control non-working-class subjects and hence he tended to fall into line with Roy's position two years earlier. Moreover, like the young colonial comrade, he still gave full revolutionary priority to the working class, ascribing the fact that the revolution had so far failed to spread to other countries to 'the ideological crisis of the proletariat'.

This he typified as caused by the continuing influence over workers of 'old capitalist forms of thought and feeling' and to the influence of reformist (he said 'Menshevik') parties and unions. What Engels in his *Anti-Dühring* had termed the 'leap from the realm of necessity into the realm of freedom' could therefore not be seen as an abrupt act but as a process which would be 'repeated and intensified until the time when the final crisis of capitalism has been reached, the time when the decision comes more and more within the grasp of the proletariat'.

At the time Lukács was writing, the Comintern was moving over to its 'Second Period' of building up strength for a 'world revolution' in which formations on the periphery would figure much more prominently. The centre-piece of this policy remained the idea of shifting class alliances, appropriate to various revolutionary stages, with the local communist parties therefore being involved in various 'united fronts' with other organizations. These might shift between two forms: the front 'from above', with more or less equal cooperation in at least immediate tasks, and that 'from below', in which the communists would try to win away their partner's members and in effect subvert the alliance.

In terms of both strategy and tactics, the Comintern Fourth Congress held in November–December 1922 marked an important consolidation. It took the 'catastrophist' view that '[w]hat capitalism is passing through today is nothing but its death agonies. The collapse of capitalism is inevitable.' As a result, it therefore adopted a more critical stance towards what it now termed the 'bourgeois-democratic' as opposed to 'revolutionary liberation' movements against colonialism, the latter involving parties leading the workers and peasants. The Fourth Congress's 'Theses on the Eastern Question' declared that the 'objective tasks of the colonial revolution go beyond the limits of bourgeois democracy if only because a decisive victory for this revolution is incompatible with the rule of world imperialism', and predicted that 'the indigenous bourgeoisie and intelligentsia', although the 'pioneers of the colonial revolutionary movements', would 'turn away' the more the 'proletarian and semi-proletarian peasant masses are drawn in' and their interests came to the fore. Peasant subjects were not to be the revolutionary key, of course; local communists were enjoined to regard the 'struggle for influence over the peasant masses' as one which would train the workers to lead politically. As for alliances,

> [t]he workers' movement in the colonial and semi-colonial countries must first of all win for itself the position of an independent revolutionary factor in the anti-imperialist front as a whole. Only when its

importance as an independent factor is recognized and its political independence secured, are temporary agreements with bourgeois democracy permissible and necessary.[17]

Nevertheless, despite such talk of independence, the revolution remained dependent on the strategy and tactics of the united front of communists with other organizations, of which, as we shall see in Chapter 4, China in the period 1921–27 is the central case. The Fourth Congress therefore clearly reasserted Lenin's 1920 principle of preserving organizational autonomy when entering a front and came close to Trotsky's idea of permanent revolution in postulating an inevitable move beyond bourgeois-democratic tasks and a loss of bourgeois allies.

Whatever the strategic re-evaluation, by the time of the Fourth Congress there was little concrete experience on the periphery, as at the centre, which could support revolutionary optimism. Such enterprises as the Soviet Socialist Republic of Ghilan in northern Persia, set up in May 1920 by Red Army units in alliance with a local pan-Islamic and anti-dynastic movement under a *mollah* (Muslim preacher) and wiped out by the shah's troops in October 1921, proved that – for different reasons – expanding the revolution in Asia would prove as difficult as in the West. (One of its results was the murder of the entire central committee of Persia's new communist party by their religious ally.)

Claudin makes the point that it was no accident that the Comintern met with severe reversals in the Middle East, where the Muslim peoples were closely related to those of the Soviet Union and the bourgeois-nationalist leaders, like Kemal Ataturk, could make the most of the failure of the Turkestanis and others to gain self-determination. In notes dictated in December 1922 Lenin, obviously with the Russian Socialist Federal Soviet Republic in mind, actually spoke of 'internationalism' in terms of relations among 'nations' *within* states. In such composite social formations the 'oppressor' nation should not only treat the others equally but should accept 'an inequality' in its own position 'to make up for the inequality which obtains in actual practice'. In a message to the Party Central Committee also dictated in December 1922 but only finally read out at the Thirteenth Party Congress in May 1924, after his death, Lenin blamed Stalin's 'haste and his infatuation with pure administration, together with his spite against the notorious "national-socialism"' as playing 'a fatal role' in alienating people in the Caucasus.[18] Uncomfortably for Marxists, 'Great Russian' chauvinism continued to plague the Soviet Union up to its final collapse.

Generally, in fact, the shift in mid-1920 raised new issues but went no real distance to solving them. For the next 15 years, through another five Comintern Congresses, the issue of leadership of nationalist movements in the 'colonies and semi-colonies' was to be central and was in fact to outlive the demise of the organization in 1943. Roy's views, for example, had struck a chord; in 1921 the 'Will' group in Turkestan argued that, in spite of their present weakness, working-class socialist parties in the colonies were the only possible vehicles for raising the independence struggle to 'the level of the common struggle of all the oppressed elements and of the world proletariat' (quoted, Bennigsen and Wimbush 1979, p. 172).

Again, right from November 1917 the issue of the relationship between the spreading of the world revolution and the foreign policy of the new Soviet state had its effect. Although the subordination of the former to the latter is most often ascribed to Stalin, it must be emphasized that the principle was already well-established before he took control. Thus, on the same day in March 1921 the communist leaders signed treaties with both the government of Kemal Ataturk in Turkey and that of Britain. The former gave Kemal the money and arms needed to win his war with Greece and stabilize his control; this was despite the fact that not long before he had arrested all the Turkish communist leaders, murdered half immediately, and saved the rest for trial. The latter treaty secured acceptance of Soviet gold payments for necessary imports and services. In return the Soviet government recognized in principle the British compensation claims for nationalized property, while both agreed not to undertake hostile action against the other; the point here was specification of 'the British Empire' and not just the United Kingdom itself as thus to be immune.[19]

In his last major pronouncement on policy, in March 1923, Lenin turned to the international situation. The imperialist powers, he admitted, had blocked the capacity of the Soviet Union's socialist regime to move forward rapidly, while Germany, through enforced reparations payments, had been 'enslaved by the victor countries' which were economically in a position to make some concessions to their workers. There was also a very significant formulation by Lenin in line with his earlier analysis of imperialism; capitalism was continuing to develop, he continued, not by 'maturing' (that is, developing its productive forces by efforts at the centre) but by exploiting Germany and 'the whole of the East'. On the other hand, the 'first imperialist war' of 1914–18 had drawn the latter countries into the world revolutionary movement, and '[t]heir development has definitely shifted to the general European capitalist lines'.[20]

Lenin saw the world as now divided into 'two camps', a formulation which was to become standard for Soviet international policy, but in 1923 characterized these as the 'thriving imperialist countries of the West' and the 'thriving [sic] imperialist countries of the East', although he saw the latter as being much weaker. From the standpoint of the present study, this reduction of centre and periphery to the same terms was quite impossible, and reveals the fact that Lenin was still bound by Marx's view of capitalist development as ultimately uniform, which in the end prevented him from getting a grasp on the real future dynamics of imperialism. It should come as no surprise, therefore, that the seriously ill Soviet leader in effect had no clear strategic recommendations, maintaining that 'the answer depends upon too many factors'. He was prepared to say only that '[i]n the last analysis' the outcome would be determined by the overwhelmingly greater populations of 'Russia, India, China, etc.', and even then, having apparently committed the future of the world revolution to developments in the 'East', he now represented its 'thriving' countries as 'Orientally backward' and in need of a preliminary move to 'civilized' status, by which he meant moving to a developed capitalism.

All in all, therefore, what we have here is a failure to launch a theoretical and strategic debate in the immediate aftermath of the October Revolution which might have led to an abandonment, or at least radical reformulation, of basic ideas of Marx and Engels on such matters as the universally progressive nature of capitalism in world historical terms, the monopoly of true revolutionary potential by the working class, and the place of nationalism in the struggle against it. Of course, it is not to be expected that the necessary debate could have taken place in a context of civil war and consolidation of the new Soviet state, but only if this had been done could a full theoretical and therefore strategical grip have been taken on the issue of 'world revolution'. Only on such a basis could the follow-up issue, the possibility of building socialism without a prior full development of capitalism, have been worked out. In consequence, these problems – and this is a central motive behind this study – remain with Marxists today. We should therefore move to a consideration of the theoretical developments which did actually take place to consolidate a new Marxist formulation as an exportable discourse ultimately controlled by Soviet agents.

# 3 Comintern and Other Perspectives

In the two preceding chapters we have seen how Lenin and lesser Marxist luminaries attempted to come to terms with the immediate aftermath of the October Revolution and the period in which it became clear that 'orthodox' revolutions in the capitalist centre were not going to give the supposedly indispensable support to the Soviet regime. That left the member parties of the Comintern, and that body as a whole, faced with the continuing issue of planning, organizing and carrying out other 'unorthodox' revolutions in untheorized circumstances. Leninism/Stalinism in fact emerged and was shaped from Lenin's death in January 1924 onwards in this context. At the same time, a sort of dialectical interplay between theory and practice was launched by the concrete application of the Comintern's attempted theorization in individual countries.

In order to come to grips with that process, we need to examine key issues of revolutionary practice which had to be situated by Comintern tacticians in terms of the longer-range theoretical and strategic issues which followed from the opening of another potential revolutionary world on the periphery, and which were listed at the end of Chapter 1. These related to the problem of action taken across the revolutionary terrain: what had actually to be done, and by whom, at any specific point in time in a given social formation in order to bring the revolution closer? Dealing with these issues became a central part of the emergence of Stalinism-Leninism.

Also in Chapter 1, the reader was asked to grasp a number of concepts which could be used as levers to move our understanding. Thus, to recapitulate: revolutionary situations require, on the one side, *agents* who will interpellate a *discourse*; the object of that is to create the necessary consciousness among potential *subjects* and so form a social *terrain* for the necessary action. Clearly, accomplishing this was the basic issue where the political strategy was to extend the revolutionary seizure of power in Russia into revolution on an international scale. (As it will be in the future in conditions of the new 'globalism.') Agents and subjects for this had to be found by creating revolutionary terrains in social formations even less like those in and for which the original theoretical positions were developed than the Russia of the early twentieth century. This brings us back yet again to the issue of appropriate revolutionary theory and strategy. The actual creation of agents and subjects and interpellation of discourse may best be seen in the case studies presented in Chapters 4 and 5.

## FOUNDATIONS FOR A DISCOURSE

Throughout the coming discussion, it is crucial to keep constantly in mind the point that Marxism-Leninism was in effect created by Stalin as part of his consolidation of his own power after Lenin's death. In April 1924 the general secretary gave a series of lectures, which were then published as *The Foundations of Leninism*, and in January 1926 there appeared his *Problems of Leninism*. Stalin thus asserted his position as the leading Soviet theorist, although at first in the guise of Lenin's faithful disciple, not as an original thinker. It is in this sense that the new leader can be seen as creating 'Leninism'. This establishment of a monopoly over the interpretation of Lenin's ideas was the context for what we shall see to have been in effect the interpellation of a new internationalist discourse, but which arose from the internal politics of the Soviet Union and was then projected onto the entire international revolutionary movement.

The key theoretical formulation in those internal politics was Stalin's concept of 'socialism in one country', specifically the Soviet Union, which we shall see becoming the core idea of the Leninist discourse as it shaded into Stalinism, replacing that of 'world revolution'. This line was officially adopted in April 1925, in between Stalin's major formulations of Leninism.

In a sense, the Soviet Union-centred concept was the 'down-side' of the postulate of necessary revolutions in the periphery; given that world revolution was not spreading as expected/hoped, it said, we can go on to begin the building of socialism in the Soviet Union by drawing on its own resources while developing the revolutionary movement elsewhere. This in turn linked back to another issue, of explaining not only why it was that the 1917 revolution had occurred in a relatively underdeveloped part of the capitalist world system but had also put it in the position to become the first 'socialist' country while waiting for supporting revolutions.

In fact, Stalin had already moved at least halfway to his 1925 position even before the October Revolution. In July 1917 he had argued that '[y]ou cannot rule out the possibility that precisely Russia will be the country that paves the way to Socialism.... We ought to discard the obsolete idea that only Europe can show us the way' (quoted, Deutscher 1960, p. 154; further dicussion, pp. 153–4). This was in one sense in line with Lenin's analysis in his work on imperialism published a few months before, but its reference to socialism, rather than the prior necessity of working-class revolution, faces Janus-like in the direction Stalin later took. Although Lenin had treated the Russian Revolution as the pivot in the coming world struggle, the concept of actually building 'socialism in one country' was, in fact, Stalin's major break with the man he claimed as mentor. The senior leader believed to his death that the building of socialism in the Soviet Union depended on the success of revolutions at the capitalist centre and the aid which new socialist regimes there would give, and in *The Foundations of Leninism* his successor had repeated this. After Stalin's reversal of views, he of course defended the new idea in *Problems of Leninism*.

Building socialism in a Soviet Union surrounded by hostile capitalist regimes – and this was undoubtedly the situation faced by any leadership in Moscow after November 1917 – made defence of the revolutionary gains seem a priority. (Indeed, whatever the horrors of Stalinism's actual working-out in the Soviet Union, we cannot even now simply reject the possible validity of this position.) We have seen that the consequent gut-reaction of Lenin and the others was to reassert Russian control over non-Russian peoples. The extension of this was that, increasingly, the question of international revolution, of spreading it beyond the confines of the Soviet Union, became embroiled with, and subordinated to, the demands of Soviet foreign policy. That in its turn reflected the exigencies of fostering and protecting domestic changes, the 'building of socialism' in the way chosen by Stalin.

'Socialism in one country' was in fact a profound realignment of the national and international revolutionary spheres, since it postulated that the construction of a mighty, advanced socialist Soviet Union was not in fact dependent on rapid advances of the struggle elsewhere and necessarily delayed until they occurred. Rather, after 1925 the existence of such a socialist heartland was taken as a *precondition* for international advance. The concept of international revolution was thus in effect turned inside out. The postulate became that what was bad for the Soviet Union was bad for the world communist movement, and so to understand the latter we must come to grips with what happened in the former.

Moreover, first in the Soviet Union and then generally, the leadership's perceived need to 'read' all phenomena in terms of defending the Soviet base reinforced and consolidated characteristics of Marxist doctrine which had been shaping since the beginning of the century and were in fact an implicit possibility from the first formulation in the 1840s.[1] They appeared already in Soviet Russia in Lenin's lifetime. Marxism's dark side in practice proved to be its potential for authoritarianism and divorce from any basic democracy and respect for human rights, which became focused above all through the concept of the vanguard party and the fateful process, associated above all with Stalin, of substitution of party for working class and of party leaders for the organization as such. Coupled with this was the idea of a complete subordination of the state to the party.

The point is that these principles were imbued into the whole world communist movement, beginning with the 'thesis on the Bolshevization of Communist Parties' promulgated by the ECCI in May 1925.[2] The overall result, in the words of Claudin, was the 'transformation of the Communist International into an alienated and alienating institution, at the service of the new [Soviet] ruling class' (Claudin 1975, p. 641).

Clearly, therefore, the shift in attitudes towards Soviet development was in fact the macro-context for the thinking of the Comintern after 1925, or at latest 1927, when Stalin broke his domestic opponents. In terms of that aspect, it should be clearly understood that the following argument will not locate itself directly in the debate which lay behind the creation of Stalinism. This is because our task is to situate that reformulation of Marxist theory in a particular historical epoch and to assess the problems which arose out of it, not to bog ourselves down in a debate which at the time gave, and still gives, an impression of 'endless and bizarre quibbling and hair-splitting'.[3] We must rather grasp from the beginning the concrete nature of Marxism-Leninism in the full dialectical sense.

This means, firstly, that we must keep in mind that it was forming in the concrete historical reality of the Soviet Union in the second half of the 1920s, and hence we have to see the first formulation of Leninism as an expression of internal Soviet politics, in fact as the consolidation of control by a new bureaucratic elite, of which Stalin's personal manoeuvrings were in fact the expression. In another dialectical aspect, we may see Leninism/Stalinism as the concentration of many determinations (isolation of the Soviet Union, shift of the revolutionary impetus to 'the East', internal Soviet developments, etc.) which was therefore a very complex unity of cause and effect, at once the result of all those determinations and a point of departure for further developments.

Obviously, we need also to approach the official doctrine dialectically in the full *critical* sense, since, as we shall see, it led to multiple confusions and errors of judgement. In taking such a stance, we shall necessarily move close to the position of the other major protagonist in the 'quibbling' debate, Stalin's mortal enemy Leon Trotsky, whose advocacy of 'permanent revolution' implied that extension of the revolution on a world scale was a prerequisite for the success of the socialist enterprise in the Soviet Union. From 1928–29 onwards, of course, Trotsky's ideas became a 'deviation' which was literally mortal for many, including Trotsky himself in his Mexican exile. This does not mean that his conceptualization of permanent revolution or any other of his formulations will be immune from criticism.[4] The point is rather that, irrespective of their ultimate validity, we may understand the Stalin–Trotsky debate as one over rival core ideas for the new discourse.

Stalin basically attempted to handle the problem of the shift of major struggles to the periphery by reformulating the position pioneered by Lenin in the Russian context, postulating revolution in underdeveloped formations penetrated by capital as marked by stages, which would have different class goals and in each of which the main actors would be different class blocs, in the terms of this study a shifting constitution of subjects. Evidently the role of the party as the agent of revolutionary discourse would be determined by such constitutions, but with a view always to securing its leadership.

In December 1924, almost a year after Lenin's death and as the jockeying for political dominance began, Stalin made two key moves. In a series of articles he attacked Trotsky's 1906 concept of the permanent revolution, formulated in effect in debate with Lenin over the failed uprising in Russia, and at the same time declared that the necessary preconditions existed in the Soviet Union for 'the organizing of a socialist economy'.[5] The ensuing theoretical debate led already in March–April 1925, when the 5th enlarged plenum of the ECCI was held, to condemnation of the international dissemination of Trotsky's ideas (Sobolev *et al.* 1971, p. 228). This was consolidated after Trotsky had lost the political battle and been forced into exile abroad in February 1929, and was given its arcane form and content by the desire of both sides to legitimize themselves as agents of a discourse by constant citation of, and hair-splitting over, pronouncements by Lenin from 1905 onwards. Although we must avoid the same trap in evaluating the discourse, concrete history necessarily makes us locate that exercise in Trotsky's critique, because the latter was occasioned above all by the Comintern's failure in China, undoubtedly its most serious blow between 1920 and 1939, which we shall examine in the next chapter.[6] For Trotsky, the loser in the domestic political battle, completing a socialist revolution within national boundaries was 'unthinkable'; of necessity, the 'socialist revolution begins on the national arena, it unfolds on the international arena, and is completed in the world arena'. Therefore, 'the permanent character of the socialist revolution as such' meant that the seizure of power by the workers, whether in a developed or 'backward' country, must lead inevitably to international revolutionary wars and civil wars (Trotsky 1962, pp. 154–5). Once more, therefore, the issue of the relationship between nationalism and socialist revolution returns, and we shall also see this reflected in Stalin's key argument that a socialist Soviet Union would provide the indispensable base for such struggles.

Trotsky commented in 1928 that Stalin's position on world revolution was based on 'the two trinkets which constitute his entire theoretical baggage: "the law of uneven development" and the "non-skipping of stages"'. The latter was in fact the basis of Stalin's critique of his opponent's concept of 'permanent revolution'. The general secretary held that stages could not be jumped over, while Trotsky maintained that

> [i]t is nonsense to say that stages cannot in general be skipped. The living historical process always makes leaps over isolated 'stages' which derive from theoretical breakdown into its component parts of the process of development in its entirety, that is, taken in its fullest scope (ibid., pp. 116–17).

Stalin, on the other hand, went back to the original exchange between Lenin and Trotsky in 1906, to claim that the founder of Bolshevism had laid down once and for all the necessity of a sequence of set stages.

For Trotsky the second aspect of the 'permanentist' position related to the nature of the socialist revolution itself, which he saw as a transformation of social relations lasting for 'an indefinitely long time and in constant internal struggle'. This of course had a major bearing on Stalin's 'socialism in one country' doctrine, as had the third basic idea in the Trotskyist discourse, that

> [t]he maintenance of the proletarian revolution within a national framework can only be a provisional state of affairs, even though, as the

experience of the Soviet Union shows, one of long duration. In an isolated proletarian dictatorship, the internal and external contradictions grow inevitably along with the successes achieved. If it remains isolated, the proletarian state must finally fall victim to these contradictions (ibid., pp. 8 and 9).

Trotsky was undoubtedly correct when he noted that the 'epigones' (his rather recondite use of the term for Alexander the Great's successors for Lenin's) took different positions on all three counts. Stalin and his lieutenants, like Karl Radek, and temporary allies, like Nikolai Bukharin, both of whom he would later bring to their deaths through the labour camp or the firing squad, separated the democratic and socialist revolutions into distinct stages, leaving the role of the working class in the former tactically open. They played down, or at least truncated, the period of social struggle which would constitute the socialist revolution.[7] They in effect separated the national construction of socialism, at least in the Soviet Union, from the international revolution.

Let us first examine the concept of permanent revolution, which was in effect the basis of the core idea of 'world revolution'. This was essentially determined by the broader concept of 'combined and uneven development'. Trotsky's formulation of this is of great importance as an attempt to sum up the impact of expanding capital on the world outside Western Europe.[8] Since that process began, he argued, we should no longer think of history as moving in cycles, since capitalism 'prepares and in a certain sense realises the universality and permanence of man's development', and under its hegemony '[a] backward country assimilates the material and intellectual conquests of the advanced countries' without having to reproduce their experience. Trotsky further advanced the very interesting, and key, idea of the 'privilege of historic backwardness', which 'permits, or rather compels, the adoption of whatever is ready in advance of any specified date, skipping a whole series of intermediate stages'.[9]

Unevenness, 'the most general law of the historic process', is thus revealed 'most sharply and complexly in the destiny of the backward countries', which are 'compelled to make leaps' through 'the whip of external necessity'. Their ability to do so is 'by no means absolute', but dependent in the long term on the specific 'economic and cultural capacities of the country', which often 'debases' what it borrows because of 'its own more primitive culture'. There is a dangerous Enlightenment ethnocentricity here, which we may counter by discounting the language of 'advanced', 'backward' and 'primitive', which is not essential to the approach if we see the relationship in terms of the technological and organizational bases of capital's power and the resources necessary to counter it. Much more important for our immediate and long-term discussion is the idea that 'backward' countries are subject to 'the law of combined development', which implies 'a drawing together of the different stages of the journey, a combining of separate steps, an amalgam of archaic with more contemporary forms'.

In terms of the immediate issue, of revolution on the periphery, and at risk of putting it too simply, it might be said that Stalin tended to use the 'uneven and combined' view of the capitalist world system as a justification for his line of first building socialism in the Soviet Union, as a base for world revolution, by emphasising the unevenness. Trotsky, on the other hand, saw the combination aspect as determinant. Thus, the former could argue that, as an uneven structure, the world economy left a space open for the Soviet Union to develop a socialist system in isolation, just as in 1917 it had displayed a weak link in Russia and opened a way to the Bolshevik Revolution.

Further, if we move on now to the issue of stages, Stalin was arguing that, in spreading the revolution, the uneven development of different countries meant that the colonies and semi-colonies could not be ready for an immediate socialist revolution, requiring that 'stages' approach to make allowance for their varying levels of development. This proposition was less flexible than it seems, since it also postulated that the revolution would follow basically the same set of stages in each country. This was central to Stalin's – and hence the Comintern's – reading of the revolutionary struggle and in fact followed from the idea, laid down by Marx and Engels, that history unfolded through a sequence of such stages, which Stalin adopted and made a dogma.

Following the founders, but above all Lenin's analysis of Russia in 1905, Stalin's concept of necessary revolutionary stages mechanically transposed the supposed economic tasks of each historical stage to a stage of the revolution. The 'national democratic' revolutionary stage was therefore equated with capitalist struggle against 'feudalism', or at least 'feudal remnants', and the 'socialist' (of course) with workers' struggle against capitalism. After a successful revolution, completion of each stage's economic tasks was held to be necessary for the success of the next stage's.

This would be the role of the 'dictatorship of the proletariat' in the socialist one, another central element in 'socialism in one country'. Outside the Soviet Union, the key proposition was that one revolutionary class's tasks – specifically, the bourgeoisie's – could be carried out by the proletariat, in alliance with the peasants, prior to the actual socialist stage. This view in effect went back to the RSDLP congress in 1903 and Lenin had coined the formula of a 'democratic dictatorship of the proletariat and peasantry' in 1905 to characterize the politics of such a stage. In June 1923 the 3rd plenum of the ECCI introduced, apparently quite casually, the counterpart concept of a 'workers' and peasants' government' as the political form for this execution of the bourgeoisie's class tasks in the 'colonies and semi-colonies' (Degras (ed.) 1960, p. 27). Such reasoning incorporated the class struggle into an abstract and deterministic paradigm of necessary economic and political development which, through the idea of substitutability of classes, in effect obscured the nature of that struggle.

Stalin's opponent did not distinguish formations in terms of historical/revolutionary stage reached, but held rather that 'national peculiarity is nothing else but the most general product of the unevenness of historical development, its summary result'. This in turn meant that 'the law of uneven development... does not replace, nor does it abolish the laws of world economy; on the contrary, it is subordinated to them'. This global determination meant that 'theoretically "inevitable" stages can be compressed to zero by the dynamics of development, especially during revolutions, which have not for nothing been called the locomotives of history' (Trotsky 1962, pp. 24, 25 and 117).

In taking this 'permanentist' view, Trotsky was concerned not to give his rival the possibility of dragging up his own pre-revolutionary criticism of Lenin. He stated that the original heart of the problem of strategy was the fact that, even though both Bolsheviks and Mensheviks agreed in 1905 on 'the bourgeois character of the revolution', this did not 'answer in advance the question of which classes would solve the tasks of the democratic revolution and what the mutual relationships of these classes would be'. Trotsky maintained that Lenin's 'democratic dictatorship' formula had 'an intentionally algebraic character', and did not determine in advance the actual political relationship of the two class allies, in particular whether the peasants would be 'represented' by their own party. Trotsky reaffirmed his own position, that the dictatorship would be of the proletariat with the support of the peasants and would pass directly to the socialist revolution; '[t]hus there is established between the democratic revolution and the socialist reconstruction of society a permanent state of revolutionary development' (ibid., pp. 3, 4 and 8).

In his debate with Stalin, Trotsky could regard himself as closer to the later Lenin. We noted in Chapter 2 how, in his late 1918 polemic against Kautsky, Lenin distinguished between the first, 'bourgeois-democratic' revolution and the second, socialist one, and attacked any attempt to build 'an artificial Chinese Wall' between them. On the other hand, as we shall see in examining our cases, Trotsky's formulations were also too overriding and did not leave enough room for the great variations among formations within the peripheral totality. Both Stalin and Trotsky, therefore, shared a methodological tendency to subsume all realities within an overriding formula, creating a general leaning towards idealism which we shall take up later. The former, however, was above all subordinating the whole to its Soviet part as a reflex of his political drive to power in the one socialist country, itself the expression of the emergence of a new ruling elite. Here the key point for 'world revolution' is that, although Stalin emphasized unevenness as a characteristic of peripheral formations, he did not permit a view of 'specific features' to suggest that local communist parties could follow their own distinct paths; each must follow the general line laid down in Moscow. The set of theses adopted by the ECCI in April 1925 on the 'Bolshevization' of Comintern member parties had already established this. Trotsky contrasted such 'Messianic nationalism', which permitted immediate socialism for the Soviet Union, with the 'bureaucratically abstract internationalism' which prescribed a uniform pattern everywhere else (Trotsky 1962, p. 25).

In the context of China Trotsky in fact accused his opponent of the opposite flaw, in effect pragmatically creating revolutionary 'stages' to try to explain away reverses in the mass struggle as gainings of experience.

[E]very institution set up by the propertied and ruling classes, which is an obstacle to the revolutionary mass movement, becomes according to this theory, a great historic stage to which our policy must be adjusted until such time as the 'masses themselves' will overthrow that obstacle.[10]

I shall later discuss the combination of dogmatism and pragmatism as a general problem in Comintern thinking.

Here we should rather pick up another aspect of the dogmatism of the Comintern leadership as Stalin increasingly came to dominate it, an economistic reliance on the inevitability of capitalist crisis. As Poulantzas pointed out, 'the development of the contradiction peculiar to the capitalist mode of production, a contradiction which is *reproduced* at the same time as the conditions of capitalist production itself' is a tendency not a law.[11] This enables us to put class struggle into a much more prominent and necessary position as something which pushes the tendency forward. The opposite thinking, expressed in economism, made class struggle, which we may see as central to the revolutionary war of position, merely a reflex of capital's fortunes – economic crisis equals a phase of proletarian offensive, 'economic stablisation' equals a 'proletarian defensive' phase.[12]

The idea of a 'weak link' in global capitalism, which Stalin derived from Lenin's analysis of imperialism, in fact brings us close to excluding class struggle and politics altogether, since it shifts the argument to the macro-level and posits that the specific location of the given formation in the global economic structure determines its propensity to revolution. Political factors, what this study terms the constitution of revolutionary subjects through discourse and resultant struggle, now become very much secondary. This is especially so given that the weak link idea ties in directly with Poulantzas's main concern, economic 'catastrophism', which he rightly considers to have characterized Comintern thinking, by postulating economic crisis as appearing first at international capital's conjuncturally weakest point.

The analytical effect of these theoretical weaknesses, an economistic reading of universal stages, 'weak links' and crisis, was to make it difficult to come to grips with the class content of struggle in different conjunctions. Tied to the shift in our discourse's core idea from 'world revolution' to 'socialism in one country', they hampered developing strategies for its interpellation. The resulting actual politics of Leninism/Stalinism and testing of its theoretical content were to find their most important location in the attempt in the late 1920s and early 1930s to build a revolutionary terrain in China. In addition, examining the cases of India and Brazil will bring out further aspects of the attempt to apply the new doctrine of revolution in a variety of peripheral formations. That variety was in the first place an expression of the macro-issues of uneven and combined development which we have so far examined. The main purpose of the case studies, however, will be to take us to where it is clear we must go, namely the class, and other, struggles in which the basic historical movements and structural features found their actual expression.

In line with this move from the more theoretical to the more concrete, we need to examine two conjunctures in which the Comintern's application of strategic principles based on theory underwent basic shifts. These were its Sixth Congress, held in July–September 1928, and its Seventh, in July–August 1935. Although it is not the intention of this study to review Comintern history as a whole, if we are to establish the historicity of Marxism-Leninism those two events constituted key shifts in strategy, without which, as we shall see, the case studies and the general validity of basic theory cannot be understood.[13]

## CHANGING THE LINE

July–September 1928 was an important conjuncture in the development of Marxism-Leninism as a theory of world revolution, with a new effort being made to situate the struggle in a macro-context. With Trotsky having lost the domestic contest over power to Stalin (he was now in internal exile), the Comintern held its Sixth Congress.[14] From the perspective of theory, this can be seen as understandably reasserting Stalin's view of combined and uneven development, stressing the latter feature.

Unevenness of economic and political development is an absolute law of capitalism, and is even more marked in the imperialist epoch. Hence the international proletarian revolution cannot be conceived as a single act taking place everywhere simultaneously.

Given this plurality of struggle, and since '[i]n order that revolutionary work and activities may be coordinated and given appropriate guidance, the international proletariat requires international class discipline', it followed that this 'must be expressed in the subordination of local and particular interests to the common and enduring interests of the movement' (Degras (ed.) 1960, pp. 491 and 525).

Of course, it was the Comintern's ECCI, dominated now by Stalin's man, Dmitrii Manuilskii, which would provide the common perspective. This was not a new idea, but it now became linked to Stalin's introduction of the doctrine of 'socialism in one country', with the global scene held to be marked by 'a new basic contradiction' between the Soviet Union and the capitalist centre. The former had become 'the base of the international movement of all oppressed classes, the centre of the international revolution, the most significant factor in world history' and hence 'a driving force of the international proletarian revolutionary' (ibid., pp. 486 and 511–12). Of course, this claim to authority was also not new, but the limiting of socialist construction to the Soviet Union meant that, now more than ever, Moscow's word was law and its interests supreme.

The word which went forth in mid-1928 was a return to a 'catastrophist' formulation, that '[t]he capitalist system as a whole is approaching its final collapse', demanding a more militant posture (ibid., p. 481). This was a reversal of the line taken since mid-1921, that a gradualist approach to building up revolutionary potential should be adopted by member parties of the Comintern, which raises the issue of why such a radical shift took place in mid-1928.

That is in fact a complex issue, which has occasioned speculation by historians. Borkenau linked the change to the fear of attack by the imperialist powers after the British government broke off diplomatic relations in June 1927 using Chinese events as a pretext, the launching of the First Five-Year Plan in 1928, and the 'Wall Street Crash' in October 1929, followed by general capitalist economic depression (Borkenau 1962, pp. 336-7). One thing is clear, that although the Comintern chiefs assumed a rapid approach of general capitalist crisis, such had not yet actually begun when the Sixth Congress was held; the 'Crash' occurred a year after it. Nor are we dealing with an impressive prescience on the part of Comintern economic theorists, but rather with use of a central Marxist assumption to justify a change in line.

Nevertheless, a number of factors did come together in the period 1927-28. On one level, Borkenau's predicate of a 'change of tactics' to a more militant line as being 'the same as that of every previous turn to the left' and arising from the dynamics of the policy of 'united front' alliances with non-communists has validity.[15] Domestic Soviet political developments also played a part in the Comintern shift of line. We have to remember that the general secretary broke the Trotskyist opposition and that centred round Kamenev and Zinoviev in December 1927, after Trotsky, Zinoviev and other opposition leaders had taken advantage of the ECCI Presidium meeting in May 1927 to try to mobilize foreign comrades against Stalin, citing the failure in China (to which we shall come) as a major point of criticism. Borkenau cited the rivalry between Stalin and Bukharin, who headed the Comintern apparatus, as one reason for the Comintern's shift, and Stalin used the Sixth Congress as an opportunity to campaign against Bukharin and his foreign supporters in what became known as the 'congress in the corridors' (Reiman 1987, pp. 20-1 and 91-2).

Nevertheless, despite the dialectical interplay of internal Communist Party politics with broad issues of global strategy, I am inclined to follow Sobolev and his fellow authors in giving particular weight to the global factor of Stalin's fear of attack by Britain and perhaps other capitalist powers, which ties in with his overriding concern with building a socialist base in the Soviet Union. Significantly, already in June 1927 the ECCI 8th plenum had spoken of the recent disaster suffered by the Chinese Communist Party as 'the war which has already begun in China' and linked it to 'the war which is being prepared against the Soviet Union' (quoted, Sobolev et al. 1971, p. 264).

This has to be seen in the context of the economic crisis which had begun to effect an over-stretched regime and which was to lead to the shift between late 1928 and mid-1929 to the basic Stalinist strategy of building socialism in one country through crash industrialization and forced collectivization of the peasants. Up to early 1928, it had been believed that, despite the formal commitment to self-sufficiency, deals could be made with foreign capitalists and their governments to secure resources; in 1926, for example, a 300 million mark credit was obtained from Germany. In December 1927 Stalin himself argued that 'our financial and economic situation is extremely serious' and that it was in line with the policies laid down by Lenin to 'create some breathing space, that is, concede to the wishes of foreign capital to some extent'. The Soviet government hoped to be represented at the conference to be held in Paris in August 1928, at which the US sponsors hoped to secure a treaty renouncing the use of force in international relations.[16]

In February 1928 a secret circular to Soviet diplomats spoke of a sharp deterioration in the economic situation and serious shortfalls in food collection and therefore supplies to urban areas; 'the situation is now more serious than it has been for a long time', it said. In this situation, 'the workers' and peasants' government places a very high value on reaching agreement with the capitalist groups' and it was necessary to 'set aside all dogmatic considerations at the moment'.

The Sixth Comintern Congress was held a few months later and, as we have seen, took a 'catastrophist' view of global capitalist fortunes. Although the Soviet government ratified the non-aggression pact in September, in can be no coincidence that the prolonged Congress discussions took place precisely during the period when, in the words of a quite recent study, Stalin and his lieutenants decided on a policy of 'financial self-defense' and defiance of foreign powers (Reiman 1987, *passim*). Given that draft Congress statements would have had to be prepared well in advance, the policy lines guided through by Stalin's supporters on the ECCI in effect represented contingency planning if foreign relations did not improve. Apart from the 'theoretical' content added by predictions of forthcoming capitalist crisis, therefore, the swing to militant action envisaged for Comintern member parties was more conjunctural and expedient than principled.

In its theses on the world revolution which was now to be more actively encouraged, the Sixth Congress distinguished three situations: in 'highly developed capitalist countries'; in those at a 'medium level of capitalist development' (examples were Spain, Portugal and Poland); and in 'colonial and semi-colonial countries' (India, China) coupled with 'independent countries' like Argentina and Brazil. This gives some theoretical problems, firstly by grouping politically sovereign countries like China and Brazil with colonial possessions like India, and, secondly and more basically, raising the general issue of whether, say, Argentina was any less 'semi-colonial' (i.e. basically under the control of foreign capital) than China.

In any case, it is this 'less developed' general category of Comintern analysis which concerns us, and here it is very relevant to the postulate of a shift of Marxism to another revolutionary world that delegates at the Congress in fact complained of 'criminal neglect' of these formations on the capitalist periphery, and the special theses for them noted that 'too little has been done in this connexion'. Communist parties, where they existed, were described as having leaders but no followers, being ideologically weak, and having no trade union cells (Degras (ed.) 1960, pp. 526 and 543).

To characterize these formations generally, the formula was used that '[i]n the transition period colonies and semi-colonies are also important because they represent the village on a world scale *vis-à-vis* the industrial countries, which represent the town in the context of world economy'.[17] This formulation, metaphorical rather than analytical in nature, was clearly not intended to give world revolutionary initiative to the colonial and semi-colonial formations. Moreover, it above all seems to set the struggle in a 'national' context, and therefore perpetuates the problem of relating national struggle to class struggle and determining priorities.

The peripheral formations were in fact seen as divided into two. In some, 'feudal' relations or the 'Asiatic mode of production' (later to be deleted by Stalin from the Marxist-Leninist lexicon) prevailed, along with control by foreign capital of the main productive units, trade, banking and transport. There 'an entire period of the transformation of the bourgeois-democratic into the socialist revolution' through 'a series of preparatory stages' would be needed. In this period the role of the 'national bourgeoisie' was downplayed, since its most militant part was only 'vacillating and inclined to compromise'. The other part was the 'compradore bourgeoisie', especially the merchants, who were most directly attached to imperialism. We shall see the significance of this division in the case of India, to which, along with China and Egypt, this discussion of the national bourgeoisie was especially directed.[18]

In 'still more backward countries (for example in parts of Africa)', which were basically 'tribal', a national bourgeoisie was said to be absent. There imperialism 'appears primarily as armed conquest and seizure of land', so that 'the struggle for national liberation is the central task'. In an audacious postulation, the 1928 theses proposed that even these, like the more advanced class cases, could move to socialism while bypassing capitalism if adequate help came from countries which already had a 'proletarian dictatorship'.

As for the subordinate classes, the peasant struggle was now emphasized. Specifically the bourgeoisies of India, China and Egypt were said to fear 'even the open formulation of the agrarian question', lest it stimulate peasant revolution. Given that the peasantry was by far the largest part of the population, it was noted that 'the proletariat can only lead the bourgeois-democratic revolution to victory in union with the peasantry' who, conversely, could only be liberated under proletarian leadership. However, in a situation of increasing internal differentiation of the peasantry, some of them would pass over to 'the camp of counter-revolution'. Moreover, workers were mostly of rural origins and first generation migrants, and likely to bring with them 'the narrow craft sentiments and ideology through which national-reformist influence can penetrate the colonial labour movement'.

All this put special weight on the 'petty bourgeoisie', by which was primarily meant the 'new' Western-educated middle-strata element, often in the early stages 'spokesmen of the national struggle' and tending to gravitate towards the labour movement and frequently assuming a socialist or even communist ideological tint. Although they still played a 'revolutionary role' in India and Egypt, their tendency was to carry with them 'hesitating and irresolute' ideology. 'Only a few of them in the course of the struggle are able to break with their own class and rise to an understanding of the tasks of the class struggle of the proletariat.'

Given this view of the drawbacks of all the subordinate classes in mid-1928, it is clear why the overall strategy would be seen as using the 'revolutionary movement of the workers and peasants' to push forward the tasks of the bourgeois-democratic revolution and then those of the socialist revolution, which in any case would have to carry out some of the former's tasks. In this variant of 'permanent revolution', which Stalin now endorsed (it was in any case Lenin's), the communist parties would carry out this strategy in a sense cut loose from these defective classes. Political autonomy was strongly enjoined on them; 'temporary' cooperation or even alliances were permissible, but only with a 'genuine revolutionary movement' of the petty bourgeoisie (not, be it noted, of the bourgeoisie), and then great care had to be taken to avoid this 'degenerating into a fusion'. Anticipating my next chapter, it may be said that Chinese experience had struck home and was extending its negative influence even to cooperation with 'Jacobin' national democracy.

It has seemed worthwhile to examine the class analysis of the Sixth Comintern Congress in some detail because it was the most thorough attempted and based on a quite considerable accumulated experience (of failure). Moreover, in the sense that it emphasized building one's own class base and avoiding compromise it made sense, compared to a too tight hitching of the revolutionary star to a supposed 'national-revolutionary' bourgeoisie, or even petty bourgeoisie, as in 1920 and thereafter. Communist parties' organizational autonomy was also in principle desirable; the problem was that the whole issue carried with it the historical contradiction of substituting party for class as in effect the 'true' revolutionary subject.

As Borkenau first pointed out in 1938, the shift after mid-1928 to a more militant international line took some time, and we may date the general shift to the militant 'Third Period' (which lasted until 1935) as following the 10th ECCI plenum in June 1929. As Claudin has pointed out, this macro-level prediction of capitalist collapse appeared to be coming true in the next few years, but only in the sense of something 'so many times announced and so long awaited' (Borkenau 1962, p. 339; Claudin 1975, p. 608).

Moreover, it only *appeared* to be an accurate prognosis; fascism (Italy and Germany), military authoritarianism (Japan), the New Deal (the USA) and muddling through (Britain and France) saved capital, and the Great Depression's ultimate lack of finality has reverberated down to the present time with its new expansion of global capitalism.[19] In the meantime, however, the 'catastrophist' prediction confirmed the pressure from Moscow to attack capitalism more intensely and seek allies more circumspectly.

Even then, the commitment to unqualified militancy lasted less than two years. At its 11th plenum in March–April 1931 the ECCI condemned the view of the present capitalist crisis as inevitably its final one and 'exaggerated appraisals' of workers' militancy. The 'slogan of the dictatorship of the proletariat' was 'the ultimate aim of the workers' struggle' but 'did not meet the very complex and contradictory situation' at that time. This comment was made in the context of the struggle against fascism in Europe, and the shift away from a hard revolutionary line over the next few years in fact derives from the ultimate priority which the Soviet leadership still assigned to the centre in the global struggle. The 12th ECCI plenum in August–September 1932 linked 'the armed struggle for the partition of China' (the Japanese had occupied Manchuria in September 1931) with 'intervention against the U.S.S.R.', but in effect Stalin's concern to defend the Soviet Union acted as a counter-force to the making of a major revolutionary investment in the periphery (Sobolev *et al.* 1971, pp. 309–10 and 327).

The new period and problems were actually inaugurated by the coming to power of the Nazi Party in Germany in January 1933, which signalled not only the complete failure of Comintern policy there but a new threat of a Germany which would rearm and enter into an expansionist foreign policy. ECCI overtures to the rival social democratic Socialist International in March 1933 for joint anti-fascist action, despite current denunciation of these rivals on the left as historically playing a pro-fascist role (which earned rejection of the approach), and instructions to the French communists to form a broad anti-fascist front in June 1934 again signified Soviet true concerns.[20]

Beginning in that month, meetings of various committees preparing the agenda of the Seventh Comintern Congress, scheduled for late in the year, were held in Moscow. These were marked by such statements as the Bulgarian Georgii Dimitrov's endorsement of united fronts against fascism, and not necessarily under communist leadership, and the Finn Otto Kuusinen's criticism of those who overrated the possibility of capitalist collapse (Sobolev *et al.* 1971, pp. 357–9). These comments met with resistance, among others from the chief Chinese delegate, Wang Ming, who we shall meet again, and in September the ECCI praesidium decided to postpone the Congress. Disputes in member parties concerning appropriate tactics in the new era, along with Stalin's indecision concerning on whose side to come down, in fact caused the Seventh Congress to be delayed until mid-1935, and there is even evidence that the possibility of dissolving the Comintern altogether was mooted (Claudin 1975, pp. 123–4).

When it did meet, in July 1935, Dimitrov in his keynote speech maintained the emphasis on fascism as the main enemy, portraying it as the most reactionary form of finance capital, which 'has undertaken to bury Marxism', but was in fact creating its own gravediggers 'as a result of the dialectics of life and the class struggle' (Dimitrov 1935(b), p. 23). The defeat of capital as a whole was in this way effectively subsumed into the struggle against fascism and the key international struggle became the 'fight for peace and for the defence of the USSR'. The Italian communist Palmiro Togliatti, reporting on the dangers of world war, noted that 'certain comrades' doubted whether it was correct for the Soviet Union to make such defensive alliances with capitalist countries, as it had in May 1934 with France. In a remarkable subordination of world revolution to Soviet foreign policy, he claimed that this was desirable because relations with what was after all a major colonial and imperial power would 'enhance the prestige' of the Soviet Union internationally (Claudin 1975, pp. 184–5 and 186–7).

The Dutch delegation, coming from another colonial power, was assured, when it pursued the matter, that if Germany attacked their country they could fight a war of national defence, even though the Netherlands was a colonial power, provided it did not mean abandoning the class struggle (ibid., pp. 188–9). This gives us a clue to the main line now taken, namely in effect – although not in words – to subordinate revolution through class struggle to a national struggle of all classes against foreign aggression. The Comintern theorists thus recognized what we have seen as the problem of the 'polyvalent' subject, but in a particular conjunctural form which subordinated the revolutionary meaning. Dimitrov also attempted to state the problem within an orthodox class framework, when he said that although 'Communists are the irreconcilable opponents on principle of bourgeois nationalism in all forms', anyone who sneered at 'all the national sentiments of the broad toiling masses is far from genuine Bolshevism' (Dimitrov 1935(b), p. 66).

> The interests of the class struggle of the proletariat against its native exploiters and oppressors are in no contradiction whatever to the interests of a free and happy future of the nation. On the contrary, the Socialist revolution will signify the *saving of the nation* and will open up to it the road to loftier heights (Dimitrov 1935(a), p. 80, original emphasis).

In a follow-up to his 1935 report Dimitrov raised the question of the attitude which should be taken towards the foreign policy of governments and the 'defence of the country'; the 'monopoly of the bourgeoisie' in this sphere, he said, 'must be demolished once and for all'. However, clearly this was to be achieved through alliances not overthrow. Moreover, it was 'completely wrong to depict *all* countries as aggressors at present', and quite clearly France and other colonial powers were included within this category (quoted, Dornhorst 1977, pp. 17 and 18, original emphasis).

In general, therefore, the Seventh Congress and its follow-up had much more meaning for the countries of the centre than for the 'colonies', 'semi-colonies' and 'dependent' countries, where the fascist threat was rather remote (except for Ethiopia, invaded by Italy in October 1935). For communists in the periphery a resolution of the Congress did prescribe a significant variation, the formation of 'an anti-imperialist people's front', drawing in 'the widest masses' and working with not only 'national-revolutionary' but even 'national reformist' organizations, provided this meant 'a definite anti-imperialist platform' (Degras (ed.) 1965, p. 367). In the latter category of temporary allies we may clearly see a reflection of the broad popular front policy adopted in the developed countries.

It is hopefully clear that the shifts associated with the Sixth and Seventh Comintern Congresses link us in strategical terms with the broad issue of the 'permanent' nature of world revolution, which we saw to be raised in the debate on uneven and combined development. Dimitrov clearly stressed the unevenness, for example, when he declared that

> [n]*ational* forms of the proletarian class struggle and of the labour movement in the individual countries are in no contradiction to proletarian internationalism; on the contrary, it is precisely in these forms that the *international* interests of the proletariat can be successfully defended (Dimitrov 1935(a), p. 80, original emphasis).

Comintern shifts in 1928 and 1935 also link the theoretical issue of revolutionary stages to the concrete strategies to be adopted in any given country. That has necessarily brought us to the question of the revolutionary significance of various class elements, and so back to propositions made in Chapter 1 on revolutions as necessarily involving formation of complex blocs of class and other social forces. Clearly, the closer we come to the concrete application of theory-translated-into-strategy the tighter grip we shall also need to take on the other proposed factors: rupture between dominant classes and subordinated classes and groups; ideologically and politically autonomous spaces created for the latter to occupy as their own revolutionary terrain; regime crisis; and a vanguard party able to organize and interpellate a discourse.

In order to take this grip while maintaining our own autonomous posture regarding the Leninism/Stalinism which this study seeks to evaluate, it is desirable to develop at least the outlines of an alternative (Marxist) approach. This may be done by bringing into the picture the most original Marxist theorist writing in the period of the Comintern's major activities, the Italian intellectual and activist Antonio Gramsci, who was imprisoned by Mussolini's Fascist government from 1926 to 1935 and died in April 1937 as a result of the collapse of his health in prison. Ironically, his incarceration (he was allowed to write, although not in overtly Marxist language) gave him the opportunity to pursue basic theoretical issues at a time when discussion in Comintern circles was falling away into dogma.[21] This situating of Gramsci's ideas makes them especially important if we wish to develop what seems to be the most appropriate approach to key cases, and one which will have to be developed in the future, namely a view which allows us to postulate varying revolutionary terrains, upon which intending revolutionaries have to move. This will permit emphasis upon the diversity of concrete cases, while trying to keep theoretical absolutes such as characterized theory in the earlier period to a minimum.

POSSIBLE ALTERNATIVES

Faced in his own country in the 1920s and 1930s, like Lenin earlier, by class and other conditions which did not match exactly with what Marx and Engels had postulated, Gramsci attempted a theorization which gives a basis for a more flexible explanation, although one which neither he nor any successor fully developed. In examining it critically, I ask readers to be patient in the face of more concentrated theory, because of its potential relevance for future movement-building.

Basically, Gramsci raised the issue of what we may see as an alternative to a fixed view of stages: the building in a given formation of a specific revolutionary terrain. He used the analogy of military operations and postulated two patterns of revolutionary struggle for state power to be fought across the given terrain, which he distinguished as the war of position and the war of manoeuvre. Moving beyond analogy, by 'terrain' this study's conceptualization means a configuration of social forces which can be used as a base for political and perhaps also military action to win state power. That terrain may occupy a distinct physical space within the social formation's boundaries. However, we may also speak of a space for action which is not actually physically demarcated but distinguished by the nature of its political and ideological contents, which express some actual or intended autonomy from the existing regime. Space of this non-physical kind must be created in the forms of autonomous organization for political activity, otherwise there could be no manoeuvring for power, and cognitive space, inside people's heads as it were, is certainly also involved. Clearly, this brings us into the sphere of 'discourse' and 'interpellation'.

True to his overall concern with 'superstructural' factors, Gramsci gave great weight to the '"voluntary" and organisational elements', criticizing Rosa Luxemburg, for example, for 'iron economic determinism' in her theorization of a seizure of power through the 'mass' general strike, inspired by the Russian failure in 1905–6. He also considered that her view overrated the quickness with which the struggle could be brought to a head, 'operating with lightning speed in time and space'. This was a key issue in developed capitalist systems, 'where "civil society" has become a very complex structure and one which is resistant to the catastrophic "incursions" of the immediate economic element (crises, depressions, etc.)'. These characteristics, Gramsci held, in fact implied a relatively protracted 'war of position', since even if 'the State trembled', behind it would be revealed 'a sturdy structure of civil society', 'a powerful system of fortresses and earthworks' which would also have to be taken (Gramsci 1971, pp. 233 and 235).

In contrast, in Russia in 1917 – and by inference generally in the 'East' – 'the State was everything, civil society was primordial and gelatinous'. As often with Gramsci (since he was writing under the eyes of his gaolers), we have some problems with use of language here, namely the adjectives applied to peripheral (in my language) society, but his conclusion is clear enough, namely that in the 'East' a relatively *rapid* 'war of manoeuvre' could capture the state apparatus and civil society with it.[22]

The Italian Marxist's conceptualization is valuable in part because he attempted to distinguish between basically different sorts of capitalist system which require quite different revolutionary struggles, and partly because he reminds us that some of the action-space filled by the regime ('civil society') lies outside that of the state itself and must also be conquered. Basically from the last point follows my own, that whereas Gramsci saw them as alternatives, in fact *any revolutionary movement whether at the centre or on the periphery has to – and will have to – fight both a war of position and a war of manoeuvre.* The former is a matter of creating a social terrain outside the state's immediate apparatus although within space which it formally physically controls, necessarily prior to launching the actual political/military manoeuvres which will take the revolutionaries to power because they need a firm footing for that action.

If we take the view that both (redefined) wars of position and wars of manoeuvre will be necessary, it is likely that the former will be protracted, whether at the centre or on the periphery, because of the intrinsic difficulties of constructing the necessary terrain and capturing or creating action space, among other things involving 'interpellation' – creating cognitive space for a revolutionary discourse and constituting its subjects. The war of manoeuvre, on the other hand, may be rapid, as in the November 1917 Russian case. On the other hand, in the Chinese case the war of manoeuvre proper lasted from July 1946 until October 1949, and in Viet Nam from mid-1959 (resumption of armed struggle in the South) until the 'Great Spring Victory' in April 1975; significantly, both the latter cases were full-scale military struggles. Given other post-Second World War cases, it may well be that we can postulate protracted wars of both position and manoeuvre in peripheral formations.

Clearly, in line with discussion in previous chapters and this one, a major part of the necessary war of position involves shifting class consciousness in the direction of creating revolutionary class subjects. Gramsci was orthodox enough to concern himself above all with workers, and, like Luxemburg, posited an initial state of 'contradictory consciousness' on their part. One moment of this, which we may identify with his 'common sense', is 'superficially explicit or verbal' and has been 'inherited from the past and uncritically absorbed'. The other 'is implicit in [the worker's] activity and ... in reality unites him with all his fellow-workers in the practical transformation of the real world'. Like all contradictions, this one is a unity which 'influences moral conduct and the direction of will' but as such also produces 'moral and political passivity'. That unity, according to Gramsci, can be broken by 'a struggle of political "hegemonies" and of opposing directions, first in the ethical field and then in that of politics proper'. Hegemony implies intellectual unity and 'a conception of reality that has gone beyond common sense'.[23]

The problem with Gramsci's conceptualization is that it is not clear whence the second, oppositional element of the contradiction derives. We may take it that exploitation and the other basic structures of class strike resonances in elements of the common sense, formal knowledge and culture which workers accumulate. A very clear problem then becomes the questions, where does the necessary 'conception of reality' come from and how is the process of acquiring class consciousness begun?

Gramsci thus opened the door again for the vanguard party to enter, linking the acquisition of a critical consciousness with a hegemony established by intellectuals as organizers, 'a group of people "specialised" in conceptual and philosophical elaboration of ideas' (Gramsci 1971, p. 334). He therefore takes the same view as Lenin on the importance of elements 'outside' the immediate 'economist' worker struggle, but goes even further in stressing the contribution by intellectuals. He verges on the undialectical view that movement comes, not from the opposition of the two united moments of a contradiction, but from a source outside it. The issue, therefore, becomes the source from which the intellectuals of the working class (or any other from which revolutionary subjects are to be drawn) are recruited.

In his key 1902 work on revolutionary organization, *What Is To Be Done?*, which became the classic text, Lenin in fact took two conflicting positions. On one side, recognizing internal class divisions, he maintained a position taken in 1899, that 'everywhere and at all times the leaders of a certain class have always been its advanced, most cultivated representatives'.

> The ignoring of the interests and requirements of this advanced section of the workers, and the desire to *descend* to the level of understanding of the lower strata (instead of constantly *raising* the level of the workers' class-consciousness) must, therefore, necessarily have a profoundly harmful effect and prepare the ground for the infiltration of all sorts of non-socialist and non-revolutionary ideas into the workers' midst (quoted, Landau 1977, p. 28, original emphasis).

On the other side, Lenin slipped in 1902 into the position that has become notorious, namely that revolutionary consciousness would have to be brought to workers from *outside* their class. We may see this in terms of ideas and of agents. Clearly, if the knowledge available to workers, peasants or whatever subordinated people is limited, one condition, in fact, of that subordination, then consciousness-raising could operate only with new inputs (and new interpretations of existing knowledge).

Gramsci postulated two kinds of intellectual in this context, an 'organic' version produced within a class and a 'traditional' one recruited from outside. In the case of the working class, the former would come from within the skilled stratum. As for 'traditional intellectuals', Gramsci's argument was that

> every 'essential' social group which emerges into history out of the preceding economic structure, and as an expression of a development of this structure, has found . . . categories of intellectuals already in existence and which seemed indeed to represent an historical

continuity uninterrupted even by the most complicated and radical changes in political and social forms (Gramsci 1971, pp. 6–7).

The important point here is that, as an '"essential" social group', workers (and we may add peasants) would thus be finding traditional intellectuals formed by definition outside their own class. Writing on Italian history, Gramsci noted that where 'the impetus of progress' was 'the reflection of international developments which transmit their ideological currents to the periphery', these being 'born on the basis of the productive development of the more advanced countries',

... then the group which is the bearer of the new ideas is not the economic group but the intellectual stratum, and the conception of the State advocated by them changes aspect; it is conceived of as something in itself, as a rational absolute (ibid., pp. 116–17).

Given that this was written in early 1935, it is difficult to resist taking the passage as a comment on Stalinism, which took the Soviet Union as the advanced centre. Even more important from our point of view, this conceptualization of ideas moving from a developed centre to an underdeveloped periphery enables us to stress the likelihood of leadership of class subjects in the 'East' by intellectual agents from outside the former's own ranks.[24]

Lenin clearly brought out the nature of organic intellectuals in a working-class context when, already in an article written in 1899, he noted that

[a]t a time when educated society is losing interest in honest, illegal literature, an impassioned desire for knowledge and for socialism is growing among the workers, real heroes are coming to the fore from amongst the workers, who, despite their wretched living conditions, despite the stultifying penal servitude of factory labour, possess so much character and will-power that they study, study, study, and turn themselves into conscious Social-Democrats – 'the working-class intelligentsia' (quoted, Landau 1977, p. 28).

Lenin clarified his own preference in 1902 as being for organic intellectuals, but his position, as Leon Trotsky among others noted, raised the danger that intellectual agents recruited from outside the working class because of their initial superior knowledge and interpellative skills would attempt to monopolize leadership and take the organization, as another 'rational absolute', in a direction ultimately inimical to liberation.

Gramsci, writing this time before the emergence of Stalin and in fact about pre-revolutionary situations, also noted that

[i]ndeed it happens that many intellectuals think that they *are* the State, a belief which, given the magnitude of the category, occasionally has important consequences and leads to unpleasant consequences for the fundamental economic group which *really* is the State (Gramsci 1971, p. 16, original emphasis).

It seems plausible to suggest that intellectuals coming from outside that 'group' would be most likely to make the identification with the state after leading its advanced elements in the war of manoeuvre to capture it.

Prior to that must come the war of position, a major part of which would be the shifting of consciousness within a new cognitive space by the intellectual agents. In a key piece on strategy and tactics, 'The Modern Prince', written in 1933–34, Gramsci discerned three 'moments of collective consciousness': the 'economic-corporate' based on occupation, but not yet on class; the consciousness of a solidarity of interest among all members of a class (which I would see as strictly speaking not possible); and 'that in which one becomes aware that one's own corporate interests, in their present and future development, transcend the corporate limits of the purely economic class, and can and must become the interests of other subordinate groups too'.[25]

Politics and power enter the picture already at the second level, since the state, Gramsci says, is an object of concern, and the class with conscious interests claims a right to participate in policy decisions. Beyond this, the third level 'is the most purely political phase', where 'ideologies become "party"' and the various forces contend until one, 'or at least a single combination of them', becomes dominant economically, politically, intellectually and morally. Clearly this is a reference in the workers' case to revolutionary consciousness, which poses the issues of struggle 'not on a corporate but on a "universal" plane' and thus creates its own hegemony over subordinate groups. Where class subjects from the working class and peasantry can establish hegemony over a (potentially) revolutionary bloc, this is a universalization which is essential to revolutionary action. On the part of dominant classes, hegemony implies use of the state for their own purposes, but portraying it as 'the motor force of a universal expansion'.[26]

The hegemony may also be over non-class social groups, given that unequal power may invoke, say, national identity. When looking at 'politico-military' factors, Gramsci in fact took the 'limiting case' of 'a nation seeking to attain its national independence', where the 'social disintegration of the oppressed people, and the passivity of the majority among them' requires political action with a military content (ibid., p. 183). We shall see that 'limiting cases' of combined class and national struggle were in fact to prove to be the norm even during Gramsci's lifetime.

Clearly, for revolutionary political and military action to be possible in a particular social formation at a particular conjuncture, openings in the distribution of power must exist, making it possible to create or take over a space for revolutionary action. In this respect, Gramsci was absolutely correct when, in the same key work, he criticized the tendency to cast analysis in terms of 'favourable, or unfavourable' relations of forces as taking key questions as if they were already answered, namely what are those forces and how did they come about? He distinguished three 'moments or levels' which have to be analysed.

First comes the concrete question of the development of productive forces and the place of each class in production, which he saw as being measurable 'with the systems of the exact or physical sciences'. From this reading, Gramsci felt, it is possible to see whether or not a particular society can be transformed and therefore judge the realism of current ideologies. Secondly, 'an evaluation of the degree of homogeneity, self-awareness, and organisation attained by the various classes' is needed. Gramsci saw this as proceeding through several levels 'corresponding to the various moments of political consciousness', and we have already noted his analysis of these. Thirdly, he said, our investigation would have to take into account 'the relation of military forces, which from time to time is directly decisive'. In fact, this question must be viewed in two ways, 'the strict or technical military sense' and the 'politico-military', in which basically political action necessarily has to have a military content (Gramsci 1971, pp. 180–3).

It may readily be agreed that measurement, evaluation and politico-military strategic judgement have to be carried out, but another factor has to enter the balance of forces. Above all, what is implied here in terms of revolutionary seizure of power is the existence of an organization which can do these things. This brings us back to a key part of our theorization already considered in the context of Lenin's, Luxemburg's and Lukács's views. I have distinguished class membership from becoming a class subject, which is essential if we are to avoid a mechanistic and teleological view of class and revolution, and we have seen that several levels of class consciousness are involved. The organizational factor also cannot just be subsumed into class, and certainly is not identical with the revolutionary subject. We come back again to the issue of the vanguard party.

Using the general theoretical postulates made on the basis of Gramsci

# Comintern and Other Perspectives 73

and in Chapter 1, it should be possible to analyse any case on its own merits and at the same time to have a basis for comparison, whether one is a would-be Marxist revolutionary or a student of history (hopefully both). In order to prepare ourselves both for the case studies which will explore the issue of revolution on the periphery in the next chapters, and for grasping how Marxist theory concerning revolution actually evolved, I (adapting Gramsci) have postulated necessary wars of position and manoeuvre. The former involves primarily the questions of fostering consciousness in class subjects and building a class bloc to support revolutionary action, the latter the questions of communist party alliances with other political forces and the carrying through of a 'permanent' revolution. Both involve the issue of appropriate organization.

When the party, as an organizer and 'bearer' of a discourse, takes its interpellated subjects into the field for manoeuvres, it enters into a series of movements. Both of our 'wars' are dynamic processes directed to a goal; that of manoeuvre, which brings us to the revolution proper, aims at the capture of state power. Of course, in our historical period no communist party came anywhere near such a success, and in the case studies I shall be using the above-outlined approach to try to show why not, and to evaluate the place of Leninist/Stalinist discourse in that failure. That exercise may now begin.

# 4 Semi-Colonial Complications

The Comintern leaders from 1919 faced the problems of finding revolutionary agents and subjects in a wide variety of concrete situations, which required building a communist party and therefore a practical testing of Marxism's privileging of the working class and a vanguard party.

The combined effects of capitalist penetration had reduced all peripheral formations to some degree of dependency by that time, but the uneven nature of the process, combined with regional and historical differences, meant great variations among them. It still does today, but in that epoch the most basic *political* difference was the distinction between actual colonial possessions and the 'semi-colonial' formations which were dominated by foreign capital but in which indigenous power blocs directly controlled the regime. Marx had already noted this phenomenon in the third volume of *Capital*, writing of the impact of British rule on the Indian peasantry that 'the English lost no time in exercising their direct political and economic power, as rulers and landlords, to disrupt these small economic communities'. Even then, he commented, 'this work of dissolution proceeds very gradually. And still more slowly in China, where it is not reinforced by direct political power' (Marx 1971, pp. 333–4). In dealing with China and Brazil in this chapter we shall examine contrasting cases of the latter situation, while in the next India will give us one of the most important colonial cases.

## THE CHINESE REVOLUTION: RELYING ON THE WORKERS OR THE PEASANTS?

The Chinese Communist Party (CCP) was formed in July 1921 by a small group of intellectuals, including a young teacher from Hunan province, Mao Tse-tung. Like many other young people, he had been caught up in the ferment of ideas following the 'May 4th' movement in 1919, which spread from demonstrations against Japanese imperialism to a general demand for modernization in face of foreign pressure. Anarchist and Marxist ideas were among those which caught attention; already in September 1918 the pioneers Li Ta-chao and Ch'en Tu-hsiu, inspired by the October Revolution, had set up the first Marxist study circle and the new upsurge led to the founding of socialist groups in various cities.[1] Nuclei of potential discourse agents had thus been created, but fighting the war of position was to prove complex and hard. Its key features were to prove to be an abortive attempt at alliance with an already-established party and a shift after that failure towards a peasant rather than a working-class base.

In the period now under review, China was in desperate need of good government and reform, if not yet ripe for revolution. That of October 1911, which ended the imperial regime in the name of a democratic republic, had led to a divided country. Sun Yat-sen, the Western-educated doctor who had been one of its leaders, had consolidated control in Canton and the south by 1917, but Peking and the rest of the country were in the hands of various warlords, with whom Sun's Kuomintang (National People's Party – KMT) had also to cooperate, even in provinces theoretically under its governance.[2] Grouped into shifting coalitions backed by different foreign powers, the warlords fought constantly among themselves. Between 1924 and 1930 an average of 14 provinces a year out of 18 were racked by local conflicts (Chesneaux 1973, p. 79).

The position of most peasants, already often precarious, now went into an unremitting decline in large areas.[3] Previously, except in times of crisis, the old imperial system had ensured some sort of class stand-off. Although sometimes corrupt, the bureaucrats had maintained some limits on landlord oppression in the name of Confucian concepts of duty and could be called to order themselves in its name. Realistically, with no strong military presence in most rural areas, there was often a sort of tacit agreement between peasants and landlords which kept a limit on exploitation and even meant remission of rents in bad times. In addition, a system of imperial grain stores meant some hope of relief in periods of famine. On the other side, local peasant rebellions were a historically established sanction which could sometimes widen enormously; the Taiping Rebellion (1851–64) was the biggest in world history.

However, during the heyday of the warlords, up to the late 1920s, 'the general balance of the countryside was upset'.

There was no court to rebuke or decapitate a greedy official: there was, instead, a horde of soldiers, vagabonds in uniform, without discipline or pay, who fattened on the land. They were allowed to pillage, to rob granaries, and slay without punishment. The landlords fled to the cities from these disorders. They left bailiffs behind to collect their rents. The bailiffs found that the only way to live, and to grow rich at the same time, was to go into partnership with the military. If both agreed to collect from some village, good times or bad, all opposition could be overcome. Those who resisted would be shot. The soldier with his rifle and machine gun could lord it over thousands of peasants (Fitzgerald 1964, pp. 51-2).

All this was made much worse by the warlords' increasing extraction of food and cash to consume themselves and pay their armies, the latter vital in the situation of constant war among themselves; taxes were extracted years in advance, with Szechuan by 1926 actually running 31 years ahead. The consequent increase of debt and loss of land brought the estimated number of those farming their own land down from half in 1918 to a quarter by 1927 (Ch'ên 1965, p. 105).

After 1911 the situation thus became one of nearly 40 years of decline for the peasants in many regions, increasingly making them open to interpellation of a revolutionary discourse. The situation for most workers was at best only marginally better. With a total population of around 380 000 000, the best scholarly estimate for the size of the working class is 1 489 000 in 1919, with 655 000 of them employed in foreign enterprises (Chesneaux 1968, Table 5, p. 42). Mao estimated the industrial working class to contain some 2 million members early in 1926, mostly in textiles, mining, transport and ship-building enterprises predominantly owned by foreigners, with alongside them an unspecified number of 'coolies' – rickshaw pullers, street cleaners, porters and such like (Mao 1963(b), p. 177). Especially among the latter, competition for jobs was swelled by desperate migrants from the rural areas, and slum life and all the results of exploitation were the general condition.

Particularly when combined with anti-foreigner sentiment, there could be considerable labour militancy. The May 4th movement evoked strikes in Shanghai and the south, and the wave continued into 1921. At this stage these stoppages were often spontaneous, and at the Comintern Fourth Congress in November–December 1922 Karl Radek, a Polish German who was now a leading Soviet polemicist, noted that 'comrades who are working in Canton and Shanghai have not had much success in establishing links with the masses of the workers. . . . Many of them shut themselves up in their chambers to study Marx and Lenin just as formerly one studied Confucius.' The real landmark was the

## Semi-Colonial Complications

epic strike and boycott of foreign goods in Canton and the nearby British colony of Hong Kong from June 1925 to October 1926. This brought many new members into the CCP, which was estimated to have grown from 1000 to 10 000 during the second half of 1925. The An-yüan coal miners in Hunan province were also notably militant. On the other hand, repeated attempts to mobilize peasants to support the strikers in 1925–26 failed, and the CCP had already sought a fateful broader alliance.[4]

The original position of the new CCP was that an attitude of 'independence, aggression, and exclusion' should be adopted towards other parties. However, no less a figure than Lenin had proclaimed in April 1920 when attacking 'infantile' leftism that 'to reject compromises "on principle," to reject the admissibility of compromises in general, no matter of what kind, is childishness, which it is difficult even to take seriously'. In August 1922, sponsored and prodded by the Comintern, which had been negotiating with Dr Sun since the previous December, the CCP leaders decided to direct party members to join the KMT. This move was ratified by the ECCI in January 1923 and the Third CCP Congress in June. In November the ECCI endorsed the KMT programme of 'nationalism, democracy and public welfare' with its own glosses, viewing the last, for example, as implying the nationalization of foreign enterprises and taking over landlords' holdings.[5]

Sun's organization was thus taken as China's 'revolutionary liberation' movement, which we may see as tending under him to a 'Jacobin' position, with a radical non-class programme (the three principles just noted). During 1922–23 the KMT and CCP moved together on the basis of joint individual memberships. Communist cadres among workers and peasants aligned their followers behind the nationalists; in July 1923 Mao was put in charge of coordinating this. In this way, the strategy of founding a workers' and peasants' party was sidelined and Soviet arms, money and advisers were given to the Canton government. In March 1924 Sun Yat-sen died and leadership of the KMT passed into the hands of the military commander Chiang Kai-shek. He had close contacts with capitalist circles through his wife and now the right wing of the KMT began to dominate over its radicals, but cooperation with the CCP went on; in August, for example, Mao became head of the KMT college for peasant cadres and later deputy head of that party's Propaganda Department.

In October 1925 the CCP Central Committee laid out lines for future work with the KMT which illuminate the ambiguities of the united front strategy. The general tactic was to support the KMT's left wing but oppose Chiang's right. In a rather vague formulation, communists were now told they must not 'completely become members' of the KMT, while new comrades should not join at all, except in the KMT headquarters, which is 'completely under our influence' (whatever that meant, given that Chiang controlled the armed forces). At the same time, the CCP's own local organization was to be expanded and the masses of workers and peasants won over; conversely, no help should be given to the KMT to expand into new areas (Wilbur and How 1989, p. 534).

Mao was not involved in this move. In January 1925 he had lost his place in the CCP Central Committee; he was ill, but probably more important was his firm alignment to the peasant movement when orthodoxy insisted on the pre-eminence of the proletariat.[6] He now turned to peasant organization in his home province of Hunan. At its Second Congress in July 1922 the CCP leadership had described the peasants as 'the most important part of our revolutionary movement', but took a more orthodox stance as Comintern influence increased (quoted, Schram 1963, p. 28). By July 1926 they were more carefully distinguishing between revolutionary stages, with peasants seen as 'the principal force in the national liberation movement' (Wilbur and How 1989, p. 745). The strategists in Moscow who advised them no doubt took their cue from Lenin, who, despite recognising the importance of the peasants to the revolution in Russia, had written early in April 1920 in the context of spreading it that small producers

> encircle the proletariat on every side with a petty-bourgeois atmosphere, which permeates and corrupts the proletariat and causes constant relapses among the proletariat into petty-bourgeois spinelessness, disunity, individualism, and alternate moods of exaltation and dejection. The strictest centralization and discipline are required within the political party of the proletariat in order to counteract this ...
> (Lenin 1953(f), p. 367).

The CCP policy towards peasant amelioration in mid-1926 was also notably moderate. In keeping with the 'national' stage of struggle, only 'very reactionary big landlords' were to be attacked, and rents up to half the crop and interest rates of up to 30 per cent accepted (Wilbur and How 1989, p. 745). Nevertheless, by June 1927 the communist-led peasant associations in China had an estimated 9 million members, half of these in Hunan (Chesneaux 1973, p. 74).

In the meantime, Chiang had moved against the communists in March 1926, excluding them from high positions, weakening the control of

Soviet advisers over his army, calling off the Hong Kong-Canton strike and boycott and seizing control of the latter city. CCP secretary Ch'en Tu-hsiu tried to persuade its Fifth Congress in April to end the tactic of dual membership in the KMT while retaining the alliance, but failed. On the Comintern side, Stalin's rival Grigorii Zinoviev, then still ECCI chairman, tried to persuade it to push for a CCP break with its dubious ally in May, but failed. He was dismissed from his post at the 7th enlarged plenum in November–December.

In the meantime, the 6th enlarged ECCI plenum, held in February–March, had given its advice/recommendations/orders to the CCP leaders. 'The most important question of the Chinese national liberation movement is the peasant question', it said, and the victory of 'the revolutionary democratic tendency' depended on their participation under working-class leadership. The working class was thus assigned the key role, but the CCP was warned not to 'try to skip over the revolutionary-democratic stage of the movement straight to the tasks of proletarian dictatorship and Soviet power'. Moreover, at the 7th plenum late in 1926 Stalin was instrumental in modifying the draft theses to ensure that part at least of the KMT leadership was regarded as progressive (quoted, Ch'ên 1965, p. 109; Sobolev *et al.* 1971, p. 250).

In July 1926 Chiang had begun his major offensive against the warlords, weakened by fighting among themselves. KMT armies moved north, with communist cadres spreading out in front of them to mobilize peasant and worker support, and in October captured Wuhan on the Yangtze River. The obvious next move was to thrust down-river to the major port and industrial city, Shanghai. On 21 March 1927 the workers there seized the city in anticipation of the advance of Chiang's army. Nine days later the Comintern's ECCI denied the possibility of a split between the two forces, describing the KMT leader as a 'revolutionist'. Two weeks later Stalin declared that 'we need the [KMT] Right. It has capable people who still direct the army and lead it against the imperialists' (quoted, Löwy 1981, p. 78).

On 12 April Chiang and his troops entered Shanghai and, having made a deal with the Federation of Commerce and Industry, foreign consuls and local criminal leaders, carried out an appalling massacre of workers' organizers and communists and other activists. Li Ta-chao and other leaders were executed by the chief northern warlord. Mao only just escaped and in May his Hunan peasant movement was smashed. The CCP leadership, under pressure from Moscow, tried to continue in alliance with the left wing of the KMT, now based in Wuhan, but in July this turned against them also. Next month there were communist-led risings in the city of Nanch'ang and Hunan, the latter led by Mao, which both failed.

In August 1927 Mao wrote to the CCP Central Committee that '[o]bjectively, China has long since reached 1917, but formerly everyone held the opinion that we were in 1905. This has been an extremely great error.' For this view of revolutionary preparedness, which hinted at a 'permanent revolution' stance, he was reproved and expelled from the Politburo, on which he had regained a place. Unsurprisingly, therefore, in a report to a party conference in the new Hunan-Kiangsi liberated area in October 1928 he took the orthodox line that '[b]ecause the proletariat was not firm in asserting its leadership in the revolution of 1926–27 ... the comprador class, the local bullies, and the bad gentry seized hold of it and changed the nature of the revolution'. This defeat 'of historical significance' was of the 'bourgeois-democratic revolution' and 'on the whole similar to the defeat of the Russian Revolution in 1905'.[7]

China's 1917 was still to come, but in the meantime the role of the working class as the sole revolutionary subject had been put in question, while Stalin's policy on alliances had shown what might happen to a 'vanguard' party which in effect surrendered that position. It had also revealed the problems of attempting an overriding direction of international struggle from one centre, the Soviet Union, where by 1928 the building of 'socialism in one country' had been launched.

With the ending of the first phase of the Chinese Revolution by the defeat of 1927, the issue arises as to what Chinese events since 1921 actually meant for the shift of Marxism to the periphery and as the main test case for the new Leninism. In Chapter 3 an approach was postulated which uses the idea of laying down a revolutionary terrain of class and other social forces for the wars of position and manoeuvre. This raises the general problem which is still with us: class analysis in formations where the overall impact of capital and the incorporation of them into global structures had created complex constellations without the predicted polarization between capitalists and proletariat. Mao's use of the model of Russia in 1905 and 1917 serves as a reminder that, once communist revolutionary history passed beyond the original breakthrough, concrete situations and their analysis became even more difficult. Let us see what we can learn from the Chinese experience.

**Lessons of the Chinese First Period**

Let us take the war of position first, involving the basic theoretical issue of the class nature of revolutionary stages. Keeping it in mind that a Gramscian view of 'wars' does not actually *require* a 'stages' approach, we should remember that the latter raises the question of the revolutionary class subject in an extreme form when it actually posits taking position by sliding historical 'tasks' over from one class to another.

We have already seen in the context of the debate over Russia that the concept of stages evolved postulation of some sort of revolutionary 'anti-feudal' and democratic potential among the bourgeoisie, even though this might have to be taken up by the petty bourgeoisie and working class. The Chinese case, like others 70 years later, is one in which there was a quite powerful bourgeoisie, some parts of which had impulses towards a 'national' stance, and which through the KMT controlled a state which was politically sovereign in dealing with foreign powers. In terms of the role of the Chinese bourgeoisie as expressed through the KMT in 1922–27, in a speech given to Asian students at their special university in Moscow in May 1925 Stalin actually described that party in 'Jacobin' terms, as a workers' and peasants' party which replaced a 'united national front' because it already included the 'revolutionary' part of the bourgeoisie (Carrère d'Encausse and Schram 1969, p. 226).

The relevant resolution at the 7th plenum of the ECCI in December 1926, with Chiang Kai-shek on the march to the north, declared that 'at this present stage of development, the Chinese revolution is historically bourgeois-democratic in nature', but saw its nature as changing. Its class content had been a four-part bloc of part of the big bourgeoisie, the urban petty bourgeoisie, the peasants and the workers, led by the KMT and the Canton government. However, it was 'bound to acquire a broader social character' and the CCP must move towards securing working-class hegemony over a bloc in which the bourgeoisie would become weaker in a period in which 'the agrarian struggle begins to take on acute forms'. The CCP was enjoined to remain in a supposedly radicalizing KMT and support the Canton government, and at the same ECCI session Stalin declared that 'to speak of soviets now would be running too far ahead' (Degras (ed.) 1960, pp. 340–5 *passim*; quoted, Löwy 1981, p. 76).

Even after the Shanghai, Nanch'ang and Hunan débâcles, in May 1927 the 8th ECCI plenum distinguished between the 'left' Wuhan government and 'the feudal-bureaucratic regime', and described the KMT as a meeting-point for the workers, petty bourgeoisie and peasants. At the same time, Stalin insisted that the progressive wing of the Chinese capitalist class could form part of the revolutionary terrain. He attacked

Trotsky for calling for the formation of Chinese soviets, making the remarkable assertion that what I characterize as the 'Jacobin' Left KMT was 'performing approximately the same role in the present bourgeois-democratic revolution in China as the soviets performed in the bourgeois-democratic revolution in Russia in 1905'. Even Trotsky in March 1927 had still seen the Chinese Revolution as being national democratic, and soviets, should they be formed, as instruments for 'national liberation and democratic unification' rather than the basis for a 'democratic dictatorship of the proletariat and peasantry' (Datta Gupta 1980, p. 104; quoted, Löwy 1981, p. 79, ibid., p. 82).

Since the bourgeoisie can never produce revolutionary subjects in a socialist sense, the problem Stalin and all Leninists (including Trotsky, despite his 'permanentism') were up against was their assumption, based on a rigid view of historical stages and class contents, that the organized bourgeoisie would be either willing to identify their interests with those of workers and peasants and other deprived groups because of some apparent short-term advantage or too stupid to realize they were being manipulated. Both conditions were (and remain) highly suppositious; we shall see the workings of this factor clearly in the Indian case, but it was also present in China. Moreover, the stagist theory assumes that there *is* a 'national' bourgeoisie, clearly distinguished in interest from 'feudal' landlords and foreign capital. None of this was clearly true in 1920s China or beyond. We shall, however, find a different situation in India and to some extent in Brazil.

Perhaps unconsciously recognizing this bourgeois weakness, Trotsky brought in his 'petty bourgeoisie' (which, it should be remembered, actually conflates *two* different elements, the petty bourgeoisie of small propertied artisan producers and traders and the employed middle strata). Writing in 1928, he noted that the Stalinists distinguished among three 'dictatorships', of the bourgeoisie, of the proletariat, and a 'democratic dictatorship', but the last of these 'must be of an intermediate character, that is, have a petty-bourgeois content'. If the Kuomintang regime was supposed to represent the third case, his next question is valid: is the petty bourgeoisie capable of 'playing a leading revolutionary rôle'? In asking this, Trotsky was in effect raising the problem of 'Jacobinism', namely an alternative radical position to that of the communists constituted on a non-class, probably nationalist platform. He in fact saw the leading role of the petty bourgeoisie as possible only when the proletariat was its 'fighting core', in other words in situations where capitalist development had not yet fully separated workers from artisans and put the former into direct confrontation with capital (Trotsky 1962, pp. 125–6).

That confrontation was already clearly the case in China by 1927, making it unlikely that a form of radical Jacobin politics would develop beyond what already existed through the left wing of the KMT (and was soon to be suppressed), and this is one of the senses in which the revolutionary situation might be said to have been quite far advanced in the mid-1920s. Such a situation, Trotsky wrote, 'condemns the petty bourgeoisie to nullity and confronts the peasantry with the inevitable political choice between the bourgeoisie and the proletariat', while in fact '[e]very time the peasantry decides for a party which on the surface appears petty-bourgeois, it actually offers its back as a support for finance capital'. Trotsky remained orthodoxly Marxist: only the two basic classes of capitalism could take a lead, he felt; 'the petty-bourgeoisie, including the peasantry, is incapable of playing the rôle of leader in modern, even if backward, bourgeois society', while '[i]ntermediate forms are only disguises for a dictatorship of the bourgeoisie' (ibid., pp. 126–7).

Jacobinism and the possible radical role of the 'petty bourgeoisie' therefore muddied the revolutionary class waters even more, by introducing another intermediary class (in fact, two). However, in the conditions of peripheral capitalism this was (and is) very likely to be the case. If, as Trotsky and the Comintern theorists maintained, the 'petty bourgeoisie' would always tend to follow a bourgeois lead, this tacitly admits that the overwhelming weight of the supposed allies was indeed anti-revolutionary, opening the question of under what exact circumstances might it be otherwise? In fact, in case after case (as we shall see in India and Brazil), the more one looks the more difficult it is to find a truly revolutionary combination of that kind.

It is clear that the prototypical case of China did bring out a key class in the formation of Leninist/Stalinist theory on revolution in the periphery, and one which remains important for any reformulation of Marxism for future struggle. For the KMT, with its strong landlord and rural capitalist connections, the rural movement was one of 'vandals, scoundrels, and idle peasants' (quoted, Rue 1966, p. 51). Although the Comintern at that stage held the KMT's role to be positive, it should be noted that its Fourth Congress in December 1922 called in its 'Theses on the Eastern Question' for revolutionary parties to 'formulate a clear agrarian programme ... for the complete abolition of the feudal system and survivals of it in the form of large landownership and tax farming' (Degras (ed.) 1956, p. 387). However, even in a situation of emerging confrontation with the Right KMT, we saw that the CCP Central Committee in July 1926 committed itself to the broadest rural front, including all but big landlords, and prescribed only rent and interest reduction, not land redistribution.

Moreover, as we have also seen, formation of soviets was not part of policy, but as the peasants and local trade unionists rose in advance of the KMT forces from mid-1926 they took control of local government and in effect if not in name formed soviets backed by the peasant associations. In some areas these executed local oppressors, confiscated land, and commandeered rice stores and sold them cheaply to the poor, using the money to set up schools (Ch'ên 1965, p. 115; Rue 1966, pp. 53–4). This indicates a rather high level of constitution of peasant class subjects, a definite passing beyond 'economism' and transcending the class structures which still determined the issues involved.[8] Mao Tsetung rather nicely described this in his analysis of the peasant movement made at the beginning of 1926, although speaking of a stratum, the landholder 'just able to meet his needs', which he did not regard as the potentially most revolutionary (in fact, as likely to remain neutral).

As a result of his recent oppression and exploitation by the imperialists, the militarists, and the landlord class, he feels that the world is not what it used to be. He realizes that if he now works only as hard as before, he will not be able to maintain himself. He must work longer hours, rise earlier, work longer, and devote more attention to his job, simply in order to maintain his standard of living. He begins to become somewhat abusive, calling the foreigners 'devils,' the militarists 'money-grabbing commanders,' and the local bullies and bad gentry 'the heartless rich' (Mao 1963(a), pp. 173–4).

Of course, especially in terms of such 'middle' elements, we must remember that, in China at this time as elsewhere (and still in the periphery), the context of peasant (as of worker) radicalism puts us in the presence of a complex sociological phenomenon. In terms of class, deep cultural themes could be involved. Thus, during the second half of 1926 peasant associations in some areas held feasts for poor peasants in the clan temples which were the centres of the local power structure, symbolizing its overthrow by breaking the monopoly of the rich over such ideological occasions. Mao noted how in Hunan poor peasants 'raise their rough, blackened hands and lay them on the heads of the gentry. They tie the evil gentry with ropes, put tall paper hats on them, and lead them in a parade through the villages.'[9]

Mao introduces another dimension in writing of the potential revolutionary qualities of 'declassed elements', which he sees as 'soldiers, bandits, robbers, beggars, and prostitutes' which 'each have a different way of making a living: the soldier fights, the bandit robs, the thief steals, the beggar begs, and the prostitute seduces'.[10] Although Mao does not put it this way, what these all have in common is the expenditure of labour power for a return so uncertain as to give them 'the most precarious existence of any human being'. In still postulating that these could become revolutionary subjects, the Chinese theorist unwittingly raised for us the issue which will loom large in the twenty-first century, the role of the huge and growing masses of the newly urbanized ex-peasants.

Again, the future like the past struggle will involve not only class identity and material factors; the gender issue is also central. Interestingly, Mao noted that poor peasant women in 1927, 'for financial reasons compelled to engage more in manual work than women of the wealthier classes, have obtained greater rights to speak and more power to make decisions in family affairs' than their more affluent sisters. In any case, 'women have begun to organize rural women's associations in many places; they have been given the opportunity to lift up their heads, and the authority of the husband is tottering more and more with every passing day'.

In class terms, Trotsky in the late 1920s saw the peasantry in general as the key class not only in the agrarian question but the national, giving them 'an exceptional place in the democratic revolution', which 'cannot be solved, nor even seriously posed' without a working class–peasant alliance (Trotsky 1962, pp. 152–3). This is very important from the point of view of the revolutionary subject, because it in effect shifts from a class to a national role for peasants, and hence to invocation of a different consciousness. We shall see how this issue emerged more strongly with the Japanese incursions beginning in 1931.

However, Trotsky would not grant the peasants any initiative, arguing of Russia, for example, that 'the fact that the *agrarian* revolution created the conditions for the dictatorship *of the proletariat* grew out of the inability of the peasantry to solve its own historical problem with its own forces and under its own leadership'. Moreover, capitalist penetration in the periphery gave the peasants an even less independent role than 'in the epoch of the old bourgeois revolutions'. Account had also to be taken of the fact that rich peasants would always join the big bourgeoisie 'in all decisive cases, especially in war and in revolution'. On China he noted in 1928 that '[t]he dispute is not over the decisive rôle of the peasantry as an ally, and not over the great significance of the agrarian revolution, but over whether an independent agrarian democratic revolution is possible in China' (ibid., pp. 70, 124 and 154, original emphasis).

Some four years later he was clear it was not. In a piece on 'Peasant War in China', he noted that a peasant war would have a 'tremendous revolutionary democratic significance', but 'the communist banner hides the petty-bourgeois content of the peasant movement'. Communists, therefore, should not 'scatter their forces among the isolated flames of the peasant revolt' but concentrate in the factories and workers' districts (quoted, Löwy 1981, pp. 94 and 95, n. 78). This return to Marxist orthodoxy was of course very far from the way in which the CCP was eventually able to build its revolutionary terrain and manoeuvre to power.

This verdict demands that we should move back again in time and note the special place of Mao's views on class in the evolution of Marxism in China. In February 1926 he saw the working class as the 'major', but not the 'leading' force of 'the national revolutionary movement'.[11] In February 1927, in his classic 'Report of an Investigation into the Peasant Movement in Hunan', he went further, declaring that 'if we allot ten points to the accomplishments of the democratic revolution, then the achievements of the urban dwellers and the military rate only three points, while the remaining seven points should go to the peasants in their rural revolution'. For its part, the ECCI in May 1927 went so far as urge the CCP 'to take the leadership of the organized movement of the peasantry into its own hands and ruthlessly combat every effort to restrict the extent of that movement' (Mao 1963(c), pp. 181–2; quoted, Datta Gupta 1980, p. 104). By 1930, in fact, the trajectories of Mao's own career and of the whole revolution were set on a course of fighting a war of position through rural base areas, soviets and peasant armies. The same features were in time to mark China's war of manoeuvre.

As we have seen, the major orthodox precept on manoeuvring one's way to state power, again cast within the 'stages' view, was to make alliances with non-working-class organizations in a 'united front'. The Comintern Fourth Congress in late 1922 clearly reasserted Lenin's 1920 principle of preserving organizational autonomy when entering a front. The failure to follow this line after 1922 gives us two of the lessons of the Chinese Revolution in its first period: organizational autonomy within an alliance was essential; and the role of the bourgeoisie within such was bound to be contradictory.

On the alliance issue we may note Rue's point that the CCP's link with the KMT was 'unique' in the history of the Comintern's united front strategy, because it was neither one 'from above', where the party shared direction with other organizations, nor 'from below', the more radical move of taking over the other organization's followings, but 'from within' (Rue 1966, p. 118, note). Despite its attempts to shade towards a 'from below' approach in late 1925, by permitting dual membership and placing its cadres in high KMT positions the CCP trapped itself in a contradiction between immediate influence and restraint on action, along with complete exposure of its leading activists. There are no clear indications that much was gained from this move in the crucial sphere of building the mass base for a revolutionary terrain. Until early 1927 the main working-class centres, which should have been major spaces for revolutionary manoeuvring, Shanghai and Wuhan, were not in KMT hands anyway, while activities among peasants were either Mao's private initiative in Hunan or possible because the KMT underrated that class.

## Groping for a New Strategy

The CCP's problem after the defeat in 1927 was how to pick up the pieces and devise a workable strategy for both the war of position and that of manoeuvre. The latter had not been a clear issue before, since the image seems to have been one of riding to power on the back of the Left Kuomintang. Here the key factor, decisive for the whole future of the revolution and later to affect that in other countries like Viet Nam, was the split between Mao, who since October had been ensconced in a remote mountain base area in Kiangsi province, and the Central Committee dominated from July 1928 by Li Li-san, a former labour organizer, who had ECCI backing. Both now followed their own lines, Mao seeking to coordinate his Chingkangshan rural base development with others being established and to build a Red Army, Li following the orthodox worker and urban-oriented strategy.

However, the organizational base for the latter was now much weakened. In March 1927, on the eve of defeat, the CCP was estimated to have some 58 000 members, with 53.8 per cent of them workers, 18.7 per cent peasants, 19.1 per cent 'intellectuals' and 3.1 per cent soldiers. Although figures are uncertain, various sources indicate a serious drop in worker membership of the party; one said from 66 per cent in 1926 (sic) to 8 per cent in 1930. When Li attempted to organize strikes after mid-1927 he could muster only 2000 workers in Shanghai, for example, and 1000 in Wuhan (Sobolev *et al.* 1971, p. 254; Ch'ên 1965, p. 149). Although it was in no sense either clear or accepted by the majority of the leadership, a shift was on hand to reliance upon the peasantry, who now became in effect an alternative source of revolutionary subjects to the Chinese workers.

In the meantime, the ECCI assessment of the situation was realistic. In February 1928 its 9th plenum declared that 'no mighty upsurge of the revolutionary mass movement on a national scale' existed. There was no condition of permanent revolution; indeed, not even bourgeois-democratic goals had been attained. The Chinese comrades were urged to avoid 'playing with insurrection' and to concentrate on drawing the masses into struggle and organizing a Red Army. Prefiguring a different strategy, the ECCI maintained that peasant demands should be met by confiscating landlords' holdings and soviets set up as a basis for a dictatorship of workers and peasants (Sobolev *et al.* 1971, pp. 256–8).

In July 1928 the CCP held its Sixth Congress in Moscow, concurrently with the Comintern's own sixth assembly. The latter's instructions to the Chinese comrades modulated February's class line: they were to break with the bourgeoisie and concentrate on building a workers' party; no more peasants were to be admitted, but they could be mobilized through separate associations. Eventually, when mass uprisings began, soviets of workers and peasants would be created. Hsiang Chung-fa, formerly a coolie on the Shanghai ore barges and only semi-literate, now became party general secretary, a token of emphasis on 'proletarianization'. On the other hand, in a letter to party members in October Li estimated that peasants numbered 70–80 per cent of them and raised fears of the bad effects of a 'peasant mentality', declaring that '[o]nly a proletarian mentality can lead us onto the correct revolutionary road' (Rue 1966, pp. 100 and 138).

However, Mao maintained his own Front Committee, which linked the base areas and served as his independent power base against the Central Committee. In April 1929 the Front Committee answered the latter's criticisms of its banking on the poor peasants and not also allying with the rich against the landlords by asserting that building strength in the urban areas as laid down by the party's Sixth Congress was not enough, since 'the revolution will develop swiftly'. Main necessities – and now the war of manoeuvre was under debate – were to help the urban struggle and hasten 'the rise of the revolutionary tide' by developing the rural struggle, establishing small soviet areas and building the Red Army. In addition, adopting only guerrilla tactics and pulling

Mao himself out of base area work, as the Central Committee wanted, was incorrect. In general:

> it would be wrong to abandon the struggle in the cities, but in our opinion it would also be wrong for any of our Party members to fear the growth of peasant strength lest it should outstrip the workers' strength and harm the revolution. For in the revolution in semi-colonial China, the peasant struggle must always fail if it does not have the leadership of the workers, but the revolution is never harmed if the peasant struggle outstrips the forces of the workers (quoted, Mao 1964(a), p. 123).

In the last sentence two important points come out. First, 'leadership of the workers' has to be read in fact as 'party leadership'. Second, Mao (whose letter it really was) was in effect now postulating the peasantry as the leading class – of course, under CCP leadership – in the Chinese Revolution.

In a letter to the CCP Central Committee in June 1929, the ECCI attempted to lay down a line for agrarian struggle and, reflecting the more aggressive international line after the Sixth Congress, moved closer to Mao's position. The 'severe and prolonged agricultural crisis' was bound to radicalize the peasantry, the Comintern leadership declared, so that the prospects for CCP work among the 'exploited peasant masses' were 'extremely favourable'. On the other hand, that category did not include the rich peasant 'kulaks', with whom an alliance was in no circumstances permissible. (We see here a reflection of Stalinist typification of the main enemy in collectivization in the Soviet Union itself.) Nevertheless, Chinese comrades should not draw 'wholly incorrect and purely Trotskyist conclusions' that the Chinese Revolution was anything other than bourgeois-democratic in its present stage (Degras (ed.) 1965, pp. 32–6 *passim*).

For its part, probably not even having yet received the ECCI letter, the Central Committee plenum the same month remained somewhat ambivalent on the peasant question, but did run counter to the ECCI line by stating that it was 'still a mistake to oppose rich peasants unconditionally'. It also opposed premature rural uprisings, which it termed 'putschism and impatience' (Rue 1966, pp. 162–4). Meanwhile, Mao's Front Committee had passed a land law for the base areas in April and begun to redistribute land.

Mao further stated his own position in January 1930 in the document which became known as 'A Single Spark Can Start a Prairie

Fire'. In this he noted that 'China is a semi-colonial country for which many imperialist powers are contending'. From this two key distinctive features followed: only in China was there currently 'prolonged and tangled warfare within the ruling classes'; and the 'peasant problem' had produced country-wide uprisings. The basic task was to establish rural base areas, deepen the agrarian revolution and build a Red Army 'which will become the chief weapon for the great revolution of the future'.[12]

Seeking to challenge pessimistic views among comrades, Mao distinguished China from Western Europe (and prefigured post-2000 issues). In the latter, the 'forces of the counter-revolution' were much stronger than in the Asian case, so even though European revolutionary organizations might also be stronger, 'the revolution will undoubtedly move towards a high tide more rapidly in China'. Acknowledging that the Chinese revolutionary forces had been much weakened since April 1927, Mao thus placed most weight on the weakness of the CCP's opponents. His analysis of the multiple contradictions then existing, which he felt comrades were not discerning clearly enough because they saw only 'superficial appearance' and did not penetrate to the 'essence', meant that he saw a situation in which a workers' strike, peasant uprising, student demonstration or army mutiny could serve as the single spark which set the prairie on fire. At least in the short term, therefore, Mao was postulating multiple, and not necessarily directly class, revolutionary subjects.

For his part, Li Li-san declared in April that '[a]ll the talk of "encircling the city with the country" or of relying on the Red Army to take the cities is sheer nonsense'. He criticized Mao for in fact proposing protracted 'boxing tactics'. Nevertheless, both factions were agreed that revolutionary possibilities would soon open, and Moscow encouraged this. In June 1930 the ECCI passed a special resolution on China, which declared that 'events are moving in a direction which will create a revolutionary situation in the near future if not throughout the whole of China, at least in a number of the most important provinces'.[13] The workers' and peasants' struggles needed to be 'merged into one' and the Red Army 'must be made into a genuine national army'. Directives were given for policy in the base areas, especially in land reform. Outside those areas, peasant guerrilla war was to be fostered.

The ECCI went much further than this, by now moving the Chinese Revolution out of the 'bourgeois-democratic' category. Rather than allying with the bourgeoisie, workers and peasants were now 'engaged in direct struggle against them', opening the possibility, if successful, of initiating a 'non-capitalist road of development which will provide the material economic foundation for the gradual and steady transition of the Chinese revolution, by a series of intermediate stages, into the socialist revolution'. For its part, the CCP Central Committee also in June 1930 actually designated China as 'the weakest link in the chain of world imperialism', where the revolution might be the first to occur and 'spark off world revolution and decisive class war in the world' (Degras (ed.) 1965, p. 119; cited, Claudin 1975, p. 290).

This CCP leadership resolution laid it down that in order to take power in several urban centres strikes and insurrections would be necessary; it was 'a wholly mistaken idea not to pay attention to urban work and to count on the villages to surround the towns'. However, rather than undertaking a patient rebuilding of urban organizations, and in the spirit of China as the immediate weak link, the Central Committee ordered the Red Army into action; in August–September its units twice captured Ch'angsha and lost it again. At a September plenum Li Li-san recognized that his line had failed; on the other hand, the Central Committee could see no immediate alternative (cited, Claudin 1975, p. 291; Ch'ên 1965, pp. 157–9).

After the first capture of Ch'angsha, the Comintern hailed the victory as beginning 'a new chapter of the Chinese revolution', but in October it had to backtrack, censuring Li and claiming poor party control over the Red Army, which had been infiltrated by 'kulaks'.[14] The unfortunate Chinese leader was called to Moscow and subjected to an ECCI inquiry, after which he was relegated to a minor position in the Soviet capital while he re-educated himself. In January 1931 a new Central Bureau for the Chinese soviet areas was set up, with Mao as a member. This gave him more influence in the Central Committee, which in that month was purged by the ECCI's emissary, Pavel Mif, who had arrived in mid-1930 with the '28 Bolsheviks', mostly his former students from the Moscow Chinese university, to get a Stalinist grip on the CCP.

The dominant Chinese among this new leadership group was Wang Ming (actual name, Ch'en Shao-yü), who became acting party general secretary when Hsiang Chung-fa was betrayed to the Shanghai police and executed in June 1931. In his *The Two Lines*, published in February, Wang had reasserted the militant Comintern line by denouncing any policy of forming alliances, of which, as Rue points out, anyone could retrospectively be found guilty other than the 28 Bolsheviks, who had been out of China during the period of working with the KMT. At a party conference in November Mao's land law was actually attacked as favouring rich peasants and he was accused of 'opportunistic pragmatism' and 'general ideological poverty'. The agrarian revolution, it was reaffirmed, must be led by the proletariat (that is, the CCP Politburo) (Rue 1966, pp. 244, 247-8).

This was in fact an application of a resolution by the ECCI's 11th plenum, which in August 1931 had set out the tasks of the CCP in class terms as recruiting 'the best elements among the workers' as 'a matter of top priority'. Party organizations were to be re-established in the big urban centres and contact reopened with groups in factories which had gone on struggling even after repression. The power of a future Soviet government was seen as dependent on developing the 'hegemony of the proletariat' in the revolution, including over the peasantry, as 'an incipient and transitional stage on the way to the dictatorship of the proletariat'.[15] This was in effect a swing back towards the Li Li-san line, and after decisions in September 1932 preparations again began to be made for an assault on KMT-held cities.

Mao and his supporters apparently went along with this, and although they still controlled the soviet government established in Kiangsi in October 1930 and the Red Army, these had been under increasing KMT military pressure since the launching of Chiang Kai-shek's first 'encirclement' campaign in December 1930. Others followed in February and April 1931 and a fourth from June 1932 to March 1933. During the same period, under the direction of the new CCP general secretary, Po Ku, the other leader of the 28 Bolsheviks (Wang Ming returned to Moscow in late 1931), dissidents were being purged.[16]

In October 1934 the Kiangsi base, which by then included about 3 million people, had to be evacuated, under extreme pressure from the fifth KMT 'encirclement', begun a year earlier. Some 100 000 men, 20 000 of them cadres and the rest soldiers, and 35 women escaped through a gap forced earlier in the KMT lines.[17] This was the beginning of the epic Long March, which ended for Mao and the First Red Army in October 1935 in the remote Yenan area of northern Shensi province, just behind the Great Wall and safe from KMT reach. Only 4000 of the original 87 000 (including trainees) survived a march of over 12 000 kilometres under frequent attack, but the arrival of the Second and Fourth Red Armies a year later brought strength up to perhaps 80 000.[18]

Meanwhile, in January 1935, in the middle of the march, a conference held in Tsun-yi in Kweichow province had enabled Mao finally to assert his authority, although it could be argued that this only became absolute after the party's Seventh Congress elected him Politburo chairman in April 1945.[19] From the beginning of 1935 he and his supporters controlled the party's Central Military Committee and Secretariat, but it must be borne in mind that another of the 28 Bolsheviks became general secretary at the same time, and their influence continued in some areas outside the Yenan base.

From late 1935 Mao's dominant part of the CCP therefore had a secure base in a remote region, but was faced with the problem of how to build a terrain of class forces which would permit a war of manoeuvre extending into the key central and coastal regions.[20] By this time, that issue had in fact become effectively tied to the patriotic anti-Japanese struggle. We have already noted that in September 1931 the Japanese had invaded Manchuria, still held by a warlord and therefore not a key KMT region. In April 1932 the CCP soviet government based in Kiangsi actually declared war on Japan, and in January 1933 Mao's faction offered an alliance with 'any armed force' which would join them. However, this did not include the KMT as such: in July 1934 Mao issued a proclamation describing Chiang and the KMT as 'the most faithful running dog of Japanese imperialism' and 'the greatest traitors in all Chinese history', although the offer was again made to work with 'all armed forces in China' to defeat the invaders (Schram 1963, pp. 37–8 and 152–3).

The most important feature of the overall Chinese situation after the establishment in Yenan, therefore, proved to be Mao's adoption of his own line in the direct confrontation with the Japanese. The point is that, as we saw in the previous chapter, the French and other communist leaders, supported by the Bulgarian veteran Georgii Dimitrov in the ECCI, were now arguing in Comintern circles for the broadest possible front against fascism (opposed by Manuilskii, Mif and – significantly – Wang Ming). In the Chinese context this identified the Japanese regime as fascist and implied allying with Chiang against the invaders, but in June, just before the Seventh Congress finally met, Mao's Yenan government again issued an appeal for a 'united popular front' against both Chiang and the Japanese (Sobolev et al. 1971, p. 367).

The Seventh Congress had specific prescriptions for China, which were more radical than for the 'colonies and semi-colonies' in general. The development of the 'people's anti-imperialist movement' was linked in the analysis of Chinese conditions with 'the armed people' and soviets as 'the unifying centre of the whole Chinese people in its struggle for liberation'. Development of these elements and the communist armies was to be coordinated with the movement (Carrère d'Encausse and Schram 1969, p. 248). This gives an impression of a direct revolutionary struggle led by the CCP, which would mean against Chiang, but, on the other hand, Dimitrov in his Seventh Congress keynote speech gave the stamp of approval to the formation of a front of all organized forces 'ready to wage a real struggle for the salvation of their country and their people' (Dimitrov 1935(a), p. 68). In the wake of the Moscow meeting – with the ECCI actively involved in drafting it – the remaining non-Maoist CCP elements issued an appeal to all patriots, including in the KMT, for an alliance against the foreign enemy.[21]

This kept China formally within the more general line, but in December 1935 the CCP Politburo reasserted the position of fighting both the local version of 'fascism', Japanese imperialism, and Chiang's Kuomintang regime. The now-dominant Mao reported to a party conference and laid down the line for the coming wars of position and manoeuvre. Thus, he spoke of bringing together not only workers, peasants and the petty bourgeoisie but also those parts of the 'national bourgeoisie' which had little or no affiliation with foreign capital or Chinese landlords. In fact, he envisaged that even landlords and compradors might come to 'engage in a veiled strife or even an open conflict with the Japanese imperialists and their running-dogs'. The party's task, therefore, was to form a 'broad national revolutionary united front' to represent all these class elements; 'closed-doorism' was 'an infantile disorder'. Mao now spoke of the immediate goal as a 'people's republic' (Mao 1964(b), pp. 162–5 *passim*).

A Central Committee resolution adopted a few days earlier seems to represent the views of Mao's rivals; it spoke of a 'government of national defence' and, more orthodoxly in Marxist-Leninist class terms, stressed the need for the support of 'the majority of the working class'.[22] Such a government need not have excluded Chiang, whereas Mao still spoke of the KMT president as the 'chieftain' of a 'camp of traitors', the 'big local tyrants and evil gentry, the big warlords and the big bureaucrats and compradors'. This actually provoked an ECCI critique, arguing that it was impossible to conduct two struggles simultaneously and that priority must be given to the 'anti-fascist' one (Sobolev *et al.* 1971, p. 426).

On the other hand, there was a very pragmatic issue in play for Mao at this time, namely the fact that, as he admitted in an essay a year later, after the Long March only one base area remained (the Shensi-Kansu border region), party membership was down from 300 000 to 'a few tens of thousands', with parallel figures for the Red Army, and the CCP organization in KMT-held areas was almost destroyed. This obviously implied political manoeuvring to reduce the pressure, and, while we can probably take it that the Central Committee's letter of invitation to the KMT leadership in August 1936 calling for a united front and a 'united democratic Chinese republic' came from Mao's opponents, during that year he shifted himself (Mao 1964(c), p. 195; Schram 1963, p. 38).

The opportunity to take a new stance came with a rather bizarre affair. Chiang Kai-shek, who had been able to weaken the remaining warlords while campaigning against the communists, was in fact kidnapped by two of the former in December 1936 and the communists played a part in securing his release in return for a promise to cooperate in resisting the invaders. In January–February 1937 there were discussions on this between the KMT and CCP, during which the latter undertook to abandon armed insurrection, designate the liberated area a 'special region' of the (KMT) Republic of China and place the Red Army under the Republic's control.[23] The CCP also now abandoned land reform although retaining rent and interest reductions.

In July the necessity of unity seemed confirmed by Japan's all-out assault; Shanghai was captured by its armies in November and Nanking in December, with an appalling massacre of the latter's population. In August Mao issued a 'Ten-point National Salvation Programme' calling for a 'national defence government' to include all parties, but expecting it to carry out 'revolutionary policies for resisting Japan and saving the nation' (Ch'ên 1965, p. 225). However, party leaders were not yet agreed on important parts of strategy. In December 1937 Wang Ming returned to China, and, in a report to the ECCI, came out for a united front with the KMT in a 'national revolutionary alliance', but with organizational independence for the party and Red Army and continued vigilance against betrayal by Chiang. We may take it that the various factions of the CCP were now in line (Sobolev et al. 1971, p. 427). In March 1938 the Politburo accepted this as policy, but also Wang's strong rejection of guerrilla warfare in favour of large-unit action, which ran against the Mao group's line. However, during the extended sessions of the Central Committee between September and November the Red Army suffered a major defeat when the Japanese took Wuhan, justifying emphasis on the guerrilla form. Moreover, in September the ECCI came out in favour of Mao (Apter and Saich 1994, pp. 56–9).

By now, in fact, the Comintern was increasingly out of the picture. Its Seventh Congress had instructed the ECCI to allow greater latitude to member parties to regulate their own affairs and 'as a rule to avoid direct intervention in internal organisational matters', but even if it had wanted to treat the CCP as an exception to the rule, the ECCI was no longer in a real position to meddle through Wang, since it was in the process of being purged as part of Stalin's drive to liquidate his real or supposed enemies (Sobolev *et al.* 1971, p. 397; Rue 1966, p. 278).

By October 1938 Mao had moved so far as to declare the KMT to be indispensable to the resistance war, as its 'leader and framework'. It had a 'glorious history' and '[u]nder the single great condition that it support to the end the war of resistance and the United Front, one can foresee a brilliant future for the Kuomintang'. Evidently he must have had a huge tongue in his revolutionary cheek in saying this, and his following remarks had more ultimate significance; the communists must strengthen themselves 'in order to assume their great responsibilities in the national war', with concrete activities 'in every domain'. In December a Politburo praesidium resolution laid down a line of party and army organizational independence, continuing organizational activity in KMT-held areas, especially the big cities, training of cadres in Marxism-Leninism, and treating the Yenan base as 'a model of the most democratic integral part of the entire Chinese Republic' (Schram 1963, p. 160; Sobolev *et al.* 1971, p. 428).

The real status of the KMT–CCP alliance was already revealed in April 1939, when KMT forces and CCP guerrilla units clashed in the north and in June in the south, and intermittent fighting continued in various provinces until the next spring. In the north this gave the party a chance to expand its territory, setting a future pattern for a completely military war of manoeuvre lasting from early 1947 until final victory in October 1949. Moreover, by their cruel behaviour, the foreign invaders often pushed the peasants into supporting the only force apparently determined and able to fight back, the CCP.

In November 1938, as part of his assertion of control of the CCP leadership, Mao set out his general blueprint for eventually winning power; having shifted the concept of war of position by positing a basically rural terrain, he now did the same for manoeuvre. In doing so he also asserted his theoretical and political independence from Moscow. The Russian October Revolution pattern of political work in the urban areas and then seizing first the cities, then the rural areas, he said, did not apply in Chinese conditions; the appropriate form for a 'semi-colonial and semi-feudal country' was to avoid 'a long period of legal struggle' and to take first the villages and then the cities. Mao's view of the war of manoeuvre was very distinct: '[t]he central task of revolution and its highest form is an armed struggle for political power. War settles the question.'[24]

The case of China is a key one for this study and for the whole history of the twentieth century. From 1921 it represented the main test for Leninism/Stalinism; it in time led to the third major communist revolution in the twentieth century (I count the Vietnamese August Revolution of 1945 as the second); and it laid the basis for major division in the 'socialist camp' from the late 1950s. However, we cannot assess either the doctrine or the work of the Comintern in spreading it on that basis alone, because China was indeed exceptional, its concrete conditions determining in effect a complete reconceptualization of communist revolution, even if this was not admitted by leaders. The wars of position and manoeuvre were radically reshaped by reliance on the peasantry to provide the main revolutionary subjects and by militarization. In that sense, it could be argued that the Chinese case was not a 'fair test' for the Comintern and Leninism/Stalinism, and there are great limitations on its revolutionary lessons for the new stage of capitalist globalization. By turning from that 'semi-colony' first to a 'dependent' country and then (in Chapter 5) a colonial possession, we may get a much better grasp on what the whole issue was about in the interwar period and set some parameters for what might be applied today.

## BRAZIL: WORKERS AND SOLDIERS

At the anti-Bolshevik Amsterdam Labour Conference in July 1919 Samuel Gompers, leader of the conservative American Federation of Labor in the USA, claimed also to represent 'the twenty-one republics of Central and South America' (quoted, Dulles 1973, p. 96). This labour extension of the Monroe Doctrine situates the Latin American countries on our periphery, but at the same time must not mask the fact that this region of independent states did become a scene of Comintern activity and a source of problems for Leninism/Stalinism which it did not encounter in the 'colonies and semi-colonies'. In token of the latter issue, in 1928 the Sixth Comintern Congress, as already noted, extended the concept of 'semi-colonial' to a third category, 'independent', expressly to cover the countries of Latin America, citing Argentina and Brazil as cases, The communist parties of these and six other Latin American countries were actually represented at the Congress (McKenzie 1964, p. 306).

The main interest of Brazil for us will prove to be as a case study in the difficulties of setting up communist parties on the basis of fragmented left political and labour movements. Beyond this comes the universal issue of 'stages' and what kind of alliances to make and with whom, in a situation where capitalist factions contested for power in a sovereign state. Moving from position to manoeuvre, in Brazil we may also consider the special question of military action, which became such a key issue in China, but in a markedly different form, namely whether to ally with radical but non-communist insurgent officers. That was to become a marked issue after 1945, above all in the Arab world.

By 1920 Brazil, like the other Latin American republics, had been independent for almost a century, although it had been ruled by an emperor (originally the Portuguese king exiled by Napoleon) until a coup in 1889. By the constitution of 1891 it was a federation, the United States of Brazil, with each of its units controlled by a local oligarchy, basically landowners allied with local merchants. Those of the two states of Minas Gerais and São Paulo dominated the national power bloc. Since the late nineteenth-century global expansion of capital, the economy had basically depended on coffee exports, and by a fiscal device known as the 'socialization of losses', adopted by the power bloc in 1906, the currency was devalued whenever world prices fell, in order to maintain sales.[25] The system was very ineffective, however, and coffee prices fluctuated considerably between 1918 and 1935. The First World War had of course severely disrupted the market, and the Great Depression also had a marked impact on prices (see Dulles 1973, Appendix, pp. 535–9). Between 1919 and 1930 the average exchange rate of the currency with the US dollar declined by around 93 per cent (Ianni 1964, p. 43; calculated from Dulles 1973, p. 546).

During the same period of integration into the world economy, and backed by protectionist policies, some industry began to develop in the larger cities, especially such basics as textiles. With a population of 30 million, in 1920 there was a total of 275 517 industrial workers, with 40.7 per cent of them in textiles and the next largest categories food (18.8 per cent) and clothing (10.3 per cent). There were only 14 147 (5.1 per cent) in the 'heavy' metal-working industries. As in Russia in 1917, the working class was highly concentrated; the Communist Party's estimate in early 1925 was over 300 000 industrial and other workers in the São Paulo Federal District, the main manufacturing centre. On the other hand, industrial workers were greatly outnumbered by the 9 million peasants and agricultural labourers.[26] The main interest of the communist movement in Brazil is in fact its attempt to take position on a terrain which it limited in effect to manufacturing workers, a sort of classical Marxist approach which ran against conditions on the periphery, and Leninism/Stalinism's faltering attempt to adapt to these.

As in Argentina and Uruguay, in Brazil the origins of leftist ideas, more often anarchist and syndicalist than Marxist, were heavily tied up with large-scale immigration from Europe in the last decades of the nineteenth and early twentieth centuries. In mid-1919 a conservative writer found comfort in the idea that '[o]rderly races' had come to Brazil, unlike Argentina's attraction of 'professional agitators' from Spain and 'dangerous' Slavs. Still, in 1912 around 82 per cent of São Paulo textile workers were foreign-born and provided at least some receptive ears to people like the German-Brazilian anarchist Edgard Leuenroth (Dulles 1973, pp. 4 and 84–5). Other leaders, like the pharmacist Otavio Brandão, had deeper roots in the country.[27]

As throughout the world, and amid increasing labour militancy, leftist elements responded immediately to the 1917 Bolshevik Revolution with a new impetus to organize. Typifying their dominance in the union movement, it was the anarchists who established a communist party in Rio de Janeiro in March 1919, with a national conference in June, and the new party's programme included what the Bolsheviks would have seen as 'ultra-leftist' features – abolition of the state, workers' management of enterprises (but without anyone assuming managerial roles) and distribution 'to each according to his needs'. Anarchist and syndicalist influences also ensured a high degree of militance, as when a trade union newspaper declared during a strike in August 1919 that '[w]e are at war against private property, the State, and the Church. The objective of the war is the complete elimination of these institutions' (ibid., pp. 79 and 88–90, and quoted, p. 105).

Anarchism was the traditional enemy of Marxism on the left (even though they shared much social analysis), and obviously a 'communist' party with such a programme would not appeal to Lenin and the Bolsheviks, while Brandão labelled Lenin a 'buffoon' and Trotsky (then commanding the Red Army) a 'coarse officer'. Almost inevitably, therefore, the Rio-based party was bound to fade away as the anarchists became increasingly disillusioned with developments in the 'first workers' state'. In November 1921 a separate group of pro-Bolsheviks, led by Astrogildo Pereira, a Brazilian-born journalist, founded a 'Communist Group' in Rio de Janeiro, and soon after three others were formed, with the expressed intention 'to defend and spread the program of the Communist International'. In March 1922 representatives of six of the now eight groups set up the Partido Comunista do Brasil (PCB) and accepted the 21 conditions of admission prescribed by the Comintern (ibid., pp. 157, 171, 173, 176–9). In November Brandão, having studied Marxism in the meantime, rallied to the new party.[28]

In November–December 1922 the PCB was represented at the Fourth Comintern Congress, and was faced by a ECCI report which criticized it for containing 'residues of the bourgeois ideology' and being 'influenced by anarchist preconceptions', with as results its decentralised structure and 'confusion about Communist theory and tactics'. As a result, the PCB was only granted 'sympathizer' status, not full Comintern membership. On the other hand, the first ECCI pronouncements on Latin America had been tentative and clearly not based on hard information. Thus, 'On the Revolution in America', published in January 1921, tried to combine all the Americas and actually made the ultimate success below the Rio Grande dependent on a workers' revolution in the USA. It did not even reach the level of discerning stages and kinds of alliance for the former. The more specific appeal 'To the Workers and Peasants of South America', issued in November 1922, also did not envisage 'national democratic' alliances, viewing local capitalist classes as hopelessly in the North American grip, but gave no indication of how peasant and worker struggles might grow over into the goal of 'proletarian dictatorship'.[29]

By the beginning of 1924 the PCB had got its local act together enough for an ECCI representative to be able to report favourably. In the meantime the anarchists and syndicalists, the former by definition less able to organize, had begun to lose ground, although they maintained a hold in some unions. On the other hand, the PCB leadership recognised that pro-management 'yellow' unions were stronger (for example, among textile workers) than either its own or the anarchists' (quoted, Dulles 1973, p. 203, and pp. 205 and 273). With such limits on labour struggle, in November 1925 the party began to compete in local, state and federal elections, trying to build a 'Labour Front' for this purpose.[30]

Although the general Comintern line specified united fronts, it must be clearly understood that the PCB was scarcely in a position to build itself a base from which to negotiate alliances. In February 1925 the party had only around 300 members, half of them in the Rio de Janeiro area. At the beginning of 1927 the party's Communist Youth had only eight members, although by May a special drive directed by Leôncio Basbaum, a medical student who became a leading party figure, had pushed this up to around 100 and to some 250 by late 1928. In 1928 the Comintern recorded a membership of 1200, which probably included the Youth and was even then exaggerated, since party membership was reported to Moscow at the end of that year as 800. The most promising feature was that 80 per cent were workers (Aguilar 1968, p. 11; Dulles 1973, pp. 272, 328, 330 and n. 15, p. 377). Small size is partly explained by conditions of repression; in August 1927, in order to secure a loan from British banks, the federal government passed a new law extending the powers to ban unions and jail labour organizers. In these circumstances, it is understandable that building a base among workers and peasants was slow and uncertain. In terms of the latter class, in February 1928 the PCB-dominated Labour Bloc was relaunched as the Worker and Peasant Bloc, and indeed some rural organization was going on, but to report to the Sixth Comintern conference, as the PCB delegation did, that a 'tremendous agrarian revolution' was about to take place was absurd (Dulles 1973, pp. 334–9, 343 and 364).[31]

During these years of trying to build the party another significant political phenomenon also appeared. In July 1922 young army officers, known as the *tenentes*, attempted a coup in Rio de Janeiro and in July 1923 in Santos, where they held out longer and secured spontaneous working-class support. Forerunners (like the earlier Young Turks in the Ottoman Empire) of a much more widespread phenomenon in peripheral formations after 1945, they may be categorized as 'Jacobins' in the terminology of this study, being nationalists and socially vaguely radical. More immediately, they were upset by the arrogance of senior officers and the army's generally low status. A more serious *tenente* rising began in October 1924 in Rio Grande do Sul and had a result which proved to be a key to the PCB's future. At the end of the year, as the rising began to collapse, Captain Luis Carlos Prestes led a column of rebels on a march which ultimately covered the interior of Brazil, fighting as it went, and on through Paraguay into exile in Bolivia in February 1927, covering an estimated 36 000 kilometres in all (three times as far as the Chinese Long March). This epic created heroes, above all Prestes, and a myth of struggle which became central to Brazilian revolutionary ideology.[32]

Nevertheless, the declared objectives of the 1924 rebels were scarcely revolutionary, involving assurance of the 1891 Constitution, uniform judicial and electoral systems, freedom of thought, free primary and professional education, punishment for 'embezzlement of the people's patrimony' and 'rigorous economy of public money along with efficient assistance to the nation's economic forces' (Dulles 1973, p. 249). Granted, actual implementation of such measures would have hit the local landlord-commercial oligarchies and their use of the federal state apparatus, and the demands were typically 'national revolutionary' in the Comintern sense. This created a potential opening for a PCB–Prestes alliance, but at first the party made no clear move in his support, although it suffered from the repression after the 1924 rising.

In April 1926 Brandão published his short book *Agrarianism or Industrialism*, the first real attempt at a Marxist analysis of Brazilian conditions and in line with Comintern reasoning. This saw the country as dominated by 'feudal' agrarian interests based on coffee and squeezed by rivalries between British and US capital, the former dominating through loans to the federal government although the USA was the biggest export market. However, a 'large industrial bourgeoisie' was emerging and being supported by US capital, even though its opposition to the system was as yet 'disorganized, chaotic'. The ex-anarchist saw the *tenente* revolts as expressing this opposition, and prescribed a united front with the petty bourgeoisie and industrial bourgeoisie, whose revolution could be made into 'a permanent revolution in the Marxist-Leninist sense' by 'prolonging it as much as possible' and pushing it to its limits 'in order to agitate the deepest layers of the proletariat' and open the way for 'the proletarian, Communist revolution' (quoted, Dulles 1973, pp. 270–1).

This analysis in fact only gave further theoretical depth to the position taken at the PCB's Second National Congress in May 1925, which specified the 1922 and 1924 risings as a movement of the military and civilian petty-bourgeoisie (what this study terms the middle strata) on behalf of the industrial capitalists against 'semi-feudal agrarian capitalism'.[33] Nevertheless, it was not until late in 1927 that the PCB leaders, evaluating their previous approach as too sectarian, decided to seek allies, and they now began to work towards a remarkable piece of substitutionism, not only of the 'large industrial bourgeoisie' by the 'petty bourgeoisie', but of the latter as a class by the exiled Prestes and his military cohort. In December 1927 an envoy was sent to Bolivia, carrying a suitcase full of Marxist texts for the education of the potential ally.

In this context, we should note that in March 1926 the ECCI reaffirmed its belief that the Latin American bourgeoisies were hopelessly subordinated to the imperialist powers, above all now to the USA, and looked towards future wars between Latin American states resulting from imperial rivalries to provide revolutionary openings (Pinheiro 1991, pp. 154–9).[34] As we have seen, in mid-1928 the Sixth Comintern Congress resolved that general capitalist conditions would justify a militant posture to create such openings in the future. In presenting a special report on Latin America, Jules Humbert-Droz, the Comintern's Swiss 'expert' for the region and author of the March 1926 line, managed to remain formally within a stages concept but in effect to abandon it. The revolution there, he said, was 'bourgeois-democratic' because it was opposed to the 'feudal' landowners backed by the imperialist powers, but the local capitalists would never be strong enough to win. National democratic demands must therefore be pushed forward by mass action. Therefore the proletariat, led of course by communist parties, must immediately take the lead of a bloc of itself, the poor peasants and the revolutionary petty bourgeoisie. Conversely, the latter were dangerous as a possible source of military coups (Cerdas-Cruz 1993, pp. 14–15; Pinheiro 1991, pp. 172–3).

The PCB began its application of the new line at its Third National Congress in December 1928 – January 1929. The 'democratic, agrarian, anti-imperialist revolution' was deemed to have begun in 1922–24, and would reach its peak in 1930, with the coincidence of a new presidential election and 'catastrophe in the coffee policy' (as predicted by the Comintern in global terms). The specific task of the PCB in the 'third uprising' (that is, following up the *military* ones) was to gain control of the 'proletarian faction' in the revolutionary movement and overall hegemony (Degras (ed.) 1960, p. 527; Dulles 1973, p. 375).

The militant line now being taken by the PCB, like other parties of the Comintern, put the ECCI to the test of keeping control of what it had itself caused. The post-Sixth Congress strategy carried the danger of moving to a 'permanent revolution' stance and opening the doors to Trotskyism. Criticism of Latin American comrades for taking precisely such 'petty-bourgeois' positions was made by Humbert-Droz at a conference of Latin American communist parties in Montevideo in June 1929. This criticism was specifically directed to a 'completely conspiratorial and military conception' of armed action. Given the PCB's later 'golpism' (*golpe* = coup), to which we shall come, it is interesting that this was accepted by the Brazilian leadership, although not by all Latin American comrades, notably the Ecuadorians (Pinheiro 1991, p. 187; Sobolev *et al.* 1971, pp. 289–90; Zaidan Filho 1985, pp. 93–5).

The Comintern's transmitted line in mid-1929 had other implications. Generally, Latin American comrades were told to look to the CCP–KMT alliance against the warlords before 1927 as a way to handle the combination of political and military action, which seems a most dubious position (but reflecting Stalin's). The Brazilians were specifically rebuked for allowing the Worker and Peasant Bloc to degenerate and, more crucially, told to take a definite position regarding Prestes, towards whom the ECCI was clearly warming (Pinheiro 1991, pp. 188–91).

At this point in time, the PCB was in fact asserting itself in the labour movement, forming its unions into the General Confederation of Labour and fomenting printers' and bakery workers' strikes in April–May 1929. However, a potentially more important strike by construction workers was wrecked by conflicts with the anarchists, who were also well-established in that sector. The PCB, on the other hand, claimed that 60 000 of the 100 000 organized workers belonged to its Confederation, and that only 2000 were anarchist adherents (Dulles 1973, p. 393).

However, this labour activity did not mean an end to electoral politics. Crucially, the party decided to nominate its own candidate for the presidential election scheduled in 1930 and not to back the challenge by the Liberal Alliance of Getulio Vargas, who as governor of Rio Grande do Sul and spokesperson for the southern 'gaucho' cattle ranchers was challenging the São Paulo domination. The point is that Vargas was seeking to put forward a radical image. His Alliance's programme called for 'the valorization of human capital' in the rural areas through better education and health facilities and 'agricultural colonies' provided with land and tools, and extension of existing pension schemes, a labour code, a minimum wage law and better education and hygiene for workers. At the same time, looking forward to a possible coup if he lost the election, Vargas secretly gave Prestes almost US$100 000.[35]

The PCB leaders' decision on an electoral strategy sat uneasily with general Comintern instructions for Latin America, circulated in February 1930, which re-emphasized the building of a worker–peasant–petty-bourgeois bloc under the hegemony of the party and a strategy of forming worker–peasant–soldier soviets (Cerdas-Cruz 1993, pp. 18–19). However, in late 1929 the Brazilians had also obeyed Moscow and set up a Revolutionary Military Committee to prepare for the 'third uprising', which was in touch with the 'petty-bourgeois' Prestes supporters and its own cells in the armed forces.

The possible alliance with Prestes was gradually becoming central to PCB strategy. A direct approach for funds to the Comintern by the 'Cavalier of Hope', now in Argentina, had been refused early in 1929, but while in Moscow in mid-1929 party secretary Astrogildo Pereira reported positively on Prestes to the ECCI, claiming that during the former's column's travels in the interior its programme had become much more radical, to include confiscation of landlord property and remission of taxes on the peasants. Prestes, having read his suitcase of theoretical works, had undoubtedly and sincerely radicalized his ideas, speaking in an interview in November 1928, for example, of the growth of a mass movement and the need for a 'popular revolution', but he rejected a proffered alliance and programme (including nationalization of land and the breakup of big holdings) by the PCB in June 1929 as too radical.[36]

In April 1930 a special ECCI resolution on Brazil was made known to PCB members. This in fact maintained Brandão's 1926 analysis on the contradiction between British-backed 'semi-feudal' landowners and the US-supported 'industrial bourgeoisie', which it said would be aggravated as the global crisis worsened and was 'the fundamental premise for the ripening of the revolutionary situation of Brazil'. Its conclusions followed the recently reaffirmed Humbert-Droz line: the PCB must prepare to lead 'the revolutionary insurrection of the great masses' which might result from the presidential election (which was thus brought, somewhat uneasily, into line with the militant strategy). Dmitrii Manuilskii had in fact been highly critical of the Latin American comrades at the ECCI praesidium meeting from which the message came, claiming that they were 'finding themselves nowhere in the revolutionary movement . . . dragging at the tail of other classes, losing their own individuality' and abandoning the struggle for hegemony over the revolution.

Manuilskii specifically criticized the PCB for working with the 'so-called Prestes column' through the Worker and Peasant Bloc, which it had allowed to become a parallel party. The criticism continued at a session of the Comintern's South American Secretariat in April–May, which focused on the Brazilians' 'rightist errors'.[37] This 'Brandão line' of preparing for a working-class revolution 'under cover' of a 'petty-bourgeois-democratic revolution' was described as based on a 'menshevist, anti-Leninist and anti-marxist' theoretical position which denied the necessary hegemony of the proletariat. (Afterwards most members of its Central Committee, including Brandão, were replaced.) As for an alliance with Prestes, the PCB was to avoid '*prestista*' infiltration but keep in mind that he was popular with the masses. The coming revolution must be entirely controlled by the party and based on soviets and the establishment of the dictatorship of the proletariat.

Among the successes in Latin America later claimed by the Comintern during its 'third period' was a 'sharpening of class contradictions', which 'accelerated the bankruptcy of those petty-bourgeois organizations that had tried to lead the mass revolutionary movement' (Comintern

1935, p. 119). One example given of this was the disintegration of 'Prestismo' in Brazil, with the rallying of a minority of its leaders to the Communist Party in 1930. However, this smacks of rationalization, if not falsification, after the event; in fact, the whole process of allying 'Prestismo' with communism was much more tortuous. In May 1930 Prestes circulated a manifesto which included a workers' government and councils of workers, peasants, soldiers and sailors, and prescribed seizure and distribution of land, extensive nationalizations and repudiation of foreign debt; evidently his further reading had borne fruit. After seeing the draft some of his followers became alarmed, while the PCB criticized its failure to mention the 'hegemony of the proletariat', since 'an agrarian and anti-imperialist revolution can exist only under the hegemony of the proletariat and never under the hegemony of the petty-bourgeoisie' (Pacheco 1984, pp. 155–6; quoted, Dulles 1973, p. 429).[38]

This closely followed the Comintern's 1928 line of course, which required leadership by the party to ensure the necessary conditions for revolution. Prestes's creation of a League of Revolutionary Action in July cannot, therefore, have helped the PCB's mood, even though he gave it a sort of watchdog function, of criticizing any deviations by peasants or petty-bourgeoisie. The hapless revolutionary officer now earned himself the epithets 'oscillating, nebulous, and erroneous' (Dulles 1973, pp. 432–3). On the other hand, it would seem that many party members, including some leading activists, favoured the alliance with him.

Rather than 'the revolutionary insurrection of the great masses' led by the PCB, the next decisive political move was a coup in October 1930 by military supporters of Vargas and the Liberal Alliance, which had concluded it could not win the coming election. A brief creation of a local soviet, crushed by Vargas's followers, was the communists' only contribution; the party predicted a prolonged civil war leading into a worker–peasant revolution, but the military junta rapidly handed over to Vargas as the new president. Within a month the PCB Politburo's analysis was characterizing the Vargas regime as 'fascist and imperialist' but already 'decomposing'. As for Prestes, it said, he had begun to break with his 'petty-bourgeois' followers, the great majority of whom would 'sell themselves cynically to the imperialists and become an anti-labor fascist force'. The 'most proletarianized part' of the petty bourgeoisie, under the pressure of economic crisis, would move into a united front with the workers and peasants and '[a]s long as Luis Carlos Prestes and other petty-bourgeois revolutionaries march with this united front of the masses, our united front will truly be achieved' (quoted, Dulles 1973, p. 452). The PCB leaders had now apparently freed themselves from flirting with military rebels as proxies for petty-bourgeois class allies and with 'golpism' as a strategy. Those leaders were now mostly new, with a changed Central Committee and, in November, Astrogildo Pereira replaced as general secretary of the party by Heitor Ferreira Lima, a former tailor who had just spent three years studying in the Soviet Union. His first months in office were marked by the failure of an attempt to organize a workers' hunger march in Rio de Janeiro in January 1931, which gave an excuse for further police repression. However, this was not the Vargas government's only policy towards labour. A decree in December 1930 extended old age pensions to new categories of workers and protected them from dismissal after ten years service except for a 'very serious fault' (ibid., p. 455).

Much more crucially, in March 1931 the 'unionization law' provided for the creation of unions, federations and confederations (except for state officials and domestic workers, the latter of course the largest sector of female employment). Native or nationalized Brazilians were to hold the majority of offices, which was one way of limiting penetration by the left, and more directly, the new unions were forbidden to engage in 'propaganda of sectarian ideas, of social, political or religious character' or to support political candidates. Labour Ministry officials were given supervisory control, and the unions were mandated to help reduce conflict between workers and employers. On the other side, they had power to sign labour agreements and deal with the ministry. Especially given that the possibility to form *sindicatos* was also applied to employers, it is clear that the Vargas regime was thus moving towards a form of labour organization like that in fascist Italy, as the left immediately recognised, but the point is that it met positive response; by mid-1933 officially claimed membership of *sindicatos* replacing old unions was 168 330 employees and 4349 employers, the former especially in transport, the food industry, construction and textiles (ibid., pp. 462 and 464.).

There is reason to believe that many workers in fact thought that Vargas was a better bet than revolution. The economic situation was declining; coffee prices dropped 37.4 per cent between 1929 and 1930 and another 17.1 per cent in the next year, and by 1933 were 55.8 per cent below 1929 (Dulles 1973, pp. 538–9), which affected the whole situation. With unemployment growing, workers often preferred to keep quiet.

Moreover, the PCB was hardly in a condition to campaign among them, with so many militants arrested and a power struggle in train among those who remained free. Ferreira Lima and the others were now under the direct control of Ines Guralskii, sent to take charge by her husband, the head of the Comintern's South American Bureau. In June 1931 she actually removed the hapless ex-tailor from office, replacing him with Fernando de Lacerda, a doctor and one of three sons of a wealthy family who had been active in the party who, although thus an 'intellectual', was not against the new cult of 'proletarianizing' its leadership. In early 1932 Lacerda was replaced on his own nomination by a worker whose level of education made him a doubtful head of a party's organization. The Central Committee decided (on Lacerda's suggestion) that its intellectual members should not be allowed to vote, and non-member workers were allowed to attend and vote 'because we are a democratic labor party' (Dulles 1973, pp. 490–1).

While the PCB tried to stabilize its leadership, in May 1932 a general strike did develop in São Paulo, despite the state control of unions, a number of which, like those for railway workers, metal workers and shoemakers, had been infiltrated by the PCB. As usual, loss of income and police harassment pushed the strikers back to work, while leaders were arrested. A revealing commentary on building class alliances is provided by parallel events, with crowds also brought out by local politicians smarting at the dominance of Vargas and his 'gauchos' and physically assaulting former *tenentes* who had justified the PCB suspicion of the 'petty bourgeoisie' by allying with the new regime (Dulles 1973, p. 494). It is also important in the context of labour struggle that in March and May new decrees mandated an eight-hour working day and 48-hour week, and in the latter month also equal pay for women, along with childbirth leave and a right to return to their jobs afterwards. Again in May, conciliation commissions with workers' representatives were established for handling disputes, with fines for employers refusing to cooperate.

Faced by a regime which gave a distinctly pro-labour impression, the PCB went through two more changes of general secretary in the second half of 1932. Intellectuals expelled or resigning were finding refuge in the Trotskyist Communist League, which for some time had been subjecting the PCB to strong criticism. In November Miguel Costa, senior officer of the 1925–26 column, and other old *tenentes* were active in forming the Brazilian Labour Party, which was later to become Vargas's political machine. A more ominous token of the times was the appearance of Plinio Salgado's green-shirted and overtly fascist

Integralista party. For their part, the PCB's inexperienced leaders fell back again on participating – through a legal Labour and Peasant Union and without any success – in elections, this time for the Constituent Assembly which the Vargas government, having survived a rising in São Paulo from July to September 1932, had announced to pacify the bourgeois politicians.

While the PCB leadership was rerunning an old tactic, the international context of its wars of position and manoeuvre changed. The Nazi accession to power in Germany in January 1933 seemed to presage a mass movement of the middle strata and petty bourgeoisie to the extreme right, perhaps killing forever the kind of strategy prescribed by the Comintern for Latin America. Brazilian communists, alarmed by the rise of the Green Shirts, began to reconsider the question of a broad united front against rising fascism. A long series of PCB reassessments led to the important decision to broaden and deepen entry to the official unions and to concentrate on a membership drive; the claimed result was a tripling in strength, to 5000. In July 1934 a gregarious ex-army sergeant, Antônio Maciel Bonfim, became general secretary and proved a success.[39]

Clearly, the new front strategy raised again the issue of working with Prestes, who by May 1934 had completed his break with his own past. In March 1931 he had denounced the large number of his former supporters who now backed Vargas, endorsed the position of the PCB on the class nature of the petty bourgeoisie and dissolved the League of Revolutionary Action. The PCB's leaders remained dubious about lingering '*prestismo*', which, rooted in 'the unstable mentality of the petty-bourgeoisie', lacked confidence in peasants and workers and 'proletarian' leadership and tended to turn to individual saviours.[40] In October 1931, as if to bear them out, followers of Prestes had been heavily involved in an abortive military rising in Recife state. For his part, at the end of the year Prestes announced his adhesion to the PCB, which was not yet accepted, and left for Moscow on the invitation of the Comintern. There his contribution to building socialism in one country was first of all supervising workers' housing projects, then he joined the staff of the Comintern.

In September 1933 a Comintern analysis of Cuba still contained general Latin American references to a democratic dictatorship of workers and peasants based on soviets, and this theme was repeated as late as November 1934 (Cerdas-Cruz 1993, p. 182, n. 30). However, during 1934 the ECCI in effect laid down a new Latin American line, of a 'national anti-imperialist revolution' combining not only workers, peasants and petty bourgeoisie but also 'that part of the bourgeoisie which is against imperialism' (Pacheco 1984, p. 167). In mid-1934 Bonfim and others travelled to Moscow for the subsequently deferred Seventh Comintern Congress, which we have seen take a decisive strategic turn to the Popular Front and broadest possible alliance. There they attended the third congress of Latin American communist parties in October, which laid down the new line.

The ECCI analysis in May 1935 already quoted found considerable fault in the execution of the 'united front' policy by Latin American parties. Some elements within them had resisted the move, which was 'subjected to the grossest right and left opportunist distortions', and conversely, in carrying it out, 'the leading role' had often been lost. This would certainly seem to be true of Brazil, as a prime example of 'left' distortion, but during the sessions of the Seventh Comintern Congress Brazil was actually praised as a good example. This was presumably in part because of the PCB's recent recovery, but also illustrates ECCI's lack of real knowledge of local conditions and dependence on reports by national party leaders who were all too likely to paint overly flattering pictures of their own work and often may have had only a poor grasp of the real situation themselves. (In addition, of course, the built-in image of the rise of a proletarian revolutionary movement on the crest of history dominated thinking on both sides.) Reporting on new front activities to the Seventh Congress, the Brazilian delegation claimed that people had 'rallied in millions' and were ready 'to begin the counteroffensive', with 'decisive battles for bread, land, and liberty' (Comintern 1935, p. 122; Aguilar 1968, p. 26; Dulles 1973, p. 521).

A capacity for what one scholar has called 'delirious and megalomaniacal analyses' must have been one explanation for the decision, apparently made in Moscow after the third congress of parties, to exempt Brazil from the 'popular front' strategy of broad class collaboration and instead go for an armed uprising (Pinheiro 1991, pp. 238 and 289–90). This is even more remarkable given the Comintern's recent experience with armed action in Nicaragua, where during the period 1927–33 it had first backed and then repudiated the anti-imperialist movement led by General Augusto César Sandino, and in El Salvador, where it backed the new Communist Party in March 1930 and then bitterly criticized it as it lay in ruins after the abortive peasant rising in January 1932.[41]

Internal ECCI politics was doubtless the main reason for the decision on Brazil, with Dimitrov, close to Stalin and scheduled to replace

Manuilskii, pushing for the new broad fronts and the exponent of the previous hard-line fighting for some measure of continuity. This was reflected during the congress of Latin American parties, where one 'Keirøs,' significantly described as a former Brazilian soldier, presented a report advocating a union of urban struggle with rural guerrillas, with an explicit reference to China, and predicting splits in army ranks in the face of this (Pinheiro 1991, pp. 277–9). It would be splendid if it could be established that the pseudonymous author was Prestes, who had finally been admitted to the PCB in August 1934, but it seems likely that it was Bonfim. In any case, we can see that the Brazilian leaders were backing a radical version of the line on Latin America established since 1925–26.

Their capacity to put it into practice is another matter. In May 1935 one of the Comintern's main organs published a highly critical assessment of the Latin American parties in general, which has already been cited. Even the strongest of them, it said, were 'characterized by more or less considerable fluctuation of membership, inadequate ideological maturity of the leading cadres, insufficient ability to consolidate successes organizationally'. Work in mass organizations, especially trade unions, was weak and work in rural areas poor, 'especially among the Indian peasants'. Full use of legal existence was not being made, and adaptation to illegality was weak (Comintern 1935, pp. 121–2). All of this (with the exception of the point about Indians, given the nature and remoteness of the Brazilian native peoples) certainly applied to the PCB.

In March 1935, before the delayed Seventh Congress had actually met, the National Liberation Alliance (NLA) was publicly launched in Rio to implement the national anti-imperialist revolution line, with Prestes, still abroad, as its honorary president. Its open programme did not include insurrection, of course, but took the 'Jacobin' line of cancellation of foreign debts and nationalization of foreign enterprises, protection of individual freedom, popular government, and distribution of large estates to the peasants while protecting small and medium landholdings. However, there was a kind of schizophrenic element in the NLA, since it also looked towards the rural areas, especially the impoverished north-east, as the potential site for armed action, going so far as to hail the local bandits (*cangaceiros*) as a 'true revolutionary movement' (Pinheiro 1991, pp. 275–6).

This was far less true in the Brazilian context than for Mao in China, and the key military factor was that Prestes, who returned secretly in April, was able to bring his considerable number of supporters into the NLA. In a July manifesto he now glorified the *tenentes* he had previously abused and declared that 'the idea of assault ripens in the consciousness of the great masses'.[42] A week later the government banned the NLA under a new national security law. Nevertheless, the drive to organize the Alliance seems to have brought the PCB some thousands of new members, presumably mostly *prestistas*, and perhaps another 70 000–100 000 supporters (Levine 1970, p. 79). The NLA was replaced as an open organization by the Popular Front for Bread, Land and Liberty, and in October, on the Comintern's suggestion, Prestes (now an ECCI member) was brought into the PCB's Politburo. In any case, the ECCI had sent a German communist, Arthur Ewert, one of Prestes's Moscow sponsors and an advocate of the hard line, to supervise preparations for the rising.

Some active members, however, were doubtful about the new policy of direct struggle for power and were reproved by none other than Wang Ming for their 'sectarianism' in doubting the movement to 'go forward to the highest form of struggle for power'.[43] On 23 November 1935 that struggle began with an army unit uprising at Natal in the north-eastern Recife state. In fact, the insurrection was premature, and was later said to have been provoked by the government before the originally planned date.[44] A very short-lived Popular Revolutionary Government was set up in Natal, but a second army rising in Recife city lasted less than two days and then Natal was retaken by government forces. The military rising in Rio de Janeiro was even more short-lived. Nowhere were there popular uprisings to support the military conspirators, whose PCB-inspired action thus became pure *golpismo*.

In an assessment published ten years later, Prestes, now PCB general secretary, noted of the events of 1935 that

> [i]n the fire of events, our Party was revealed in its true nature – a small party, only feebly linked to the masses, infiltrated by alien ideologies that employed ill-chosen methods of organization, and therefore incapable of surviving the brutality of reaction, which brought it to almost total extinction (Prestes 1945, p. 142).

He thus ignored the fact that the 'alien ideologies' (military insurrectionism) and 'ill-chosen methods of organization' (reliance on dissident army units) were in fact his own importation, although Bonfim and the other Politburo members were at fault in eagerly accepting them. The PCB, and for that matter the Comintern, had in effect surrendered to the old Brazilian – actually, general Latin American – tradition of politics through the *golpe*, the coup, which had nothing to do with mass action.

The result for the party was in fact brutal repression on the greatest-ever scale and a situation of painful rebuilding.[45] At the beginning of 1938 it was reported that '[t]he Party is ridding itself of its old sectarian heritage and is entering into temporary alliance with all groups, classes, parties, and associations which agree to wage the anti-fascist struggle' and also 'fighting side by side with the bourgeois-democratic governments such as the U.S.A. and France'. The mandate to 'Struggle against every form of imperialism' was now denounced as 'a Trotskyite slogan' (quoted, Aguilar 1968, n. 4, p. 33). In other words, the PCB had now gone over to the more mainstream post-Seventh Congress strategy, which in its case was a token of weakness, the need to form a protective screen of allies and give up its revolutionary appearance which followed from the failure to take position in an underdeveloped working class or alternatively to build a real bloc with peasants and others and on that terrain conduct a long-term war of political manoeuvre. These interwar failings are the important lesson of the PCB's case for twenty-first-century movements, along with its shift to military adventurism, rather than seeking to combine any necessary armed action with politics, as may well be necessary in the future.

In the interwar years, in a 'dependent' social formation as in a 'semi-colonial' one, the tasks of taking position and manoeuvring to power thus proved practically and theoretically beyond the power of local communists and conceptually ungraspable by the custodians of Leninism in Moscow. In Chapter 6 we shall look at some of the doctrinal failings more closely. Here we have seen that the terrain of class analysis and alliance-building remained extremely difficult to lay out in situations where local power blocs of landowners and capitalists had control of the state apparatus and its policies, a theme which will doubtless resonate in Latin America and elsewhere on the periphery in the twenty-first century. The failure was virtually absolute in Brazil, where a deviant tactics of golpism was adopted, a temptation which we again find catastrophically in Indonesia in 1965. Successes in China – the ability to survive and control a remote area – came because Mao opted for a terrain, strategy and tactics which were quite deviant from Marxist orthodoxy of any kind (and in a large country) but did follow the Comintern line of national patriotism after mid-1935. His reliance on building the party's own armed struggle, rather than on army officers who otherwise might have been glad to wipe it out, is also a lesson to be reconsidered in future cases. We should now turn to see how various issues of revolutionary strategy worked out in our third interwar case, Imperial India.

# 5 Confronting Colonialism: Revolution and the Raj

In 1928 Trotsky claimed that '[t]he woeful epigones ... in their hunt after a peasant party, ended up with the subordination of the Chinese workers to the Kuomintang [and] the strangulation of communism in India in the name of the "Workers' and Peasants' Party"' (Trotsky 1962, p. 71). He thus extended his views on the inherently subordinate revolutionary status of peasants into a general fault of Stalin and the Comintern, a supposed over-emphasis on them. India is an important case in the history of Marxism's shift to the periphery after 1920 for a number of reasons, not only because of the communists' failure to ground themselves among the peasants in the 1920s and 1930s. Above all it is important because there, more than in any other colonial context, the Comintern came up against something which was arguably a 'national' bourgeoisie in the sense of real opposition to the imperial rulers. Jairus Banaji, for example, noted that 'in India alone of the major colonial countries an indigenous bourgeoisie was successful in leading a mass movement against imperialism' (Banaji 1977, p. 31). We shall find that in these and other senses India is a most illuminating case in terms of the need for socialist revolutionaries to take position among class interests and create revolutionary subjects, and one which is of considerable relevance now, as indigenous capitalist classes consolidate in some Asian and Latin American countries.

## THE FOUNDATIONS

For the imperial rulers India, with its 338 200 000 people in 1931, was truly the 'jewel in the crown', but the crown was held in the metropolis and Indian riches were basically transferred there.[1] In 1928 Trotsky also noted their combined but unequal relationship:

> Britain's dependence upon India naturally bears a qualitatively different character from India's dependence upon Britain. But this difference is determined, at bottom, by the difference in the respective levels of development of their productive forces, and not at all by the degree of their economic self-sufficiency (Trotsky 1962, p. 28).

By the late nineteenth century, therefore, India was grasped within the system of realization of surplus value and accumulation centred in the metropolis. The important point was that already before the end of that century the organic intellectuals of the Indian bourgeoisie had arrived at the same basic theoretical position as Trotsky did later. As one of them put it in 1893, India had become 'a Plantation, growing raw produce to be shipped by British Agents in British Ships, to be worked into Fabrics by British skill and capital, and to be re-exported to the Dependency by British merchants' (quoted, Chandra 1966, p. 86). Dadabhai Naoroji had already stated the 'drain theory' in 1867. Well in advance of contemporary Marxist theorizing and very close to such work done in the 1960s and 1970s, he and a number of other Indian writers in the decades spanning 1900 in effect put forward a concept of 'unequal exchange', calculating that there was a net export surplus drain of nearly a half of India's net revenue. This was 6 per cent of gross national income, but nearly a third of the net social surplus (Chandra *et al.* 1989, p. 97; Chandra 1966, pp. 106, 113, 121 and 122).

Typically in dealing with the periphery, the colonial state had not held to British *laissez-faire* principles, undertaking most notably the building of the railways which fetched out Indian produce. Implementing its own version of development policy, it also set up 'pioneer' industries and those requiring very large investment, but not to replace local capitalists in anything of which they were capable, and also with the intention of handing state enterprises over to Indian capitalists who were advanced enough to take them over. All the same, India remained basically a producer of raw materials for use in above all British industries; thus, in 1911 about three-quarters of foreign investment (including in Ceylon) was in extractive industries (60 per cent in plantations) and only 3.7 per cent in manufacturing, including jute fabrics.[2]

The early Indian dependency theorists drew more than economic conclusions from their studies. As one of them wrote in 1901:

[t]he introduction of foreign, and mostly British, capital for working out the natural resources of the country, instead of being a help, is, in fact, the greatest of hindrances to all real improvements in the economic conditions of the people. It is as much a political, as it is an economic danger.

Naoroji drew the logical political conclusions. At an international socialist congress in 1904 he demanded internal self-government, such as was found in Canada and Australia, and in his presidential address to the annual session of the Indian National Congress in December 1906 he laid this down as the organization's goal (quoted, Chandra *et al.* 1989, p. 94, and p. 100).

Congress had been founded already in December 1885, as the mouthpiece of Western-educated middle-strata elements like the lawyer Motilal Nehru who stood in general for democratic, secular politics and national unity and sought such concessions as a reduction of the military budget, press freedom, and the right of Indian judges to try British offenders. By 1906, as just noted, frustration on these and similar issues caused radicalization, and Congress came out for self-government. Moreover, it broadened its social base through launching the '*swadeshi*' movement to that end, with a boycott of British imports. There were some socialist influences, often channelled through resident Britons like Annie Besant, the Theosophist mystic, but the key factor which may be related to the boycott in particular is the Congress intellectuals' class links (often directly family ones) to the Indian bourgeoisie. Above all in Bombay, wealthy trading houses like the Birlas had emerged and moved into manufacturing commodities, especially textiles, which were in competition with imports. Here we find a basis for a national bourgeoisie which was being hampered from developing into a full capitalist class by colonial rule and which therefore had a vested interest in independence and control of the state and for which Congress was to prove an excellent vehicle.[3]

In December 1907 Congress split into moderate and radical factions, and another inauspicious development was the emergence of the All-India Muslim League claiming to speak for Muslim minority religious interests against the Hindu majority. The split also gave impetus to an important tendency centred originally in Bengal, namely armed actions by some youth groups against the colonial authorities.

The First World War, fought for British and not Indian interests, was nevertheless a turning-point in the colony's development (Morris 1983, pp. 600–7). During it and immediately after, there was in particular an expansion of cotton and jute textile production to compensate for reduced imports; in the period 1919–22 the annual investment rate in cotton goods production almost doubled. This was mainly by Indian entrepreneurs, who also now went into engineering, iron and steel, paper and cement. From 1922, however, British policy ceased to favour this trend; for example, a proposal to give Indian shippers a monopoly of coastal traffic was defeated. The investment of British capital also declined, indicating a general downturn in the economy after the postwar boom.[4]

That boom period had witnessed a major upsurge in nationalist politics. In January 1915 Mohandas Gandhi had come back from South

Africa, where he had gained fame as the defender of the Indian migrant community. He rapidly became a leading Congress figure, and in February 1919, applying his concept of non-violent mass resistance, Congress launched a 'non-cooperation' movement against new repressive legislation. In April this led to a typical colonialist response, the Amritsar massacre, with 379 officially dead and probably many more in actuality.

In August 1920 the movement was renewed, this time emphasizing boycott of foreign cloth, and by January 1922 it became a mass civil disobedience, with a total of around 30 000 arrests. However, in the next month, in the Chauri Chaura incident, 22 policemen were killed by a crowd enraged by being fired on. Following this violation of his principles, Gandhi called off the campaign, writing to Jawaharlal Nehru, Motilal's son and a radical young Congress leader, that otherwise 'we would have been leading not a non-violent struggle but essentially a violent struggle'. This did not prevent Gandhi from being arrested in March and getting a six-year sentence.[5]

Clearly, national struggle could not be held separate from social issues if a mass following was to be mobilized. In 1886 Dadabhai Naoroji had in effect opposed this, maintaining that the new Congress must be concerned with 'questions in which the entire nation has a direct participation', leaving 'social reforms and other class questions' to other organizations. However, in May 1899 came the first major strike, by railway workers. The *swadeshi* movement included strikes and unions were formed. In the period 1914–19 foodgrain prices almost doubled, giving extra impetus, and in 1918 125 000 Bombay textile workers struck, while in the period 1919–20 around 600 000 workers in all went on strike. In November 1920 the All-India Trades Union Congress (AITUC) was founded (Chandra *et al.* 1989, pp. 211 and 216; Banaji 1977, p. 27). Lala Lajpat Rai, its main leader, declared that 'Militarism and Imperialism are the twin children of capitalism; they are one in three and three in one' and

> [a]n appeal to patriotism must affect the rich and the poor alike, in fact, the rich more than the poor. . . . The Indian capitalist must meet labour half way and must come to an understanding with it on the basis of sharing the profits in a reasonable and just proportion (quoted Chandra *et al.* 1989, p. 216).

The militant working-class challenge was therefore to not only the British rulers and employers but the aspirant Indian capitalists in the immediate postwar period. The Congress response, led by more radical members like the younger Nehru, was to begin to work with the AITUC in 1922. In that year more than a million working days were lost to strikes in the Bengal jute mills, and there were continuing strike waves until 1926 (Banaji 1977, p. 27).

On the other hand, Banaji makes the point that 'the social connections which were made in the first great upsurge of the postwar aftermath were not between the "rising working class movement" and Congress, but between Congress and the peasantry', and this was to prove decisive for the history of both Congress and the communist movement (ibid., p. 28). By the second decade of the twentieth century the majority of Indian peasants, the great bulk of the population, were caught in the classical mill of peripheral capitalism, ground among the pressures of commoditization, export production, taxation and land shortages.[6] Proletarianization was advancing; between the 1921 and 1931 censuses wage-labourers rose from 18.6 to 26.3 per cent of the labour force (Krishnamurty 1983, Table 6.2, p. 535). Direct confrontation came not only with landlords over in particular share-cropping and with merchants-cum-moneylenders, but with officials over tax-collection and the state's ability to exact rent through its control of all land not privately owned. As with workers, the postwar period saw important peasant organizational developments.[7] In February 1918 the first Peasant League (Kisan Sabha) was formed in United Provinces, and in October 1920 Congress organizers moved in to bring it into the non-cooperation campaign. Another important movement began among Muslim tenants in Malabar in August 1921 (Chandra *et al.* 1989, pp. 197–204).

GETTING A FOOTHOLD

As we shall see, the key Congress link to the peasantry was to be through Gandhi, not in terms of peasant organization as such, but we must now bring the communists into the picture. It is important here that there was an already-established situation of mass mobilization and struggle into which the Comintern's followers had to insert themselves as they sought to expand the world revolutionary movement after its Second Congress in July–August 1920. In October an Indian Communist Party was established, but in far-off Tashkent, in Soviet Central Asia, mainly from among Muslim opponents of British rule in exile.[8] However, M.N. Roy, whom we have already met as Lenin's theoretical opponent at the Second Congress, was able to add his intelligence and energy to the effort, and comrades were infiltrated to create five groups in India itself, of which that in Bombay led by S.A. Dange was the most important.[9]

It was implicit in the Comintern concept of the united front, adopted in 1920, that the Indian comrades link themselves to Congress, but the problem was to persuade its leaders, as already established featured players, to take note of the new actors. In a December 1921 manifesto Roy, who was banned from India and was living in Berlin, called on those in Congress who believed in mass action to form a bloc within it to push it towards more radical positions. On the other side, Comintern views on appropriate struggle were not likely to attract Gandhi, the Nehrus and other Congress luminaries. In December 1922 the ECCI took the line that 'British rule can and will be overthrown only by a violent revolution'. Dange and other communists attended Congress's annual general session in that month, but their attempt to influence the programme to be adopted was blocked by Gandhi.

The Fourth Comintern Congress held in November–December 1922 assessed progress in India. The old Bolshevik Grigorii Zinoviev spoke of 'valuable results', but another, Karl Radek, of failure to penetrate unions or use 'the rights which our British overlords are compelled to concede to us [sic]'. In an article published in October Roy had in effect challenged the concept of stages of struggle by saying that the 'nationalist bourgeoisie is not pitted against an old order of social production'. Consistent with his arguments against Lenin in 1920, he wrote that there was a need for colonial communist parties because there were inherent limits on how far the 'native bourgeoisie' would go. As a preliminary step, he advocated establishing a workers' and peasants' party. However, as an Indian delegate to the Fourth Congress he orthodoxly described the national bourgeoisie as the 'vanguard' against 'backward, antiquated forms of society', and the Congress's 'Theses on the Eastern Question' stated that the Comintern 'supports every national revolutionary movement against imperialism'.

In effect, the issue of building a class terrain for colonial wars of position and manoeuvre had been raised, and Roy continued to press for independent organizational initiative. In an article published in the Comintern's journal *Inprekor* in January 1923, he described the Gandhi movement as petty-bourgeois and predicted that it would eventually be captured by its radical minority. In mid-1923 he suggested fusing existing groups into a small illegal communist party which would work through an open workers' and peasants' party; in fact, a manifesto of the Labour and Kisan Party of Hindustan had been issued in Bengal in May. In June an ECCI message to a proposed Lucknow conference to establish such a party (never actually held) hailed it as 'the first working class party of India', but stated that the 'Indian bourgeoisie is a revolutionary factor, because its interests are objectively in conflict with imperialism'; any revolutionary party of workers and peasants must collaborate with it (Adhikari (ed.) 1974, pp. 106–8 and 153; Degras (ed.) 1960, p. 12; Overstreet and Windmiller 1959, p. 65).

By early 1924 the colonial authorities had already come to see the communists as a threat. Known communists were arrested and tried in April–May in the so-called Cawnpore (Kanpur) conspiracy case against Roy (in his absence), Dange and six others. The defendants were sentenced to four years in prison, seriously weakening organizational efforts. With this background, the Indian report to the Comintern Fifth Congress held in June–July 1924 recommended that, since the 'big bourgeoisie' had abandoned the national liberation movement, a 'national people's party' and a 'proletarian class party' should be established. This was in line with Roy's suggestion, and during the discussion he claimed that, had the bourgeois leaders not defused the peasant movement in 1922, 'the edifice of British imperialism would long since have collapsed'. From this he concluded that it was 'an utterly ridiculous stand' to maintain that 'the colonial bourgeoisie is an objectively revolutionary force which we should support and with which we should establish relations'. Nevertheless, the final resolution, opposed by him, in fact directed the ECCI to expand direct contact with 'national movements for emancipation', which could only mean with Congress.[10]

Roy's basic problem was that he was getting caught up in the internal Soviet struggle for power. At the Fifth Congress he was put in his place by the senior Soviet representative on the colonial commission, Stalin's man Manuilskii, who described him as under 'the influence of nihilist theory on the national question'. This reproof reasserted the dogmatic view of necessary stages of struggle, to which Stalin was crucially committed in the case of China, which was more important to the Comintern. Paralleling the current line of the CCP, the ECCI plenum in March–April 1925 recommended communist entry into the Congress and Swaraj Party organizations. The object was to 'create a mass national-revolutionary party and an all-India anti-imperialist bloc' and at the same time unite existing communist groups into a single party (Sobolev et al. 1971, p. 230).

The Swaraj Party was a product of intra-Congress debate following the 1922 climb-down, mainly significant because it revolved around the issue of working within the limited electoral possibilities offered by the colonial system until the mass base could be built. Congress was never intent on revolution, only on using popular movements to gain leverage while it negotiated itself into power and towards eventual independence. Swaraj, formed in January 1923 by C.R. Das (on whom the communists pinned their hopes of influence in Congress) and Motilal Nehru, therefore represented the 'pro-changers', who favoured a strategy of electoral participation against the 'no-changers' like Gandhi (released from gaol in February 1924). In the November 1923 elections (on a very limited franchise) Swaraj won 42 of 101 seats in the central legislature, got a clear majority in the Central Provinces assembly, and was the largest party in Bengal. Gandhi came round, and in November 1924 a Congress agreement with the Swarajists recognized their work as part of Congress's.[11]

In the context of a strong and confident colonialism, with British control of the state apparatus, the bad effects of participation asserted themselves, opening up chances for the British to play off different Indian interests, including Congress factions, against one another. In March 1926 the Congress leaders decided to withdraw from all elected bodies to arrest this trend. In the meantime, their, and the Swarajists', moderation had induced an upsurge of extreme militancy. In October 1924 the Hindustan Republican Association (Army), dedicated to armed insurrection, was formed and began guerrilla operations.

This activity appeared to be an outflanking of the communists by much more militant elements who combined nationalism and Marxism. However, the strategy of leaders like Baghat Singh and Surya Sen was misplaced given the balance of forces, while communist organizational efforts were being realistically directed towards Roy's double-track strategy of open workers' and peasants' parties and a secret communist party. Since 1923 various versions of the former had been launched in Madras, Bengal, Bombay and the Punjab, sometimes within Congress or the Swaraj Party. In December 1925 a meeting was held in Kanpur on the initiative of a former supporter of the Bengal militants to create a legal party dedicated to 'national communism', but delegates from the various communist groups were able to turn this into the founding of the Communist Party of India (CPI), the first real attempt to create an integrated leadership. In principle, Roy's external party, based in Germany, now became the foreign bureau of the internal party.

## THE COMINTERN'S LONG ARM

The formation of the CPI provided an opportunity for integrated revolutionary leadership, but in practice this was still dispersed among provincial organizations separate from the party centre. This was a matter of concern at Comintern headquarters, and as a result brought another factor onto the Indian communist scene, namely emissaries of the Communist Party of Great Britain (CPGB). Since its early days, in fact, the Comintern's interpretation of internationalism had been to give the metropolitan parties a mandate to assist the building of the movement in their countries' colonies, not in principle wrong but likely to lead to extra dimensions of tension caused by paternalism or even racism. In the Indian case, the CPGB, itself only founded in August 1920, had been instructed in March 1922 to 'initiate a well organized and long term action to support the revolutionary movements in India and Egypt'. By June 1923 the CPGB was being criticized for not doing enough (Degras (ed.) 1956, p. 326; Degras (ed.) 1960, pp. 12–14).

In mid-1924 the Fifth Comintern Congress directed metropolitan parties to have 'very close contact' with colonial communists. Significantly, Roy opposed this, and in July 1925 a conference in Amsterdam attended by him and other Indian and British comrades revealed considerable tension. However, Roy was sent to China on a Comintern mission at the end of 1926 and Philip Spratt was sent to India by the CPGB, and Ben Bradley not long after, to try to get the CPI and workers' and peasants' parties (WPPs) off the ground.[12]

A first result of this Comintern attention was the consolidation of the Bombay WPP in February 1927. In the following month a leadership meeting to consider a request by Roy to disband the CPI, still not functioning as an integrated party, and leave the way clear for an All-India Workers' and Peasants' Party came to the conclusion that the former's inactivity made such an act pointless (Haithcox 1971, p. 56). However, given that in May a reorganization meeting of the CPI was held, this was probably just a means of keeping a middle way between the insistent – if distant – Roy and the supposedly authoritative ECCI, which was distant but now had British representatives on the spot. Local communist groups remained active, and during 1928 consolidated the various open organizations as workers' and peasants' parties.

This coincided with a new wave of mass militancy, which seemed to open prospects of advancing the war of position by building a mass base and opening up a political space within the colonial system for communist action. The AITUC had received external support, from the CPGB-controlled Minority Movement in the British unions, Moscow's Red International of Labour Unions and the League Against Imperialism (LAI), founded as a front at a conference in Brussels in

February 1927. AITUC affiliated to the last during 1928. In November 1927 its leaders decided to join the nationalist boycott of the Simon Commission, which was conducting hearings on new constitutional changes. There was a renewal of strike waves in 1928; 31 million work days were lost, compared with a previous peak in 1925 of 13 million.

However, strikes were now often defensive, a mark of resistance to employers' pressure to sustain profits during a downturn in business, as in the cases of the 1928 East India rail strike and the 1929 Calcutta jute strike, which cost 130 000 jobs. The biggest single struggle was the April–September 1928 Bombay textile workers' strike, led by a communist-dominated union, and CPI militants were also strong in the railway, jute and paper mills and municipal employees' unions. In December 1928 the AITUC leaders attempted to exert militant pressure on their Congress counterparts by leading a two-hour occupation of the hall where the latter were holding their annual session.[13]

Peasant discontent also began to surface again, notably the Bardoli peasant movement in Gujarat in February–August 1928, which forced the government to drop an increase in land tax (Chandra *et al.* 1989, pp. 204–9). We noted in looking at the Chinese case that the Comintern Fourth Congress in December 1922 called in its 'Theses on the Eastern Question' for revolutionary parties to campaign for the end of the 'feudal system' and any of its leftovers, like large landownership and tax farming. The latter phenomena were certainly strong in India, but the decentralized CPI had been able to do little in this respect except through local contacts by the WPPs. The basic peasant links, as in Bardoli, were to the Gandhi movement, and we must return to the significance of this.

Continuing to analyse the development of the CPI, we find that the Comintern's Sixth Congress in July–September 1928 marked a turning-point, as it did generally for Leninism/Stalinism and 'world revolution'. This was manifested in two main ways. Firstly, we have noted the strong opinion that the Comintern's previous activity in colonial struggles had been very inadequate, and from this, as well as from the general shift to a more militant posture, sprang a theoretical reassessment of the development of capitalism in India and its consequences for class formation. Secondly, and following from the last point, there was an evaluation of strategy in terms of class alliances. Both issues brought out key themes of this study's whole analysis, namely: the difficulties of applying basic Marxist tenets as solidified since Marx's death to peripheral conditions; the problems caused by an 'internationalism' which was in fact an ECCI – and increasingly Stalinist – monopoly on authoritative decision-making; and the difficulty in establishing a communist party as a viable political force with at any rate ultimate revolutionary intentions in a situation where other, nationalist, forces were strongly established.

The basic theoretical issue in the Indian context revolved around the concept of 'decolonization' through industrial development. Picked up from a casual remark by Nikolai Bukharin at an ECCI meeting in May 1927, it reflected a position taken by Roy at its session the previous December, namely that a declining British capitalism was having to rely in advanced colonies like India on mobilizing local capital 'under the financial domination of London', and 'the little child that Britain is nursing may begin to kick before very long'.[14] Roy developed this view in a book-length manuscript, and it was indeed perspicacious in view of the long-term policy of the British power bloc in granting 'dominion status' and the changes in the imperial economic base since 1914.

At the 9th ECCI plenum in February 1928 the Roy–Bukharin line was in fact attacked in a report by Eugen Varga, a Hungarian who was the Comintern's leading economist and Stalin's man (significantly, since December 1927 Bukharin's position had been slipping); British capital's policy was now said to be against industrialization.[15] Both Indian and CPGB spokespersons at the plenum resisted Varga's thesis, and 'decolonization' became a major item for debate at the Comintern's Sixth Congress later in the year.

The term 'decolonization' is in fact misleading. It was not intended to imply necessary political surrender by the imperial powers or loss of their overall economic control, but rather that they might – or, more strongly, would – move into another imperial phase by sponsoring the shift of colonies from providing basic raw materials to metropolitan industries to having industrial bases of their own. In terms of the present study, we may see this as a reorganization of the overall imperial realization and accumulation of capital, with a larger part of this done by capitalists in the peripheral formation but still under metropolitan financial control. Above all, the reasoning of the proponents of 'decolonization' sprang from a reading of Marx which was defensible given his own tendency to universalize the development of capitalism as an undifferentiated world-wide phenomenon, but simplistic in ignoring profound variations between centre and periphery which were already clear to Indians like Naoroji long before. Interestingly, the 'decolonization' thesis became the distinctive position of almost all the CPGB delegates at the Sixth Congress; one described it as a 'fundamental law of imperialism', another cited Marx on railway-building in India as implying complete capitalist development.[16] Otto Kuusinen, the Finnish colonial specialist and ECCI member who was responsible for laying down the line by presenting the 'Theses' on the 'colonial and semi-colonial countries', also made various interventions during the Sixth Congress debate. In one he argued correctly that after 1922 the British policy had rather been one of hindering industrialization. In a later contribution to the discussion, Kuusinen pointed out that what industrialization there had been in India was not a product of British policy; in the period 1919−22 only 10 per cent of imperial investment went into manufacturing (Banaji 1977, p. 33). Colonial production, it was pointed out in the 'Theses', was always shaped to the raw material needs of the metropolitan country, as with the imposition of cotton-growing in the Sudan or sugar in Java.

Real industrialization of the colonial country, in particular the building up of a flourishing engineering industry which would promote the independent development of its productive forces, is not encouraged but, on the contrary, is hindered by the metropolis (Degras (ed.) 1960, p. 534).

There still remained the issue of whether industrialization in any case necessarily implied economic and political decolonization, and Manuilskii argued at the Congress that neither the development of industry nor any turn to loosening the imperial grip were taking place. Roy's position (he was not at the Congress) combined them, but postulated also an increase in class struggle, as did the CPGB delegates, who believed that industrialization would have to be forced over into decolonization through such action (Datta Gupta 1980, pp. 117–22).

This debate must be set against actual concrete development in the interwar period, which reveals a contradiction which in the end made both sides partly right and partly wrong. India's manufacturing output in that period *was* growing, at a rate higher than world average and faster than that of the United Kingdom, the USA or Germany (Morris 1983, p. 609). Moreover, this was being done by a labour force whose growth rate fluctuated; it went down from 8.8 to 8.5 per cent of the total working population between 1921 and 1931, implying increased exploitation. Artisan production, at least in weaving, increased along with factory output, although some petty producers were being forced out, especially women.[17] On the other side, such persons were not necessarily entering the working class, upon which communist theory insisted the revolution must be built. Moreover, although the most stable part of the class, those in larger plants, increased from 1 101 000 in 1918–19 to 1 854 000 in 1938–39, even after massive manufacturing growth during the Second World War that sector was to total only 2 per cent of the whole labour force by 1947 (Krishnamurty 1983, Table 6.2, p. 535 and pp. 538 and 540; Morris 1983, p. 642, Table 7.23, p. 643 and p. 645).

Roy and the CPGB comrades were therefore incorrect in assuming a direct long-term flow from increased industrialization to a larger and more militant working class. Moreover, as noted above, there was a mid-term *political* trend in British imperialism towards the 'dominion' system of internal self-government pioneered in Canada, which was to prove the key in the Indian case. The Comintern leadership was also accurate in saying that it was out of the original process of subordination of pre-existing modes that the typical manifestations of colonial class struggle emerged, since the destruction of 'old forms' of agricultural and handicraft economy put pressure on the peasantry. Overall, it reamined true that 'the retarded industrial development puts narrow limits on the process of proletarianization'.[18]

As for the upper-class levels, the Comintern theorists distinguished between the 'anti-national, imperialist point of view' of the 'so-called compradore bourgeoisie', which meant especially the commercial bourgeoisie, and the 'other parts of the native bourgeoisie, especially those representing the interests of native industry', whose tendency, 'vacillating and inclined to compromise, may be called national reformism'. Characterizing 'China, India and similar colonial countries', the 1928 'Theses' on the colonial and semi-colonial countries said that the 'reformist bourgeoisie' were 'closely bound up with landlordism, usury capital, and the exploitation of the peasant masses in general'.

> In every conflict with imperialism they attempt, on the one hand, to make a great show of their nationalist 'firmness' of principle, and, on the other, to spread illusions about the possibility of a peaceful compromise with imperialism. In both respects the masses are doomed to disappointment, and in this way they gradually outlive their reformist illusions.

It followed that 'this bourgeois-reformist opposition has a real and specific significance for the development of the revolutionary movement and this in both a negative and a positive sense – in so far as it has any mass influence at all'.

As we already saw in looking at the Sixth Congress, in this Comintern ground-laying for the militant Third Period the role of the 'national bourgeoisie' was thus downplayed. It was seen as especially associated with 'native industry', which might be only 'rudimentary' or 'fairly well developed'. Although such elements still might play a 'revolutionary role' in India and Egypt, their tendency was to carry with them 'hesitating and irresolute' ideology. 'Only a few of them in the course of the struggle are able to break with their own class and rise to an understanding of the tasks of the class struggle of the proletariat.' We shall see the significance of this division in the case of India, to which this discussion of the national bourgeoisie was especially directed (along with China and Egypt).

In a later speech Kuusinen noted on the positive side that 'pressure from below makes the bourgeoisie indulge in oppositional gestures'. However, negatively,

[t]he fact that there exists an objective and even profound contradiction between the class interests of the national bourgeoisie and imperialism, and that this bourgeoisie has its own political main line which is not without significance, does not at all mean that it is capable of representing its objective class interest in a more consistent, more independent manner. The national bourgeoisie of the colonies is not able to do this (quoted, Banaji 1977, pp. 34 and 36).

Two generations later, Banaji was correct when he argued for a kind of Indian exception to this generalization. In so far as the more advanced 'national' elements of the Indian bourgeoisie backed Congress, they did so, as he said, because they were compelled to fight their own war of position (in my terms) in order to impose their hegemony on a mass movement for independence if they were to gain control of their own independent state and thus ensure favourable policies. He was also correct in arguing that their recent experience with the Kuomintang was an immediate conjunctural influence making the Comintern leaders downplay the nationalism of the bourgeoisie. However, we shall see that the actual political relationships of Congress to both the Indian capitalists and the key basic class, the peasants, in the 1930s make much more complex his picture of direct hegemony over a mass movement and instrumentalism, and in this sense call it into question.[19]

Obviously, these questions of how to analyse the development of capitalism in India and its consequences for the class struggle were basic to forming a line on building a communist-led mass movement and dealing with Congress. In terms of the first of these issues, although Roy, threatened by Spratt's and Bradley's work, had attempted to reassert his control over the CPI groups in a letter to them in December 1927, the CPGB delegation to the Sixth Congress in effect backed his position on the need for a secret communist party leading a mass legal one. The Soviet delegation was against this position, the Indians divided. One of them reported that the various communist groups had still to be brought together into one party, and it was noted that they had not been able fully to penetrate the four workers' and peasants' parties which were about to amalgamate. The ECCI report stated that the WPPs in practice acted as a left wing of Congress, which had been extending its influence over the petty bourgeoisie, proletariat and peasants through the 'nationalist Left wing, with its slogans of independence, social equality and socialism'. It was 'absolutely out of the question' to substitute a united WPP for a communist party, 'the organization of which is absolutely necessary' (Overstreet and Windmiller 1959, pp. 102–6, 110 and 114–19; Degras (ed.) 1960, pp. 526 and 557).

The 'Theses' on the colonial and semi-colonial countries finally adopted specified that the 'union of all communist groups and individual communists scattered throughout the country into a single, illegal, independent and centralized party is the first task of Indian communists'. The WPPs were unacceptable on the classical Marxist grounds that there was only one revolutionary class, the proletariat, so a 'two-class' policy must be avoided. On the other hand, the CPI could use the existing mass connections of workers' and peasants' parties. The need was for an anti-imperialist struggle to free India from 'all survivals of feudalism', carry out an 'agrarian revolution' and establish a soviet republic under the dictatorship of the workers and peasants (Degras (ed.) 1960, p. 544).

An ECCI letter to a meeting of Indian comrades in December 1928, attended by Spratt and Bradley, spoke of the need to form an independent workers' party. However, a 'two-class' policy was still followed, with the fusion of the four WPPs on the basis of a political resolution drafted by the Britons. It was decided to work with the Independence for India League, formed during that year by Jawaharlal Nehru and Subhas Chandra Bose, even though it was 'fundamentally bourgeois, even fascist, and ultimately counter-revolutionary', which runs against the general thrust of the Sixth Congress analysis (Datta Gupta 1980, pp. 181–2; Degras (ed.) 1960, pp. 558–9). However, in one respect the Indians did follow the Moscow mandate; after the WPP unification meeting, the communists refounded their party and requested Comintern affiliation, thus formally setting into place both parts of Roy's strategy. The effective result of this was not increased organizational work but polemic among comrades. In July 1929 the ECCI 10th plenum attacked the WPPs for not doing 'practical revolutionary work among the peasantry' and Indian comrades for delays in their 'liquidation'. 'The tasks of the Indian revolution can only be solved', they were told, 'through struggle for the revolutionary democratic dictatorship of the proletariat and peasantry under the banner of Soviets'. The denunciation of Roy was also in train; at the ECCI plenum his old associate G.A.K. Luhani, for example, attacked him as another Nehru and a counter-revolutionary. In December the ECCI in effect wrote Roy out of the international and Indian movements by declaring that he had 'placed himself outside the Comintern' (Overstreet and Windmiller 1959, pp. 133–4, 139; quoted, Datta Gupta 1980, p. 181; Degras (ed.) 1965, pp. 21, 22).

The comrade who had not feared to contradict Lenin and had been respected for this thus became the victim of a changed climate in the Comintern, although he escaped the fate of the many foreign comrades who, having taken refuge in Moscow, were later shot by Stalin or died in labour camps.[20] Nor was he so important after his excommunication that the long deadly arm needed to reach out to him as it did to Trotsky.

As for the continuing struggle in India, the communists had still not succeeded in carving out their own political space. By mid-1929 the workers had passed their militant peak. An article in *Inprekor* by Luhani in May 1928 had put the strikers' situation accurately: '[b]y coming out on strike, workers face instantaneous death from bullets or slow death from starvation in the distant villages to which they must return in default of work' (quoted, Banaji 1977, p. 38). During 1929 the AITUC split, with the CPI-influenced part affiliating to the Pan-Pacific Secretariat of Moscow's Red International of Labour Unions and the other to the social democratic International Federation of Trade Unions. The colonial authorities had armed themselves with new repressive legislation, and in March 1929 arrested 31 CPI and union leaders, including Spratt, Bradley and Dange, who became known as the 'Meerut conspirators'. This organizational decapitation reinforced police violence and starvation; between the end of 1928 and the end of 1929 membership of the communist-controlled Bombay textile union fell from around 54 000 to some 800.[21] Sporadic, sometimes large-scale strikes continued in 1930–31, but the militant phase was temporarily over.

In March 1929 an ECCI manifesto attempted to put the best revolutionary face on events. The WPP, it said, was being brought under 'the executioner's axe', but India remained a major scene of struggle. 'On the stability of English rule in India depends the strength of English imperialism on the world stage.' Again China was the reference point: '[t]he great lessons of Shanghai, Wuhan, and Canton were not given in vain. The slogan of Soviets is already inscribed on the banner of the Indian proletariat.' Moreover, it was said that the 'agrarian revolution is the pivot of the Indian revolution'. With these developments,

> [t]he advance of the Indian revolution will instil new life into the revolutionary movement of China, Indonesia, and Egypt, will sound the tocsin for all oppressed humanity. The day is drawing near when proletarian revolution and colonial revolt will in India fuse into one (Degras (ed.) 1965, pp. 22–3).

Given that the CPI was leaderless and its members basically grouped into the WPP, this was an extraordinarily inflated image of the communists' organizational ability to combine both the national and social revolutions. It is also a cue to look again at what Congress was doing while the Comintern and its supporters tried to reassess and take position.

## THE COMPETITORS

As already noted, in December 1927 Congress remained true to its nationalist position by declaring a boycott of the Simon Commission, and in February 1928 began direct protest action against this new political manoeuvre to split Indian opinion, which led among other things to the police beating and subsequent death of Lala Lajpat Rai. In August a report prepared by a group under Motilal Nehru was submitted, demanding dominion status, but at the Congress session in December Jawaharlal Nehru and Subhas Bose led a demand for complete independence. The compromise, negotiated by Gandhi, was a demand for a dominion to be granted within one year, otherwise full independence would become the goal.

The CPI comment was that

> [i]t is obvious that people who can vote for Complete Independence one year and Dominion status the next year do not attach any serious meaning at all to 'Independence'. . . . Independence to the ordinary Congress leader is a 'phrase' with which to keep the rank and

file contented, and perhaps to threaten the Government (quoted, Banaji 1977, p. 36).

However, this badly oversimplified the position of Congress, both in terms of its internal divisions and, more importantly, its ability to mobilize mass support. As Indian historians have noted, Gandhi's followers had since 1923 'carried on laborious, quiet, undemonstrative grass-roots constructive work around the promotion of *khadi* [local cloth] and spinning, national education and Hindu–Muslim unity, the struggle against untouchability and the boycott of foreign cloth' (Chandra *et al.* 1989, p. 245). This clear creation of an autonomous space gives us a cue to look at the communists' major competitor in the war of position in terms of building a mass base among the peasantry. Here the emergence of Gandhiism, which became a fully elaborated discourse, needs to be analysed.

One scholar has noted that it 'was Gandhi's genius that notwithstanding the incoherence of his formal economic and political thought, he was able to enlist around a single issue a huge range of beliefs, aspirations and popular symbols'.[22] Gandhi's discourse offers a classic example of a 'Jacobin' alternative to Marxism which, although complex and ambivalent (because contradictory) in class terms, was able to interpellate many thousands of peasants and artisans. It was through this, not in terms of the communist alternative, that they responded and thus at least temporarily became historical subjects.

The crucial resources for discourse-building available to Gandhi and his followers were not actually derived from contemporary events, but from ancient Hindu beliefs and symbols. There, indeed, cloth had very special associations and meanings in religious (above all caste), gender and kinship, class and political senses.[23] (It also had associations with support of ruined weavers and other artisans in the Ganges valley for the great 'Mutiny' of 1857.) Village songs were composed as the campaign got under way which 'associated country cloth with images of motherhood, with thick white rice and curd, and with the good things of the unpolluted countryside'. Particularly interesting was the gender content. Mother India was the symbol of self-rule. 'Foreigners drain away our Mother's milk,/Will we simply stand and watch?', asked one popular song. Nevertheless, the views were male; women had to be rescued from nakedness and shame by making them household spinners and weavers again, as prescribed by the ancient Laws of Manu.

These ideas and all the manifold associations of *khadi* were inserted by Gandhi into his overall challenge to capital and its impact on the

Indian social formation. 'Benevolence which is inherent in human nature', he wrote, 'is the very foundation of the economics of khadi.'

> What Adam Smith has described as pure economic activity based merely on the calculation of profit and loss is a selfish attitude and is an obstacle to the development of khadi; and it is the function of a champion of khadi to counteract this tendency (quoted, Chatterjee 1986, p. 90).

With a view of benevolence as inherent in human nature, we are taken into an idealized peasant and artisan universe.

For Marxists, of course, the core of this discourse in class terms would be 'a backward-looking petty-bourgeois utopia'. Both the class reference and the description of content are quite appropriate. Thus, the utopia, in a recent account,

> is *Ramarajya*, a patriarchy in which the ruler, by his moral quality and habitual adherence to truth, always expresses the collective will. It is also a utopia in which the economic organization of production, arranged according to a perfect four-fold *varna* scheme of specialization and a perfect system of reciprocity in the exchange of commodities and services, always ensures that there is no spirit of competition and no differences in status between different kinds of labour (Chatterjee 1986, pp. 92 and 98).

Gandhi contrasted the impact of capitalism with the putative virtues of the past.

> We notice that the mind is a restless bird; the more it gets the more it wants, and still remains unsatisfied. The more we indulge our passions, the more unbridled they become. Our ancestors, therefore, set a limit to our indulgences. They saw that happiness was largely a mental condition.... Observing all this, our ancestors dissuaded us from luxuries and pleasures (quoted, ibid., p. 87).

Gandhi's emphasis on the self-contained village community clearly takes us back to a pre-capitalist, even pre-class world. This was bound to appeal to peasants and rural artisans whose experience was of 'massive deindustrialization and destitution, or unbearable pressures on the land leading to a virtually irreversible process of regressive rent-exploitation and stagnation in levels of productivity, of the crushing of peasant resistance' (ibid., p. 23).

On the other hand, Gandhi also appealed to the wealthy to develop the spirit of reciprocity, declaring that

There is no other choice than between voluntary surrender on the part of the capitalist of superfluities and consequent acquisition of the real happiness of all on the one hand, and on the other the impending chaos into which, if the capitalist does not wake up betimes, awakened but ignorant famishing millions will plunge the country and which not even the armed force that a powerful government can bring into play can avert (quoted, ibid., p. 112).

The class content of Gandhi's discourse was thus doubly contradictory. It directed the attention of the oppressed backwards to a previous golden age in which they believed because it matched an ancient concept of community authority which they still carried in their heads. If, as suggested in Chapter 1, thinking about revolution requires a necessary leap of the imagination, then Gandhiism was definitely making this backwards, away in effect from the reality of imperial capital. Again, the material basis of the leap was displaced onto the predicate that the indigenous exploiters were capable of moral self-reform. The action which was recommended to the peasants and rural artisans was labour in idealized old forms. Central to it was the idea of the hand-production of homespun cloth, which thus became symbolic of *swaraj*, self-rule, the end of the British Raj which had brought ruin to the old ways. As one commentator has put it, '[c]loth stood alongside the symbols of mother cow and freely prepared salt at the heart of the national movement of the 1920's and '30's' (Bayly 1986, p. 312).

The symbols were potent enough to secure mass support when in March 1929 Congress stepped up its campaign for self-government with a boycott of foreign goods, and in December Congress's Lahore session decided to extend the demand to complete independence. In a speech there, Jawaharlal Nehru declared that 'I must frankly confess that I am a socialist and a republican'. However, with his backing Gandhi was elected Congress president and gained control of its executive, and pushed for more militant action. His motivation was made clear by his comment that 'Civil Disobedience alone can save the country from impending lawlessness and secret crime, since there is a party of violence in the country which will not listen to speeches and resolutions ... but believes only in direct action' (quoted, Chandra *et al.* 1989, p. 267, and Banaji 1977, p. 30).

Behind Gandhi's comments lay a resurgence of armed struggle parallel to the boycott movement. The Hindustan Republican Association (Army) had reorganized as the Hindustan Socialist Republican Association (Army) in September 1928. In December 1928 its leading figure,

Bhagat Singh, had assassinated the police officer responsible for the death of Lala Lajpat Rai, and in April 1929 he organized a bomb explosion in the Central Legislative Assembly. Captured, however, he was hanged for the first deed in March 1931. In April 1930 Surya Sen's group initiated a new guerrilla struggle by capturing the Chittagong Armoury in an attempt to get weapons and other actions followed (Chandra et al. 1989, pp. 248–9, 252–3).

On the non-violent front, in March 1930 Gandhi launched a salt-making campaign to break, at least symbolically, the state monopoly, and there were merchants' strikes and anti-liquor and anti-foreign textile campaigns. Women were particularly prominent, and these campaigns, it has been said, 'marked their entry into the public space'. Peasants, especially in eastern India, were now even more significant than the urban population, moved by the pressures of exploitation; salt revenue represented only 3 per cent of government revenue, but 20 per cent came from land revenue. This was a real challenge to the colonial authorities, and especially ominous signs for them were the refusal of Indian troops in Peshawar to fire on a crowd, with the result that the colonial authorities lost control of the city to a popular administration for ten days in April, while in the following month textile workers in a Bombay district in effect established a soviet for a few days (Chandra et al. 1989, pp. 268, 276–9 and 283; Haithcox 1971, pp. 148–9).

At a cost of 90 000 people gaoled, cloth imports from Britain were cut by half and cigarettes were similarly affected. However, in July 1930 the authorities began their political manoeuvres. The viceroy offered dominion status and a round-table conference to discuss details, and in March 1931 the Congress leadership authorized Gandhi (in the meantime arrested and released again) to make a pact with the viceroy. Resistance campaigns continued in United Provinces, where Jawaharlal Nehru was arrested, and North-Western Frontier province.

In articles published in July 1930 Radek argued that '[t]he fight against the national-reformists, the fight against Gandhiism, is no less a condition of success for the Indian revolution than the fight against English imperialism'. At an April 1931 ECCI plenum a CPGB member declared that the Irwin–Gandhi truce marked 'the beginning of the end of illusions about Gandhi' (Degras (ed.) 1965, pp. 100 and 156). Radek was correct in seeing Gandhi as a formidable enemy, but his British comrade was quite wrong about the depth of the Mahatma's power over above all the rural masses. Both views came together in Gandhi's ability to interpellate his own discourse, which far outstripped any other Indian movement.

Moreover, a Marxist analysis must still recognize that Gandhi's dedication to non-violence was absolutely sincere and struck deep cultural resonances, and he had a very valid point, at least in the first part of his comment, when he said in December 1929 that '[v]iolence too often brings reaction and demoralization in its train, and in our country especially it may lead to disruption' (quoted, Banaji 1977, p. 29). We have already seen that the colonial authorities were only too happy to have a pretext for repression, and used it when necessary.

However, conversely, the imperial authorities' ultimate responsibility to a bourgeois-democratic regime in the metropolis, and even more their desire to use the colonial version of its formal legalities as a medium to manipulate the nationalists, did lay them open to pressure from non-violent campaigns. Congress leaders shared Western rational-legal thinking with colonial officials (and with the communists), and this in the end gave Congress more leverage than armed struggle would have in Indian conditions. The separate armed movement was smashed; Surya Sen was captured in January 1933 and hanged in January 1934. In this period the authorities never lost control of the armed forces (except momentarily in Peshawar) and it was most unlikely that even a powerful communist party could have organized a liberation war. India in 1931 was not China, where armed struggle had in fact not yet succeeded, or Viet Nam in 1945 or Algeria in 1954. It certainly seemed to make sense for Congress to say in its 1931 policy resolution that 'Civil Disobedience is the only civilized and effective substitute for an armed rebellion' (quoted, Banaji 1977, p. 29).

More broadly than the issue of non-violence, when the Gandhian discourse shaped peasants' (and others') consciouness it found its purchase in the material issue of their class position but created nationalist political subjects prepared to resist British rule. All the while that remained effective, it did not matter that the Mahatma led a struggle against the colonial state, not the landlords, whom he was content to admonish that they should act as 'trustees' of the land (Alavi 1975, p. 1237). A class message was not necessarily going to override a national one, and although the Comintern and CPI gave theoretical priority to a first stage in which the latter should predominate, the Indian comrades never really got to the peasants anyway. Again, it was not they who fought for the Untouchables (*Harijan*), as Gandhi did.[24]

These criticisms do not mean that the Comintern theorists were wrong when in mid-1928 they portrayed Gandhiism as originally a 'radical petty-bourgeois' movement (another was Sarekat Islam in Indonesia) which had become 'bourgeois national-reformist' through serving the 'big bourgeoisie'. Basically non-class ideologies, like Gandhiism, can change their class significance politically while continuing to recruit at the same levels, and 'radical petty-bourgeois' could in fact remain an adequate ideological characterization all the while the discourse opposed the abuse of big property by its holders and their failure to recognize moral obligations. The communists never really appreciated the power of any appeal other than that to class identities. The 'Programme' adopted by the Comintern Sixth Congress described Gandhiism as 'permeated through and through with religious conceptions' and idealizing 'the most backward and economically reactionary ways of living'. 'More and more,' it declared, 'Gandhiism is becoming an ideology directed against the revolution of the popular masses. Communism must fight against it relentlessly' (Degras (ed.) 1960, pp. 519 and 541). Objectively speaking, these things were true, but the Comintern and CPI comrades did not in practice do much more than suppose in an essentially idealist way that the march of history would sweep Gandhiism into some materialist dustbin.[25]

Jawaharlal Nehru was to write about the Mahatma in January 1936 that

> Gandhi has played a revolutionary role in India of the greatest importance because he knew how to make the most of the objective conditions and could reach the heart of the masses; while groups with a more advanced ideology functioned largely in the air (quoted, Chandra et al. 1989, p. 299).

This was correct, and applied both to the CPI and Congress. In terms of the latter, modern Indian historians have spoken of Gandhi as 'basically a 19th century liberal and believer in rational discussion'. That, however, is Richard Attenborough's film Gandhi, not India's historical one. Gandhi the London-educated lawyer was not the really significant Gandhi. The description better fits Motilal Nehru and even his son Jawaharlal, who later was to speak of Gandhi as 'a strange mixture of nationalism and politics, and religion and mysticism and fanaticism' (Chandra et al. 1989, p. 294; quoted, Banaji 1977, p. 28). For this study, it is of course much more important that Leninism/Stalinism, like its Marxist foundation, could not really cope with the power of national and religious identities and the role of the imaginary.

Nor was it only Gandhiism which gave a real impression of a meaningful alternative to communist revolution. The radical Congress leaders could talk in 'modern' terms about the overthrow of oppressors and socialism. Lala Lajpat Rai, the main link with the unions, stated that '[r]evolutions and revolutionary movements are only natural . . .

there can be no progress in the world without revolutions and revolutionary movements' and again '[w]e are in no danger from Bolshevism or Communism. The greatest danger we are in is from the capitalists and exploiters.' Congress leaders expressed solidarity with the Meerut defendants, the younger Nehru was one of their lawyers, and Gandhi visited them in gaol (quoted, Chandra *et al.* 1989, pp. 242, 244 and p. 302). Nehru was a Congress delegate at the Congress of Oppressed Nationalities held in Brussels in February 1927 and was elected to the executive of the League Against Imperialism founded there. Afterwards he travelled on to visit the Soviet Union.

In terms of Congress in general, the agents of Comintern discourse were up against an alternative radical ideology of the 'Jacobin' type. The Congress programme adopted at its March 1931 Karachi session demanded civil liberties, equality before the law, adult franchise elections and compulsory free primary education, clearly radical and egalitarian in a colonial context. Peasants were to get rent reductions and relief from debt, workers the right to organize and limited work hours and protection for women workers. Moreover, the programme contained an egalitarian economic message – 'political freedom must include real economic freedom of the starving millions' – and prescribed limitations on large property through state ownership of transport, mines and key industries. When an article in *Inprekor* in February 1931 lamented that 'the masses do not yet believe in the treachery of the Congress because they think that they are the Congress', it intended to draw attention to 'false consciousness' but actually admitted to the fact that the kind of 'Jacobinism' about to be thus formulated had secured a mass base (Chandra *et al.* 1989, pp. 284–5; quoted, Banaji 1977, p. 31).

In that context, it has to be remembered that Congress stood for the nationalism which Jacobin ideology also incorporates, and that, while its Jacobinism could not be described as a full discourse, it overlapped at the base with Gandhiism, which in effect was such. The key questions regarding Congress's relations with its basic support, therefore, related to which interests had an ultimately predominant voice in the organization. This was a complex and contradictory matter and the communists, in India and elsewhere, were ill-equipped theoretically to cope with it. Their view of class forces and struggle came down to two propositions: part at least of the local bourgeoisie has nationalistic impulses, historically typical of their class, but are objectively incapable of pushing through the national liberation struggle; only the workers can develop real revolutionary consciousness and serve as a vanguard to lead the peasants and petty bourgeoisie to push through national and socialist goals. These propositions were in effect imposed on reality in an idealist way, with the result, as Banaji pointed out, that the communists (and again, not only in India) reduced their analysis to 'a problematic of psychological subjects', with explanations in terms of 'hypocrisy' and 'betrayal' (Banaji 1977, p. 37).

Viewed dialectically, the concrete reality was quite different and certainly more complex. In leadership terms, Congress was a movement of the middle strata, above all of lawyers like the Nehrus. They clearly expressed the class contradiction of their kind, both aligning themselves with and opposing the local capitalists; the latter impulse explains their 'Jacobin', even sometimes socialist, inclinations. Two shared class interests brought the middle-strata leaders and the 'national bourgeoisie' together. Firstly, each found that British rule imposed limitations upon their capacity to develop. (Ultimately, of course, we are speaking here of the individual level, and we have to remember that only *part* of each class found the colonial limitation irksome enough to seek a nationalist solution.) The class contradiction between middle strata and capitalists came into play here in disputes over the timing of the independence process, basically the 'dominion' formula versus a more rapid change, and over the weight given to methods of direct resistance as opposed to entering and working within colonial institutions. Given the nature of Congress leadership, however, both moments were expressed through middle-strata figures, as when the two Nehrus took opposite sides in 1928–29.

Secondly, and more germane to the communist attempt to organize, the 'national' capitalists and middle strata shared a fear of the masses, which we have seen expressed by Gandhi's remarks in December 1929 on the possibility of 'disruption'. Gandhiism was in fact the key element here, because it mobilized mass support when needed to pressure the British in a non-violent and controllable non-disruptive form. (We have seen that the Mahatma would terminate campaigns if they began to become uncontrollable.) On the other hand, the fact that Gandhiism found its basic subjects among the oppressed classes, above all the peasantry, meant that there was necessarily a latent contradiction between them and the Congress leadership. Congress rode on the backs of the mobilized subjects rather than incorporating them in the way *radical* Jacobinism implied, and the historical role of Gandhi was to mediate this contradiction.

It had not been incorrect in class political terms, therefore, for the 1928 Comintern 'Theses' on colonial revolutionary struggle to say that the 1919–22 movement in India ended with 'betrayal by the Indian bourgeoisie' because of 'fear of the growing wave of peasant risings, and of the strikes against native employers'. It was quite possible to see the Swarajists after 1923 as having the effect of accelerating 'the political awakening of the broad working masses' by opposing the 'ruling imperialist-feudal bloc'. The slide into unreality began with the idea that even 'insignificant conflicts with imperialism which have virtually no connexion with revolution' might be given meaning if communists could take them over. Unlike the KMT, it was maintained in 1928, the Swarajist wing of Congress had not yet finally passed over to the counter-revolutionary side, and the task was now to 'expose the half-heartedness and vacillations' and willingness to compromise of the Congress leaders (Degras (ed.) 1960, pp. 531, 540–1).

The lack of realism lay in not appreciating the real significance of bourgeois and middle-strata struggle against colonialism, and not grasping the fact that such a leadership could inspire mass struggle by other than direct class discourses, even if class interests lay behind mass responsiveness. In consequence, with their simplified view of classes and history, Comintern theorists and their Indian acolytes believed that Marxist-Leninists could move in and take over the social terrain and political space created by Congress. That capacity was grossly over-estimated by the 1928 tactical line that no bloc must be formed with Congress, but temporary alliances could be made for particular campaigns, provided this did not prevent the communists' mass work and ability to block bourgeois nationalist influence in the labour movement (ibid., p. 541). That effective rejection of the united front strategy, the one flexible element in the Leninist/Stalinist position, ruled out any hope of reaching above all the peasants, something which, for all the price paid in 1927, Mao had earlier been able to do through the Kuomintang, as, for that matter, comrades like Li Li-san had been able to reach workers.

## FROM DISARRAY TO INFILTRATION

As it was, the Comintern and CPI strategists could do nothing else throughout the militant 'Third Period' but lament the absence of any real communist party and continue to indulge in wishful thinking. At an enlarged ECCI plenum in February 1930 Manuilskii complained that '[t]here is not even in India a communist party yet', so that the 'fate of the Indian revolution lies in the hands of the metal workers of

Manchester and the Scottish miners'. Again, in late 1930 the CPGB's chief theoretician, R.P. Dutt, himself of Indian descent, wrote that the Indian revolutionary movement was still 'at the level of primitive and sporadic class struggle' because there was no effective communist party (Degras (ed.) 1965, pp. 99, 100 and 156).

The non-functioning party did have a programme, issued in December 1930.[26] This 'draft platform of action' called for the winning of national independence through agrarian revolution and forcible overthrow of British rule, the biggest obstacle to which was seen as the illusions of the Indian masses about Congress. The programme called for 'ruthless war on the "Left" national reformists' and 'revolutionary armed insurrection of the widest possible masses of the working class, the peasantry, the poor of the towns and the Indian soldiers'. This was a projection beyond the concrete into the realms of fantasy, and wishful thinking continued to be its complement. Thus, in April 1931, reacting to the execution of Bhagat Singh and other comrades, an article in *Inprekor* declared that

> large and important sections of the population are being freed from Gandhism and brought to revolutionary consciousness. . . . Everybody in India can now see that everything that Gandhi and Nehru have done in the past year . . . was nothing else but a preparation for a betrayal of the Indian national revolution.

At the same time, ECCI 11th plenum theses declared that '[m]illions of workers, peasants, and the urban poor are breaking out of the confines of counter-revolutionary Gandhism'. 'The most important prerequisite for the triumph of the Indian revolution', they said, 'is to establish proletarian leadership in the revolutionary liberation movement of the masses', to which end Indian comrades must 'organize a strong all-Indian communist party' (Overstreet and Windmiller 1959, pp. 145-6; quoted, Banaji 1977, p. 39; Degras (ed.) 1965, pp. 160-1).

By that stage, therefore, the communist movement in India was locked into a kind of metronomic oscillation between two statements: Congress is losing its grip; we must organize an effective party. The first of these was untrue and the second in practice impossible. Such devices as the June 1932 open letter to Indian communists from the Chinese, British and German parties were again an idealist substitute for action; pieces of paper cannot stop metronomes. The letter called for formation of a centralized, illegal party (which, it should be remembered, had existed in theory since 1925), noting that up until then the running had been left entirely to Congress. If taken over by the CPI, it declared in another piece of internationalist fantasy, 'The Indian anti-imperialist and agrarian revolution can deliver a death blow to British imperialism'. A July article in *Inprekor* spoke of the WPP's existence as an obstacle to founding an illegal communist party, but left open the possibility of forming 'labour parties' if these could be used as instruments (Datta Gupta 1980, pp. 193–7; Degras (ed.) 1965, pp. 220–1).

In the meantime Congress action still determined what actually happened. The March 1931 pact with the imperial government proved to be only a truce. A shift in British politics in December put a Labour Party prime minister, Ramsay MacDonald, into a coalition with his Conservative opponents as he attempted to meet the economic depression, and Indian policy swung away from negotiation. At the end of the month, Congress leaders decided to renew non-cooperation, and in January 1932 Gandhi was arrested, while the colonial government again increased its repressive powers. Already by August the campaign was falling off and was finally abandoned by Gandhi in April 1934.[27]

Not just a halt in direct action but a deeper shift in Congress tactics now occurred, towards participation in colonial institutions as in 1923–26, with Gandhi mediating between the direct action militants and those who wished to work within the system. In May 1934 a new Congress parliamentary board was established to organize electoral campaigns, and in November 45 of 75 elected seats on the Central Legislative Assembly were won. In August 1935 the Government of India Act provided for provincial autonomy but reserved veto powers to British officials. In February 1937 Congress won a majority in most provinces and the leadership decided to take office despite the limitations on powers, maintaining this policy until October 1939, when Congress withdrew because of its opposition to helping the British effort in the new world war. During this period of office such policies as tenancy reform and improved education and health were attempted.

The respectability of office, even with intentions of social reform, inevitably raised the issue of the continuation of mass work. Peasants and workers were not necessarily happy to wait for ameliorative measures to take effect. In April 1936 the All-India Kisan Congress was created to represent the former, and at its second congress its president declared that '[w]e are organizing ourselves in order to prepare ourselves for the final inauguration of a Socialist state and society'. Peasant movements were active in Kerala, Malabar, Andhra, Punjab and Bihar. On the worker front, militant action revived in 1933–34, although far below the 1928 peak, with 2 168 961 workdays lost to strikes in the former year and 4 775 559 in the latter. Over half of those were in the

Bombay textile industry, and there was another big Bombay textile strike in November 1938. Congress provincial governments alternated between mediating disputes and, especially in Madras, legal sanctions against strikers and demonstrators (quoted, Chandra *et al.* 1989, p. 345 and pp. 336–7; Datta Gupta 1980, pp. 175–6).

In September 1938 the All-India Congress Committee passed a resolution against those who 'advocate murder, arson, looting and class war by violent means', but clearly Congress's new position and continuing class action by workers and peasants potentially opened a way for the CPI. In December 1933, following the release of some of the Meerut accused, a secret meeting had been held to reorganize the party, and in May and July 1934 draft statutes and 'political theses' for a regrouped party had been published in *Inprekor*, but before much could be done it was declared illegal in July 1934. Membership dropped to around 20, which in effect meant there was no party, then built back up to 150 (Chandra *et al.* 1989, p. 337; Banaji 1977, p. 32; Overstreet and Windmiller 1959, p. 155). This was enough to infiltrate a few local union and peasant league branches, the only way Marxist-Leninist influence might now be exerted, or, if sights could be set higher, through the Congress Committee.

In that respect, there now emerged another possible field for CPI influence. In October 1934 left elements in the Congress leadership like Jayaprakash Narayan formed the Congress Socialist Party (CSP) within Congress itself, with its stated object to 'wean the anti-imperialist elements in the Congress away from its present bourgeois leadership and to bring them under the leadership of revolutionary socialism'. However, it did not manage to recruit the self-described socialist Jawaharlal Nehru, who in the meantime had shifted away from the self-described international revolutionaries. In May 1931 the executive of the League Against Imperialism had labelled Nehru, who earlier had resigned from it in a dispute over 'national reformism', 'a traitor to the cause of the emancipation of the Indian people' and expelled him from the League (Chandra *et àl.* 1989, pp. 304–6; Degras (ed.) 1965, p. 157).

Much more important, the CSP failed to develop its own theoretical position and thus provide alternative leadership for a movement which could have been based on a potent fusion of anti-imperialism and socialism. As a group of Indian historians put it, '[w]henever it came to the crunch, it gave up its theoretical position and adopted a realistic approach close to that of Jawaharlal Nehru'. Disputes with the right-wing Congress leaders were therefore fought over issues of tactics rather than programmes, as in 1936–37 over electoral participation and acceptance of office.[28]

While elements of Congress were apparently moving leftwards, in the colonial periphery as at the developed centre the shift to a strategy of a broad united front began to be prefigured. In November 1933 an open letter from the CCP called on their Indian comrades to build a united front of workers and the petty bourgeoisie against the capitalists, but when the CPI leaders carried out a self-criticism in July 1934, just before the new repression, they found themselves guilty of isolating the party from the anti-imperialist struggle, which meant from Congress.[29] The shift in political line at the Seventh Comintern Congress held in July–August 1935, analysed in Chapter 3, confirmed cooperation as the new line. The CPI leadership had in fact already proposed a united front with Congress in December 1934, but conditional on agreement to a programme which included a 'workers' and peasants' Soviet Government' and confiscation of land without payment, which indicates either gross self-delusion or insincerity of intent (Degras (ed.) 1965, p. 357).

At the Seventh Comintern Congress Georgii Dimitrov in his keynote speech condemned the December 1934 conditions as a front and other acts as sectarian errors. In the general context which we have noted earlier in the case of China, of a major shift in tactics to the broadest possible popular front against fascism and imperialism, he held that CPI members should penetrate Congress organizations to crystallize 'a national revolutionary wing among them, for the purpose of further developing the national liberation movement'. In Wang Ming's revised report on the colonies and semi-colonies, published after the Congress, China and Brazil were used as examples. In the former, it was stated, the party was itself incorporating the four key classes (workers, peasants, petty bourgeoisie and national bourgeoisie), in Brazil an anti-imperialist coalition of the four was being formed. Indian comrades should combine both tactics, and once again they were criticized for previous 'left sectarian errors'.

> [W]ithout the active participation of the Communists in the general peoples' and national struggle against imperialist oppression it is inconceivable that the Communist groups or the young numerically small Party can be transformed into a real mass party and without this the hegemony of the proletariat and Soviet power in the country is not to be thought of (quoted, Datta Gupta 1980, p. 220).

Wang condemned premature demands for soviets and a radical land-distribution policy and held that it was inappropriate for the Indians to specify narrow conditions for a united front (ibid., pp. 213–14; Overstreet and Windmiller 1959, pp. 157–8).

In practice, however, implementing the Comintern's mandate was not a question of allying organizations 'from above' but of communist infiltration 'from below'. An article in *Inprekor* on 'Problems of the Anti-Imperialist Struggle in India' in March 1935 laid down the Dimitrov line of joining Congress 'on the basis of collective membership', but this had no real meaning. The few remaining communists could not bring their illegal party out into the open to make an alliance with the CSP, let alone Congress itself, and would have been laughed at if they had (who needs 20 or even 150 uncertain allies?), which made infiltrating the two nationalist organizations by joining individually the only practical tactic.

Already in April 1935 the communist-led and non-communist union movements had amalgamated and communists were allowed to become members of the CSP from January 1936. In February a set of 'Suggestions on the Indian Question' sent from Moscow (the ECCI no longer directly instructed . . .) included alliance with the CSP and a campaign for a constituent assembly. As for CPI cooperation with Congress itself, the publication of the so-called 'Dutt–Bradley Thesis' in the same month marked the laying of the line. Progressives were to be found, it said, in Congress, with not only 'a line of irreconcilable struggle with imperialism' but giving chance for 'an advance of the program to reflect the growing influence of socialist ideas'. Congress could therefore play 'a great and a foremost part' in building an anti-imperialist people's front and even become such itself. The key was the CSP, which they estimated as commanding a third of Congress's total support. The Indian comrades should seek amendment of the Congress constitution to allow the collective membership of local organizations, internal Congress democratization, an unambiguous demand for complete independence and abandonment of non-violence (Datta Gupta 1980, pp. 222–4; Degras (ed.) 1965, p. 389; Overstreet and Windmiller 1959, pp. 159–60).

The CPI leaders and their foreign advisers had thus committed themselves to attempting to colonize part of the Congress/CSP political space. The contradictions of this soon emerged. On one side, in late 1936 a party manifesto warned of a 'Gathering Storm' mandating active class struggle to build up the united front, but at the same time the document accepted the Congress decision to contest elections because the working-class struggle was not far advanced enough for anything else.

By July 1937 the communists had got as far as accepting Congress ministers. As for the CSP, in February 1937 the CPI Politburo, attempting to implement the Comintern line, had proposed an alliance which must also include 'certain organizations of the Indian merchants and industrialists', in other words Wang's fourth key class, and found themselves attacked by the CSP as revisionists. This was an unusual twist, although their reply, that the socialists were 'left sectarian', was a more normal part of Leninist/Stalinist abuse. Next month the CSP national executive complained of the CPI's fostering of factionalism within its ranks (Datta Gupta 1980, pp. 228–30; Overstreet and Windmiller 1959, pp. 161, 163–4).

On the other side of the contradictions, the individual membership tactic paid off; by 1939 20 communists were members of the Congress central committee, roughly a sixth of the total, including Dange, who was also president of the AITUC. As if the turnabout in accepting Congress as a worthy opponent of imperialism were not enough, in March 1939 the CPI members supported Gandhi against Bose for Congress president, and shortly after it was declared in an article that 'the time and opportunity have come... to weld even Gandhism with the new nationalism'. In May attempts to push a militant line in the trade unions in face of non-communist opposition were described as 'nothing short of disruption' (Overstreet and Windmiller 1959, pp. 167–70).

On the eve of the Second World War, therefore, where we may halt our analysis, the CPI had found a way of getting access to the Congress mass base by riding in its pocket, making very considerable concessions along the way in terms of rhetoric and some in behaviour. In this sense, and in that of the fact that by 1939 CPI membership had grown to over 3000, the shift in line by the Comintern in mid-1935 had paid some dividends (Damodaran 1984, p. 348). A basis had at least been laid for making the CPI a permanent part of the Indian political scene after independence was gained in August 1947, although it carried a Stalinist load which kept it marginalized and eventually split and considerably reduced it.

Although we have now completed our analysis of the fortunes of the Comintern's Marxism-Leninism in India, it needs to be consolidated by completing the account of Congress if we are fully to grasp the main point, namely that in that colonial possession the Comintern and its local agents were up against an unusually developed national bourgeoisie.

In the 1930s that class in fact developed further. The British government, as part of a general policy of imperial protectionism after the

Great Depression began in late 1929, gave tariff preferences to Indian-produced consumer goods. During the 1930s there was consolidation of local enterprises in iron and steel, cement, sugar and matches, with formation of manufacturing companies by expansion of groups like the Birlas, Tatas and Thapas (Banaji 1977, p. 26). These saw political independence as a vehicle for increasing their power, and often were even prepared to accept state planning as a necessary intervention to this end.

The success of the first two Soviet Five-Year Plans in a world of tottering capitalism in fact inspired a general faith in economic planning. Already in March 1931, as we have seen, the Karachi resolution had opted for a large public sector, and this eventually led up to Congress in October 1938 setting up a National Planning Committee (NPC) under the chairpersonship of Jawaharlal Nehru. The resolution establishing the NPC noted that the 'problems of poverty and unemployment, of National Defence and of the economic regeneration in general cannot be solved without industrialization'. This was entirely in line with what the Indian capitalists wanted, but it is significant in this respect that the NPC deadlocked on the issue of nationalization and deferred the decision (Chandra 1966, p. 145, n. 78, p. 147 (quotation), pp. 153 and 159).

In 1935 Nehru wrote of the Karachi resolution that '[t]his was not socialism at all', and we may take his personal trajectory in the period 1933–36 as showing the ability of the capitalists to bend the middle-strata Congress leadership in directions favouring them. In 1933, disillusioned with the socially conservative tendency among the dominant Congress leadership, including Gandhi, Nehru had begun to shift to the left ideologically.[30] In September he wrote, in a letter to Gandhi, that 'the problem of achieving freedom becomes one of revising special interests in favour of the masses. To the extent this is done, to that extent only will freedom come.' In a series of articles, 'Whither India?', published in October 1933, Nehru referred to 'the great human goal of social and economic equality, to the ending of all exploitation of nation by nation and class by class, to national freedom within the framework of an international co-operative socialist world federation'. In his address as Congress president in April 1936 he declared that, in conditions of global capitalist crisis, 'I am convinced that the only key to the solution of the world's problems and of India's problems lies in socialism'.

As to political implementation of these general goals, Nehru maintained that votes as such were useless unless the masses held power.

The obstacles to a classless society must be removed 'gently if possible, forcibly if necessary' through 'effective pressure, amounting to coercion'. This was less than explicit, and the idea that bringing into being a popularly elected Constituent Assembly would create a 'semi-revolutionary situation' was naive. Moreover, his view of the mass movement was limited, as in the call in his April 1936 address for 'active participation of the peasantry and workers', but only through organizational affiliation to Congress (Chandra 1975, p. 1308, and quoted, p. 1311).

The key point is that the capitalists had a better political sense. In May 1934 a group of them published the 'Bombay Manifesto' attacking Nehru's leftist views, and another article declared that 'though he calls his creed socialism, it is really Communism and Bolshevism of the Russian type'. This was a typical conservative reaction, and G.D. Birla, senior member of the very powerful Bombay family, reacted against it; the 'Manifesto', he said, 'has done positive harm to the capitalist system'. Two years later he was taking a sophisticated position: '[i]t looks very crude for a man with property to say that he is opposed to expropriation in the wider interests of the country', he wrote, and, to the conservatives, '[l]et those who have given up property say what you want to say' (ibid., p. 1315, and quoted, pp. 1317 and 1319).

As already noted, big capitalists like Birla could accept as necessary for their own future some parts of Nehru's message, like the need for a public sector. Nehru also shared with them a strong opposition to foreign capital; a leading business figure declared that the latter had 'stifled India's political aspirations, crippled her financial strength and contributed only to her economic subjection' (quoted, Chandra 1966, p. 142). In May 1936 the 'socialist' Congress leader (who did not join the CSP) was favoured with a series of support meetings and addresses by such organizations as the Bombay Bullion Exchange, Hindustan Native Merchants' Association, Bombay Cotton Brokers' Association and Country-Made Fancy and Grey Cotton Piecegoods Merchants' Association. He was praised for his 'unceasing efforts for the betterment of the conditions of the teaming millions of workers, labourers, and peasants of the country', and the president of the last-named body noted in his welcome speech that

> [e]ven though your theories of socialism might have stirred a section of the commercial community, we are of the opinion that our advancement is inter-dependent upon the advancement of the masses.... It is true that certain extreme views regarding Marxism

or Communism may not be acceptable to the mercantile community, but looking to the present condition of India and her teeming millions ... it cannot be denied that the reconstruction of the present form of society is needed (quoted, Chandra 1975, p. 1321).

On one side, therefore, what happened with Nehru's swing to socialism constituted a classical piece of capitalist cooptation. On the other, his fellow Congress leaders got together to block any action he might have taken. Gandhi, the revered Mahatma, was the key here. During the 1930s he was in fact moving to an acceptance of modern large industry, as long as it did not create unemployment and lightened the burdens of labour and was state-owned. He was in touch with the British authorities through G.D. Birla concerning persuading Congress leaders to participate in elected bodies after the 1935 act, which we have seen was successful. As for control of Congress, in April 1936 10 of 14 members of its Working Committee were right-wingers or, as Birla put it, there was 'an overwhelming majority of Mahatmaji's Group'. 'Through a series of carefully managed organisational crises, the Congress Right-wing ... aided by Gandhi, curbed, disciplined and tamed the fire-eating Nehru of the Lucknow Session', while 'Nehru indirectly helped by fighting, bowing down, and sulking in turn, and by fighting the Right-wing on questions of manners and styles of functioning rather than on policies'. The acute Birla noted that Nehru 'seems to be out for giving expression to his ideology, but he realises that action is impossible and so does not press for it' (Chandra 1966, p. 142; Chandra 1975, pp. 1309, 1317 and 1319).

If we wished to enter the realm of might-have-beens, we could suggest that Nehru might have got further – and shown more stamina – against the sophisticated capitalists and their Congress allies if there had been a communist party within Congress, or even allied to it from outside, strong enough to give him an alternative base. The point is that there was not. The analysis of the Indian case has amply shown this, and allows us to sustain Banaji's overall verdict even if we have needed to amend and qualify some parts of it.

> Confronting an already strong bourgeoisie and a colonial state apparatus, misguided by Comintern policies whose shifts they barely understood, and isolated from the peasantry, the Communists in India were doomed to remain a *backward insignificant* force throughout the main course of the national movement (Banaji 1977, p. 40, original emphasis).

In the language of this study, the CPI never came anywhere near building its own revolutionary terrain through a successful taking of position among, and creating revolutionary subjects from, various social forces. In this failure it resembled the Brazilian party, but it could also envisage manoeuvring around, and with, a 'national bourgeoisie' made radical by colonial rule, whereas we have seen that Vargas and his predecessors directly held state power. The British Raj had a huge vested interest in keeping India afloat economically and politically and could do so in the imperial context, despite economic depression in the early 1930s. What is more, this facilitated the growth of the Indian capitalist class, who proved useful partners of the British power bloc once the lesson of Gandhian mass campaigns went home.

In future cases, of course, this element of direct foreign rule will not be present, and the situation will resemble that of the interwar 'sovereign' Brazilian state. That was fragile and thus made unstable by world depression, the Brazilian capitalists and landowners were more politically divided than the Indian, largely by affiliation to different foreign interests. Instability threatened through potential seizures of power until Vargas actually did this successfully. The Chinese state and economy were even more vulnerable and the capitalists weaker in face of British and other foreign capital, and the regime in fact teetered on the edge of collapse until the Kuomintang united the country and then consolidated its hold after 1927. After this, it faced foreign invasion, especially from 1937 onwards and still a regional possibility in the post-1999 world.

In our hypothetical world as in the historical one, revolutionaries will have to make choices concerning class bases. The greater degree of stress in China, especially among central and northern peasants, enabled the Maoist wing of the CCP to take position by creating peasant revolutionary subjects and then to impose its unorthodox views on the party as a whole. The PCB, under Comintern aegis, stuck to a very orthodox orientation to the working class as the historically destined subject and ended up in a war of manoeuvre based on 'golpism', whereas the CCP, entirely excluded from the 'legitimate' political space after 1927, found its way, again thanks to Mao, to a military strategy which one could well argue was the only possible choice. Whether that option will be open to any revolutionary movement in the future is another matter.

Again in India, the complexities of a colonial regime far too strong to be overthrown militarily, prepared to use repressive measures when necessary, but ready to open an arena to local politicians, left the CPI leadership in the end with no strategy but to ride on the coat-tails of the 'left' Congress leaders. On the other side, foreign rule left a major opening for nationalism but Gandhi and Congress pre-empted it, whereas in China, from 1931, the communists could begin to take it on board as part of their own discourse. In that sense, the Indian comrades did not really develop a war of manoeuvre at all.

In all three cases, as with all other countries whose communist parties were members of the Comintern, that general staff of the international revolution was reacting, commenting, prodding and issuing orders, a factor which has fortunately been removed with the Soviet Union's demise. We have seen in each case in this and the previous chapter how complex and ultimately faltering the external influence was. An overall assessment of this, and of Leninism/Stalinism as a revolutionary discourse for the periphery, will be taken up in the next chapter.

# 6 Leninism/Stalinism as Theory and Discourse

The point has come at which some overall summing-up and assessment must be attempted, a placing in history of Leninism and its malign offshoot Stalinism as a theory and doctrine of revolutionary action in the periphery. This book takes it as axiomatic that such an enterprise is not dead, and the launching of retrospective analysis is therefore necessary.

## BASIC PROBLEMS

Leninism began to emerge as such only after Lenin's death in January 1924, but its basic ideas link back earlier, to the 1917 breakthrough in Russia and indeed ultimately to the 'classical' ideas of the founders. We need, therefore, to begin our summation with a brief revisit to those.

Marx and Engels, especially as interpreted by the successor theorists of the Second International, bequeathed to Lenin and others the orthodoxy that capital, in expanding as a world-wide system, would perform two historical functions. In the course of a massive development of productive forces it would create such ruptures in every form of economic and social life, and prove so incapable of managing its own expansion, that it would inevitably bring on cataclysmic crisis; and it would create the proletariat which would be the instrument of its own destruction. In September 1857 Marx had memorably declared (in the context of India) that '[t]here is something in human history like retribution; and it is a rule of historical retribution that its instrument be forged not by the offended, but by the offender himself' (Avineri (ed.) 1969, p. 224). For his successors, all historical phenomena had to be seen as moving in that single direction. Moreover, the theorists of the period between the two world wars, even Trotsky, remained trapped within the basic assumption, which had in fact never been *proved* by Marx and Engels, that the 'proletariat' was the mandated historical avenger; only it could sum up all grievances in itself, lead the revolution against capital and build socialism.

In the aftermath of the October Revolution, therefore, the deficiencies of Marxism-as-Leninism may be seen as following fundamentally from the disciples' long-term incapacity to grasp the nature of the 'permanent revolution' – another concept launched by the founders – in a global capitalist structure which had emerged with the imperial expansion and growth in the global economy since the 1880s and more directly with the impact of the First World War and Bolshevik Revolution on the periphery. Thus, the historical movement was still seen in deterministic terms, carried over from the original formulation in the European context, by which capital was bound to generate its own fatal crisis just as it was creating its proletarian executioner.

We have noted that a major token of Lenin's orthodoxy was that he never believed that the breach in world capitalism opened in 1917 could be made permanent without even bigger revolutions at the centre. In June 1921 he wrote that the growth of the 'revolutionary movement among the hundreds of millions of oppressed peoples of the East' had taken the immediate pressure off Soviet Russia, but saw the situation only as one of 'a state of equilibrium' which was 'extremely unstable and uncertain' (Lenin 1953(h), p. 570). Nevertheless, the success in Russia, even if not immediately repeated elsewhere, reinforced Marxism's 'revolutionary immanentism', and set a definite limit on how deeply any theoretical reworking could go. Claudin made an important distinction here, between the possibility for Lenin to develop a theory of the Russian Revolution based on concrete experience since 1905 and the fact that the actual behaviour of the working class in the central formations in belying belief in such principles as internationalism left Marxists without concrete material for theorizing a world revolution. 'If there are no "materials" of this order available', he commented, 'the entire works of Marx and Engels are inadequate for building the theory of the revolution in a given society' (Claudin 1975, p. 61). It is the fact that at the end of the twentieth century we do now have such materials which inspires the present study.

Another basic aspect of the thought of Marx and Engels, taken over by the successors, fundamentally influenced the nature of Leninism/Stalinism. The founders' basic approach predisposed their disciples to economistic explanation and a conversant failure to give due weight to other factors.[1] Although he did not make this more radical critique, Nicos Poulantzas pointed out that the Comintern theorists took a basically economistic approach, with dire consequences for the work of the Comintern and its member parties.[2] While accepting this argument, which focuses on the concept of capitalist crisis, I would broaden it, by also considering the centrality given in Leninism to the concepts of stages of the revolution and of the weak link. Both of these concepts, it may be argued, also led to an economistic position. This greatly reduced the capacity to come to grips with movements, which might be liberatory in content, based upon the constitution of subjects through national, religious, racial and gender identities. These might be directly shaped by economic – better put, material – factors, and would certainly be indirectly shaped by them, but could not be *reduced* to the effects of those.

Leninism's other great inherited problem also derived at least in part from its tendency to economism. That was the failure to come fully to terms with its own Enlightenment background as reformulated into a materialist concept of history and revolution by Marx and Engels. Here lay a major contradiction. On the one hand, Marxism shared much content with the bourgeois thought which had lain behind the consolidation of capitalism at the centre, the basic rationality of historical development, progress, and so on. On the other hand, capitalism's expansion as imperialism and creation of an irrational, backward periphery made the applicability of the Enlightenment–French Revolution–Modernist syndrome of liberation on the periphery impossible. In effect, Leninism was the major form in which the Enlightenment message of liberation was carried to the periphery, but the seed fell on a stony ground which was also of the bourgeois Enlightenment's making. To put it in another way, the avengers who picked up Marxist-Leninist doctrine had already been brutalized by capital, their own cultures badly damaged by it.

This raises the absolutely basic question posed in Chapter 1: given that the impact of Enlightenment thought on the periphery had been through imperialism, could – and can – its ideas carry a liberatory meaning there? The theoretical, and practical, issue here is extremely complex and central to the spirit (although not the focus) of the present study, since it involves the question of whether a democratic socialist regime is possible in a peripheral social formation which has not experienced a full capitalist development, including the political content of human rights and representative democracy which capital in fact does not always find necessary to preserve its own power.[3] Of course, on the periphery capitalism itself in no real sense sustained the rational and liberatory impulse of the Enlightenment, hence the stony ground referred to above. Conversely, from the point of view of the periphery, which had its own intellectual and cultural traditions, the destructive aspects of capital's expansion gave – and gives – an opening for alternative 'Jacobin' movements, based, for example, on an Islamic resurgence.

In the interwar period the issue was temporarily settled by the turning of the ugly Stalinist face on first of all the Soviet Union itself, then on the whole international struggle. Stalinism in the context of my argument was, therefore, a substitution for the Enlightenment tradition of democracy and enquiry. With this view of the linkages between the original Marxism and its Leninist/Stalinist metamorphosis, let us proceed to re-examine and recapitulate the issues which this study has tried to show being raised by that shift and the successors' practice.

## STRATEGY AND THE COMPLEXITIES OF CLASS

A new terrain for the war of manoeuvre became possible in Russia in practice between 1898 and 1917, but could its map be extended to a general groundplan for the other world of the periphery? The enterprise had to be undertaken as it became clear that the terrain postulated by Marx and Engels had not yet been laid down in key formations at the centre, even though Germany in particular had been very heavily damaged by the 1914–18 war. The conclusion was that, as Trotsky noted, Paris would now have to be attacked via the Punjab; in other words, the contradictions of the East must be brought in to exacerbate those of the West. This extension further to the east could not be just spatial; as we have seen, the theoretical displacement beyond even Russia required much mental labour as backing for action.

However, we must remember that, not only for Lenin but also for both his self-chosen successors, Stalin and Trotsky, the terrain of the East was meant to be subordinated to the main historical task, building that in the West and manoeuvring to power there. 'World revolution' remained the declared and even actual aim. Leninism marked no real break with the original Marxism in this respect, while the basic referents still included above all the macro-ideas that class struggle was the motor of history, that the level of development of capital and more specifically industry was the key to revolutionary development, and that the 'proletariat' was the basic revolutionary class. The attempt was rather to tackle the political/strategic/tactical side of the projection of the revolution beyond the new Soviet Union than to grasp theoretical basics.

The political task which faced the communist theorists in first laying out the strategy for the taking of power in Russia and then explaining the act involved a displacement of history, as it were, from the original standpoint of the necessary creation by capital's own development of an industrial proletariat as the privileged revolutionary subject. This displacement occurred, basically, in two ways: by preserving a concept of the proletariat as a vanguard of other labouring people (and the party as *its* vanguard) and by developing a concept of necessary alliances. As we have seen through our cases, this approach was extended when the attempt was made to project beyond the new Soviet Russia into a world revolution and is by no means dead today.

The interwar attempt to develop a political strategy was cast within a postulate of the founders made more rigid during the period of the Second International: that history must develop through set stages, with socialism necessarily following from at least a relatively advanced capitalism. To this the later theorists added, basically as a result of the Russian experience of 1905–6, the idea that, in turning the class 'tasks' of those historical stages into political tasks of the revolutionary stages, some 'skippings' and condensations might be permitted by combined and uneven development. On one hand the theorists after 1917 thus introduced an element of flexibility which permitted the Leninist discourse to absorb new information. A Peruvian Marxist could note in the period before forced collectivization in the Soviet Union that the peasants there had benefited from land redistribution *because* capitalism had not been fully developed: 'in Russia, the rural class has gathered the first fruits of the Bolshevik revolution, because there was no bourgeois revolution to destroy feudalism and absolutism and to initiate a liberal democratic regime' (Mariátegui 1971, p. 46). On the other hand, the Comintern theoreticians remained 'orthodox' by giving a victorious working class the role of carrying out historical tasks which would have been completed by the bourgeoisie if capitalism had finished its development.[4]

The theory of stages was closely related to that of uneven and combined development, which was on the one hand potentially very rich as an explanatory device, and remains so, and on the other open to manipulation to explain things in very different ways, as we have seen in the case of Stalin and Trotsky. Although I earlier suggested that these opponents differed in relative emphasis on one of the two basic terms, in the longer perspective the basic assumption of both seems to have been that the contradictions involved would cause the combinatory side to prevail. One implication, as we have seen, would be 'catastrophism', the assumption that capitalist crisis must spread and exacerbate, a view which dominated above all in the Comintern's crucial 'third period', 1928–35, or at least in its core years, 1929–33.

The assumption proved to be untrue in the case of the centre after the Great Crash of 1929, basically because it was sufficiently uneven as a collection of separate states to prevent an overwhelming combination of national crises. Generally, in fact, the quality of uneven development diversified situations among social formations in the interwar period, also on the periphery, and ruled out set strategic formulae for revolution. On the other side, the common effects of capitalist development everywhere overrode separate historical stages, and therefore revolutionary ones and their set class alliances. If there are no clearly differentiated stages with different class contents, then there are no set 'bourgeois-democratic' and 'socialist' tasks. It seems even more clear in the late 1990s that *the assumption that there is only one basic form of capitalism (as opposed to a single dynamic) must be abandoned.* The fact that the Comintern theorists – and Trotsky – failed to perceive the full implications of the division into centre and periphery after 1920 was one of their most basic weaknesses.

From one prime shibboleth of Leninism, that the revolution in the 'colonial and semi-colonial' formations must necessarily progress through stages, followed a second, that the different stages marked by different class-defined tasks must be characterized strategically and tactically by varying class alliances. This was the basic proposition related to the war of position in any given case, which also determined much of the war of manoeuvre. Even Trotsky did not make a basic break with this or with the general stages approach, only reading the tasks and shifts of alliances as necessarily condensed in a continuous process. Thus, although he mocked Stalin's 'idea of fixing an order of succession for countries at various levels of development by assigning them in advance cards for different rations of revolution', he made only a limited break with orthodoxy (Trotsky 1962, p. 124).

The basic point is that peripheral capitalist conditions opened (and still open) a wider possibility for various class subjects to play a part in struggling against capital and building socialism than was allowed by the 'classical' assumption. Peripheral social formations were and are marked by extremely complex and shifting class structures. The basic failure of Leninism was the lack of appreciation of these complexities in the constitution of the revolutionary subject, largely because it took as dogmas the original privilegings of capital and the working class, and as a result necessarily assigned the leading revolutionary role in successive historical epochs to each, which meant leaving a place open for a 'national bourgeoisie' in the first revolutionary stage on the periphery. Moreover, the issue of the polyvalent subject, the existence of other estranged social groups based on gender, race, religion and nationality, was only internalized by Marxism-Leninism in a secondary way, essentially subordinated to class shibboleths. Marxism-Leninism's failure to understand the nature of the bourgeoisie was perhaps its biggest single class failing in the various attempts to build revolutionary movements in the interwar period (and for that matter, later). Trotsky saw the main implication of the global diffusion of capital as being that 'the bourgeoisie rules in *all* the capitalist countries, with all their diversity in level of development, social structure, traditions, etc.', so that 'the distinction is great, but it still remains within the limits of the domination of capitalist relationships'. He also saw, however, that within those limits

> [t]he forms and methods of the rule of the bourgeoisie differ greatly in different countries. At one pole the domination bears a stark and absolute character: *The United States*. At the other pole finance capital adapts itself to the outlived institutions of Asiatic mediævalism [sic] by subjecting them to itself and imposing its own methods upon them: *India*. But the bourgeoisie rules in both places (ibid., p. 129, original emphasis).

The variability of capitalist regimes continues to be undoubtedly one of the key aspects in the reproduction of capital's hegemony.[5] Where Trotsky failed was in giving insufficient weight to a key distinction, between the relative power of foreign and local capital; in the reference to India, for example, he presumably meant foreign finance capital, but we have seen that local capital was very significant there, as it is in many contemporary 'less-developed countries'. The Peruvian Marxist Mariátegui was closer to the norm – also for today – when he noted that 'there does not exist and never has existed in Peru a progressive bourgeoisie, endowed with national feelings, that claims to be liberal and democratic and that derives its policy from the postulates of its doctrine' (Mariátegui 1971, p. 30). Yet communist orthodoxy demanded such, banking the whole success or failure of the first revolutionary stage on building an alliance with it ('united front from above'), even if that might also involve nibbling its political foundations away in the process ('united front from below').

Trotsky came closer to clear understanding than he did in postulating bourgeois universalism when he wrote that:

> [t]he fatal mistake of the Epigones, and above all Stalin, lies in this, that from Lenin's teaching about the progressive historic significance

of the struggle of oppressed nations they have inferred a revolutionary mission of the bourgeoisie of the colonial countries. A failure to understand the permanent character of revolution in an imperialist epoch; a pedantic schematisation of the course of developments; a chopping up of the living and combined process into dead stages imagined to be necessarily separated in time – all these errors have brought Stalin to a vulgar idealisation of democracy or a 'democratic dictatorship,' a thing which can be nothing in reality but either an imperialist dictatorship or a dictatorship of the proletariat (Trotsky 1967, vol. III, p. 57).

On the Stalinist side we may detect, as a response to disappointments by various bourgeoisies, a tendency to replace them with the 'petty bourgeoisie', but we have seen amply from the Brazilian case how labile they were and were perceived to be, with a tendency to pass over to the side of capital. Trotsky even saw this Janus-face of the petty bourgeoisie (in my terms middle strata), capable of inclining also to the revolution, as affecting the overall approach of the Soviet power bloc.

The compromisist – that is, petty bourgeois – conception of the correlation of classes within colonial nations, that conception which killed the Chinese revolution of 1925–1927, has even been introduced by the Epigones into the programme of the Communist International, converting this programme into a mere trap for the oppressed peoples of the East (ibid., pp. 58–9).

In terms of the peasantry, the 'epigones' – this time including Trotsky – were less open-minded than Lenin. Listening to a report on revolutionary prospects in the East at the Second Comintern Congress, for example, the senior leader had scribbled the note: 'deduction: *adjust* both Soviet Institutions and the Communist Party (its membership, special tasks) to the level of the *peasant* countries of the colonial East' (Lenin 1971(b), p. 202, original emphasis). Unfortunately, and presumably because the pressures of the situation in mid-1920 permitted no such radical rethinking, this idea was not even put into print in Lenin's lifetime and in fact not before 1963.

Events in Russia in 1905–6 had opened up a theoretical space for the peasants in the revolutionary struggle, as when Trotsky noted that the dictatorship of the proletariat 'bases itself upon the alliance with the peasantry and solves first of all the tasks of the democratic revolution'. However, 'social and political relationships' he felt must be 'mature' in a way which left the initiative to the working class; thus, in 1905 one mark of failure was that the Russian proletariat could not 'unite the peasant masses around it' (Trotsky 1962, pp. 132 and 153). We have seen, on the other hand, that Mao Tse-tung, although he always paid lip-service to working-class leadership, was beginning to shift the revolutionary emphasis in China radically by 1935. He introduced a very specific correction (from his point of view), which gave a quite different shape to the Chinese Revolution.

As for the working class, keeping faith with its mandatory leading role proved very irksome in the conditions of the periphery, where its very varied size and level of development militated against generalization. Thus Trotsky, defending his analyses of the events of 1905–6, followed the founders in the West European context of 1848–49 in claiming that the Russian working class led someone else's revolutionary drive: 'I never denied the *bourgeois* character of the revolution in the sense of its immediate tasks, but only in the sense of its driving forces and its perspectives' (ibid., p. 56, original emphasis). This view of displacement of interests from one class to another and of 'surrogate' class consciousness was likely to become pragmatism. Even then, it was much more plausible than, say, the Li Li-san/Comintern line of insistence on working-class action in China after 1927, while in another case, Brazil, we have seen a party which, prompted by the Comintern, was always very 'proletarian' in its orientation, having to scramble for petty-bourgeois/middle-strata and indeed military allies as it lost working-class support to Vargas.

For Trotsky, in fact, working-class hegemony in the revolutionary struggle was so axiomatic that the class's mere presence was enough to ensure this.

> History is not made to order. A country can become 'ripe' for the dictatorship of the proletariat not only before it is ripe for the independent construction of socialism, but even before it is ripe for far-reaching socialization measures. . . . The law of uneven development still lives, despite the tender theoretical embraces of Stalin.[6]

This qualification, in the name of a new 'law', of Marx's comment in the 1859 'Preface' on the necessary exhaustion of capital's potentialities before socialism could come onto the historical agenda is potentially valuable as a Marxist approach to twenty-first-century developments. In 1929, however, it represented a sort of idealization of a putatively revolutionary working class. Although Trotsky recognized that the dictatorship of the proletariat would 'have a highly varied character in terms of the social basis, the political forms, the immediate tasks and the tempo of work in the various capitalist countries', the exiled leader maintained that the 'revolutionary hegemony of the proletariat' was a universal necessity. Of equal significance to the level of development of the working class, Trotsky felt, was its capacity to dominate in laying down a 'national' programme on 'far-reaching and burning' problems 'in which the majority of the nation is interested'. Basically this meant the agrarian and national questions, and if these 'in their varied combinations' were acute, 'the young and relatively small proletariat can come to power on the basis of a *national democratic* revolution sooner than the proletariat of an advanced country on a purely *socialist* basis'. Again, '[b]ackward countries may, under certain conditions, arrive at the dictatorship of the proletariat sooner than advanced countries, but they will come later than the latter to socialism'. In these formulations we find not only an idealist projection of the universal significance of the working class but, in its assumed capacity to undertake representation of the interests of any other, a simultaneous danger of a kind of pragmatic 'substitutionism' in the analysis of concrete situations. In either case, we have a danger of misreading the complexities of peripheral formations which seems borne out by the manifest failures in one after another up to – and after – the Second World War.

In any event, the concept of the necessary hegemony of the proletariat over a national democratic revolution carried out by a multi-class bloc, which Stalin and Trotsky shared, and even more the post-1935 idea of a people's front against imperialism, raises the 'Jacobin' problematic again. It has already been suggested in this study that precisely such a revolution carried out by subjects mobilized from a range of subordinate classes, but not on a class basis, was the political goal of radical Jacobinism.[7]

Lenin in fact saw such a discourse as having become *identified* with the working class by the early twentieth century, writing already in his 1904 work 'One Step Forward, Two Steps Back' that a socialist revolutionary was a 'Jacobin who wholly identifies himself with the *organization* of the proletariat – a proletariat *conscious* of its class interests'. Again, '[c]onscious workers and proletarians believe that power should pass to the revolutionary class, the oppressed, and that is where the essence of Jacobinism lies' (Lenin 1953(a), p. 383, original emphasis).

However, the identification of socialist revolution with Jacobinism is an unjustifiable elision. As Gramsci noted in an early reaction to the first Russian Revolution in February 1917, Jacobin and proletarian revolutions were mutually exclusive (cited, Davidson 1974, p. 140). The reason is that the former is based on the petty bourgeoisie and middle strata (in my analysis) and its political subjects are recruited through a non-class discourse. In fact, in the Russian case the 'Jacobin' element proved to be not particularly strong and hence assimilable into a more directly working-class discourse. Elsewhere that was not so, and this will also be a twenty-first-century issue, for example in terms of socialism and radical Islamic fundamentalism.

In attempting to extend anti-capitalist revolution to the periphery, interwar communists basically ran up against a massive political contradiction, based on the incomplete and differentiating class effects of capital's penetration of the formations there. Because proletarianization was incomplete and even actively retarded and the peasantry and petty bourgeoisie still numerous, while the middle strata might be quite large but socially and politically repressed (India is a good example), democratic and nationalist impulses were often strong, while pre-colonial cultures might provide material for even radical opposition discourses. 'Jacobinism' was, therefore, a frequent manifestation of popular discontent, and even at times very strong (India again). Communists could not afford to ignore it, and its strength also serves to remind us of the importance of constituting political subjects on the basis of non-class identities.

On the other hand, 'Jacobin' movements like the Wafd in Egypt, Sarekat Islam in Indonesia and Gandhiism in India were powerful rivals of the communists, indeed much stronger and rooted deeper in the labouring people. Ernesto Laclau, in his more Marxist phase, postulated the capacity of socialist movements to challenge the regime directly as being determined by their ability to incorporate the Jacobin message in their own.

> From the socialist point of view, the periods of greatest revolutionary confrontation are not those when class ideology presents itself in its maximum purity but when socialist ideology has fused completely with popular and democratic ideology, when proletarian ideology has succeeded in absorbing all national traditions and in presenting the anti-capitalist struggle as the culmination of democratic struggles and socialism as the common denominator in a total offensive against the dominant bloc (Laclau 1977, p. 117).

This seems to be historically true, but the problem is that it simultaneously brings into play the other moment of the contradiction between

Jacobinism and Marxism, the dangers of activating ideological elements which in class and/or cultural terms may not sit well with socialism and even be inimical to it. Trotsky, attacking what he saw as a tendency to 'national communism' in Germany at the beginning of the 1930s, wrote that

> [i]n order that the nation should indeed be able to reconstruct itself around a new class core, it must be reconstructed ideologically and this can be achieved only if the proletariat does not dissolve itself into the 'people', into the 'nation', but on the contrary develops a programme of *its* proletarian revolution and compels the petty-bourgeoisie to choose between the two regimes (quoted, Laclau 1977, pp. 130–1, original emphasis).

Laclau described this as a 'complete formulation of class reductionism', and there is indeed that danger, but he failed to recognize the centrality for Trotsky's point of 'the nation'. Granted, it is ambiguous as the exiled Russian made it, because in the context of international revolution he may merely have been repeating the founders' point in 1848 noted in Chapter 1, that a 'nation' is the only objective base for seizing power. But when he says that the point is to present it differently ideologically, he leaves open the possibility of a positive fusion of nationalism and socialism – and also opens the contradictions of a multi-class movement and the yawning chasm of a quite different 'national socialism'.

All in all, it seems fair to say that the class nature of the new 'colonial and semi-colonial' formations was never fully grasped by those who were formulating the new Leninist discourse, so that the nature, relations and possible revolutionary role of even the workers, let alone the peasants, petty bourgeoisie, middle strata and local bourgeoisie, were never properly investigated. The inherited dichotomous view of key classes made it misleadingly easy to put them into a rank order of importance in taking position in a revolutionary struggle by reading them off from supposed closeness to either bourgeoisie or proletariat, and the class implications of uneven and combined development were not allowed to change this. In this situation, Comintern and other interwar theorists took refuge in the prefix 'semi-'; the effect of this, as in 'semi-colonial' or 'semi-feudal', giving as it did the impression of an opening to a shift in concept, was to block real investigation of the phenomenon.

Perhaps the most serious result of inadequate class analysis was the way in which in practice the concept of 'national revolutionary' movements subordinated the analysis of Comintern theorists and the practice of its adherents to initiatives taken by the local nascent or actual capitalists, like those represented by Vargas in Brazil. In that sense, the potential revolutionary class elements lost the initiative in two senses: they were lulled by the comforting thought that history was inevitably with them; and they ended up dragging behind bourgeois nationalists who were able to mobilize popular followings of their own.

## THE ISSUE OF THE REVOLUTIONARY SUBJECT

The preceding discussion should have given some sense of the theoretical issues involved in the macro-concept of 'world revolution' as it bore on whole peripheral social formations. With the complexities of the revolutionary subject, however, we moved towards the micro-level, in effect posing the key question of finding those who will actually act, the agents and subjects in a specific formation, and prescribing appropriate action for them in conducting the wars of position and manoeuvre. That remains the central issue in all future cases. This study has posed the issue of the 'polyvalent' subject, the possibility of resistance to powerholders on a multiple basis, appealing to more identities than that of class.

We have seen in the original Central Asian and Indian cases, and raised by the general issue of 'Jacobinism', that the Leninist attitude towards non-class factors like national consciousness was extremely problematic. Trotsky, who was more theoretically adventurous (although sometimes only ambiguous) than most, still maintained that the 'subordination of the belated national revolutions to the revolution of the proletariat follows a law which is valid throughout the world', so that '[i]n the broad historic sense the national revolutions of the East are only stages of the world revolution of the proletariat, just as the national movements of Russia became stepping stones to the Soviet dictatorship' (Trotsky 1967, vol. III, p. 56).

There is a very definite tension here, which Lenin, in commenting on the Easter Rising by the nationalists in Ireland in April 1916, potentially relieved by a more nuanced line which unfortunately was not fully developed later. Referring specifically to Europe, he noted that revolution '*cannot be other than* an outburst of mass struggle by all oppressed and discontented people of every kind', and that 'pure' social revolution did not exist.

To think that social revolution is *conceivable* without revolts by small nations in the colonies and in Europe, without revolutionary outbursts by a section of the petty bourgeoisie *with all its prejudices*, and without the politically naïve proletarian and semi-proletarian masses moving against oppression by the landlords, the church, the monarchy, and against national oppression, etc., – such thinking means *repudiating social revolution* (quoted, Carrère d'Encausse and Schram 1969, p. 147, original emphasis).

The Bolshevik leader remained on firm ground when, in his draft theses for the 1920 Comintern Congress, he postulated the Irish (following Marx) as such a 'small nation' – incidentally, both European *and* colonial – but proved to be in deep waters with the 'Negroes of America' as a 'dependent and subject' nation (Lenin 1953(g), p. 466).

Nor was national identity the only one which in reality could not just be seen as subordinated to class. Religion was a factor which the new Marxist-Leninist discourse was also unable to absorb, tending always to underrate its depth and intensity; after all, the Naqshebandi brotherhood which we saw leading Muslim resistance in Central Asia, for example, had lasted since the early thirteenth century AD, surviving considerable changes in the material, and even more political, factors which defined its operating space, and in a much more complex fashion than Marxism allowed itself to theorize.

Let us look at one more non-class identity, which we have only really learned to appreciate since Lenin's time. Were we to attempt a reading of the experience of world revolution under Comintern auspices in terms of gender the result would be gloomy. Although there were specific activities both internationally and by national parties in defence of women and to further their interests, these were cast within a male framework of partitioning off such issues from what was tacitly taken to be more important. Communist parties and linked organizations not directly intended for women remained masculine preserves; at the Comintern Seventh Congress the pioneer Vietnamese woman communist Nguyen Thi Minh Khai actually rebuked delegates for this, telling them that 'work among women is not given proper attention not only in our own country but also in many other Communist parties'.[8]

An almost farcical series of incidents among leaders of the Brazilian party in early 1932 may serve to illustrate a general problem. In a situation of loss of comrades by arrest, necessitating new blood, Ericina – Cina – de Lacerda, wife of the incumbent general secretary, was nominated as member of the Central Committee. She was barred, on the grounds that she had only been a party member for a year, which seems on the surface reasonable, but then she was assigned to do the work anyway by taking over the routine office tasks, which looks very much like male exploitation of a female to do the revolutionary equivalent of housework.

Obviously smarting, Cina claimed a right to a Central Committee vote (this was at the meeting where, as we saw in Chapter 4, her husband pushed through the removal of voting rights from himself and other 'intellectuals'). The reasons she gave are revealing: although of a well-to-do family she was a worker, since her grandfather had been a peasant, and she performed domestic tasks for her husband and four children. Interestingly she won her case, although from a 'gender struggle' point of view she had employed very mixed reasoning in order to do so. First, she had succumbed to claiming legitimacy through the male line, and had indulged in the very masculine party one-up*man*ship of legitimation by class descent. However, second, she had very properly argued that 'women's work' was 'real'.

After this, her conduct again reveals the stresses of women comrades. She it was who initiated the power play of bringing worker non-members to Central Committee meetings. Then, in the male sphere of competitive power-grabbing, when this was prohibited she wept, provoking the intellectual Leoncio Basbaum to the comment '[t]his, comrades, is not Communism, it is feminism!'. Cina's reply to that extraordinarily revealing remark was that Basbaum was 'against women', of whom he had a 'bourgeois concept'. She went on to reveal a growing command of (male) power politics in organizations by manipulating document circulation and promises of favours, but in the end lost and was relegated to her office tasks. Sadly, because it shows her typical lack of options, her final way out was to go off with a male comrade from the USA who had come to advise the PCB.[9]

## PRAGMATISM AND UNIVERSALISM

The difficulties experienced by Brazilian comrades in responding to the international lines laid down by the Comintern, and to handling problems like gender upon which they were absent or at least elusive, raise a general problem for the organization's member parties. This had directly political consequences, but was by nature methodological and with roots deep in the Marxist tradition.[10] The Comintern may be seen as schizophrenically torn between two epistemological tendencies:

the establishment of a holistic universal theory and recognition of 'special cases' in order to remain strategically flexible, which risked a decline into empiricism and pragmatism. Both tendencies raised the issue of at what level to set theoretical generalities, as universals or working hypotheses.

In terms of universalist theory, the global extension of capitalism in two main variants, postulated in Chapter 1 as basic to this study, was what conceptualizing uneven and combined development was really all about. Thus Trotsky drew an important distinction which would have to be taken up again in the context of a possible twenty-first-century internationalism, but which was far too sophisticated for the Comintern's theorists, or rather for the political needs of their masters.

If we take Britain and India as polarised varieties of the capitalist type, then we are obliged to say that the internationalism of the British and Indian proletariats does not at all rest on an *identity* of conditions, tasks and methods, but on their indivisible *interdependence* (Trotsky 1962, p. 26).

Moreover, even formations on the periphery were different from one another and required a theory which could accommodate this. Referring to Lenin's insistence on a forward revolutionary policy after his return to Russia in April 1917, Trotsky argued that '[o]ut of Lenin's "algebraic" formula his closest disciples made a purely metaphysical construction and directed it against the real development of the revolution'. Why, the dissident theorist asked in 1928, should we now apply Lenin's 1905 formula on Russian class struggle to China and India; who would intervene, as Lenin had done, with the 'class instinct [sic]' of the proletariat behind him? Would it not be better 'to introduce into this formula those specific corrections the necessity for which has been demonstrated by historical experience both in Russia and China?' (ibid., pp. 112–13). Trotsky's plea for flexibility must be seen as qualified by his motivation here, which was to argue that the revolutionary strategy should have been intensively pushed forward under working-class leadership. The reality of this has been explored above in the different historical cases of China, India and Brazil.

The significance of certain cases for Comintern theorists and strategists explains the importance given to China in this study. Not only did the debate within the Comintern and Soviet leadership tend to revolve around the Chinese case, but so also has subsequent treatment, taking it as in effect paradigmatic for the practice of Leninist theory on the periphery. While not for one moment belittling the importance of the Chinese Revolution, the third great one in human history, my point is that it was not in fact typical.[11] By the late 1920s basic conditions for a truly revolutionary war of position prevailed there; the old order had collapsed into a widespread condition of disorder, with no firm governance and the condition of the mass of the population visibly deteriorating and causing a rupture between them and established authority. Moreover, that condition was visible to many workers and peasants through their own self-reflection, so that they were open to the interpellation of a new discourse which would point their way forward to a war of manoeuvre and taking of state power. The Comintern's and CCP's failure was in providing such, and the necessary organization, leaving the way open for Chiang Kai-shek to restabilize a dependent capitalist regime form, but also for Mao Tse-tung to strike out on his own.

However, nowhere else on the periphery was there even such a *pre-revolutionary* condition. Elsewhere, material conditions of great poverty for many were still held in place by 'colonial and semi-colonial' regimes which were not losing their grip, as in India, or which could be preserved by intervention by some fraction of capital, as with Vargas in Brazil. (Here we are directly parallel to our contemporary situation.) On the non-material plane, the conditions for developing revolutionary class subjects were underdeveloped, and the forms of consciousness outside class were very complex and often ran counter to that of class.

The local handful of original converts to Marxism-Leninism had therefore to interpellate their discourse in uncongenial circumstances, to burrow their way into an unwelcoming environment and begin to try to find ways of changing it, using a supposedly universal blueprint. In India we have seen the case of inability to rival, or capture, an alternative 'Jacobin' movement based especially on the peasantry which in practice was an instrument of an unusually strong and sophisticated national bourgeoisie. Brazil gave us the case of a less national but relatively strong bourgeoisie which the communists attempted to confront most of the time in a classical way, in effect through the working class alone. When they did move to a broader alliance, it was to a 'petty bourgeoisie' which was not such at all, but a military surrogate in a 'Jacobin' tradition.

The further differentiation of types made by the Comintern's Sixth Congress in 1928 in order to encompass cases (basically African) without any real working classes or even national bourgeoisies illustrates the tendency to pragmatism, but cast within a continuing assumption of universal historical stages. Referring to the Comintern's line between 1928 and 1935, the Indian Marxist Jairus Banaji noted that the 'methodology of the Third Period was profoundly *empiricist*, and supported now by a psychological problematic, now by a mechanical analogy'. Trotsky saw the Comintern as 'eclectic through and through'. The need to remain flexible in fact resulted, not in increased theoretical sophistication, but in 'an analysis of "national peculiarities" for which, however, there was no room in a methodology of pragmatic reactions and transposed solutions' (Banaji 1977, p. 37, original emphasis; Trotsky 1962, p. 157).

In a longer-term sense, it might be said that Leninism/Stalinism had no alternative to pragmatism in a situation in which its own basic theoretical relapses into assumptions-become-idealist dogma denied it the ability to be creative. Its agents were therefore in fact reacting on a short-term basis to developments and events for which neither its sources nor its theorists' interpretation of Russian developments had prepared it.

In that sense, despite the established pattern of analysis of Comintern policies by scholars as a series of ideological shifts from 'left' to 'right', it would be better to see a number of continuities being reinterpreted in response to broad international shifts – or better yet, perceptions of supposed shifts – and then in each specific case. Sometimes the Comintern could attempt strategic formulations which appear sensitive to variations without pure pragmatism, as when the much-maligned Sixth Congress mandated the regime form for the more advanced peripheral formations as a 'democratic dictatorship of the proletariat and peasantry on the basis of Soviets' with a 'revolutionary workers' and peasants' army'. This would result from 'a prolonged period of struggle', with a later one to establish a 'proletarian dictatorship' and socialism via such measures as nationalization of land and large foreign-owned enterprises. This proved to be a quite adequate guide, for example, in the case of Viet Nam.[12] In the 1928 programme it was even envisaged that countries 'without a proletariat' might nevertheless succeed in national independence struggles, and they must organize 'a popular (peasant) Soviet regime' and nationalize foreign-owned land and businesses (Degras (ed.) 1960, p. 507).

Conversely, Comintern failures could result from not carrying out its own line. As Banaji noted:

> [b]oth in Germany and in India in this period, despite their radically different conjunctures, the absence of any significant political intervention by the proletariat resulted from an *identical omission*: in

both instances what was missing was any Leninist concept of the *united front* (Banaji 1977, p. 39, original emphasis).

We have already seen what happened in India, where even after 1935 it was not really a united front which was being implemented but deep penetration of Congress and the CSP. In Brazil, the insistence on taking position almost exclusively through the working class pushed a united front into the background. Moreover, in many countries the communist movement was so weak that it could do nothing other than attempt to follow the latest general or specific Moscow directives in a mechanical way. As in the case of India, the inability to break out of the framework of bourgeois politics meant that 'left' or 'right' turns both came down to reacting in one way or another to bourgeois parties. In other countries, important leaders might in effect ignore the Comintern's shifts, as in China, or local conditions might seem special, also to the Comintern's ECCI, and demand special applications, as in Brazil.

Nevertheless, the problem of dogmatic assumption combined with an at least implicit pragmatism was generally true of Comintern views on the 'weak link' and crisis, revolutionary stages, the united front and the internationalizing of revolution. It continued to be assumed that general capitalist crisis must produce one or more openings for decisive revolutions. There was no pursuit of the implications of uneven and combined development, the logic of which was to rule out uniform strategic lines and set tactics because of the unevenness of the differentiated peripheral totality (which had become even greater by the 1990s). The concept of different revolutionary stages remained dominant, even though on the periphery capitalism was (and is) combined with various economic forms in a way too complex to maintain some absolute historical allocation of class tasks. Trying to perpetuate the latter view led, in particular, to the distortion of allocating 'bourgeois' tasks to the proletariat, rather than situating national liberation and agrarian reform in a new context of class struggle and revolutionary socialist goals.

These questions of different circumstances and need for wide variations in strategic and tactical principles raise the general issue of a dogmatically universalistic 'international' viewpoint as opposed to the 'national' one which the complexity of social formations on the periphery implied. In this sense, Stalin's position favouring the latter had something to be said for it. Lest its source should damn it forever, we may note that in 1933, looking at the issue of strategy from the two viewpoints, Gramsci suggested that 'the international situation should be considered in its national aspect'.

In reality, the internal relations of any nation are the result of a combination which is 'original' and (in a certain sense) unique: these relations must be understood and conceived in their originality and uniqueness if one wishes to dominate them and direct them. To be sure, the line of development is towards internationalism, but the point of departure is 'national' – and it is from this point of departure that one must begin (Gramsci 1971, p. 240).

In fact, the Italian unconsciously expressed the tension between the two viewpoints when, immediately after this passage, he seems to change gears abruptly by saying that '[y]et the perspective is international and cannot be otherwise'.

Gramsci's insistence on at least a full consideration of the 'national' raises in another way a further basic (and continuing) theoretical/strategic issue. If the struggle must in actuality be at the national level, this raised the prospect of interpellating Marxism-Leninism as a discourse in a wide range of concrete circumstances, and hence the danger of pragmatism. Above all, given differences among national class structures, this in turn raised the issue of the class content of revolutions on the colonial and semi-colonial periphery, in particular given the underdevelopment of the working class. As has been restated above, such basic holistic assumptions as that of a universal replication of a particular capitalist – hence, working-class – development were faulty parts of Marxism from the start and would raise the issue of over-generalization even irrespective of the dogmatic quality later given them.

The over-generalization was expressed in the attempt to impose upon all member parties of the Comintern a universal discourse which was derived from the theorizing of the Bolsheviks and then the Stalinist leadership of the Comintern. At the same time, the basic vehicle of dogmatism, which was the major means of ensuring continuities of line in the face of pragmatic shifts and exigencies, was the vanguard party. In that sense, we may posit that *the implicit Leninist/Stalinist solution to basic methodological problems was organizational rather than theoretical.* It was also, of course, inherently authoritarian.

## VANGUARDISM AS A SOLUTION

We have seen that Marxism-Leninism had great difficulty in handling even its classical subjects, what it saw as self-conscious classes in revolutionary movement. In trying to do this, it made elisions of the supposed historical task of one class onto another and shifted – one might even say lurched –among various classes or parts of them in emphasising the significance of different conjunctures. This uncertainty in theory and Comintern pragmatism in practice were 'solved' in an idealist way by the assertion of the unvarying priority of the working class, translated into what was perhaps Leninism/Stalinism's single most damaging content, the view of the vanguard role of the party, which in effect substituted the organization for the class subjects.

Our glimpse into the internal life of the Brazilian party, with its 'proletarianization' of leadership and respect for the working class amounting almost to a cult, opens up this key question concerning the development of Marxism into Leninism/Stalinism, namely, its assumption of the leading role of local communist parties. As we have seen, this became a very acute problem in India, for example, given that the party never really got off the ground there in the interwar period but ended up riding in the pocket of the national bourgeoisie. Let it be clear that in peripheral conditions, and in perhaps other ways also at the centre, this assumption had to be made. It was the potentialities for separation of party from class and other mobilized subjects and then a turning-back of the former to dominate the latter which was so dangerous. Stalinism depended on it.

Nevertheless, it should be clearly understood that the peril was inherent in Lenin's reading of Russian necessities already in 1902. By the early 1920s certain formulations by Lukács were giving the future game away. 'The Communist Party', he wrote, 'must exist as an independent organisation so that the proletariat may be able to see its own class consciousness given historical shape.'

> The fact that the organisation of the Communist Party becomes detached from the broad mass of the class is itself a function of the stratification of consciousness within the class, but at the same time the party exists in order to hasten the process by which these distinctions are smoothed out – at the highest level of consciousness attainable (Lukács 1971, p. 326).

This was a fair comment on the unevenness of discourse interpellation and creation of subjects (in this study's language), but on the other hand clearly expresses the separation of party from class and manipulation by the former. Lukács went on to make a perfectly valid point about the relations of theory to practice: '[t]he pre-eminently practical nature of the Communist Party, the fact that it is a fighting party presupposes its possession of a correct theory, for otherwise the consequences of a false theory would soon destroy it' (ibid., p. 327). The problem was the inversion which followed from this, the assumption that *any* theoretical or strategic variation endorsed by the party leadership must be correct.

The basic problem already in Lenin's last years was the failure to grasp the issue of organization as separate from, although obviously closely linked to, that of class. Thus, it was on one level absolutely correct for Karl Radek on behalf of the ECCI to lay down the basic principle in 1921 of 'First and foremost, to the masses, by all means' and for the Third Comintern Congress resolution on 'The Organizational Structure of Communist Parties, the Methods and Content of Their Work' in the same year to insist on absolute organizational discipline (Carr 1966, vol. III, pp. 389–91). On the other hand, the result was that the Comintern and its adherents consistently substituted the communist parties as self-conscious disciplined 'vanguards' for the working class. Given the position taken in this study, that structural membership of the working (or any other) class does not lead automatically to an individual's constitution as an active subject – here of a proposed revolution – this conflation resulted in a double substitution, of class label for the actually constituted subject and of party for class.

One result of this was the use of the identification with the proletariat to justify anything the party did and a fetishization of the proletariat which was in fact a fetishization of the party, as we have seen clearly illustrated in the Brazilian case. Not only Marx's and Engels's privileging of the proletariat lay behind this, although it gave the rationale through the assumption of all the world-historical authority the founders had bestowed upon that class. Now also important was the projection of internal Soviet politics, especially after such ideological features became part of the rise of the new Stalinist elite (later carried over to China and the others) and its political use of the vanguard party concept to consolidate itself.

Leadership by the party was of course a key factor in any revolution and its preliminary struggle. Trotsky criticized Radek for forgetting that the most fundamental thing in a revolution was 'who leads it and who seizes power', since it was 'a political struggle which the classes wage *not* with bare hands but through the medium of "political institutions" (parties, etc.)'. On the other hand, the exile's attitude to organizations could be quite cavalier; already in 1916 he had asked in the Russian context 'what if there is no bourgeois democracy capable of marching at the head of the bourgeois revolution?', and answered '[t]hen it must be invented'.[13]

The inventor would of course be the working class's vanguard party, and Trotsky was aware of the problems caused by failure to distinguish between class and organization, which led inexorably to substitutionism. In an article published in October 1915 he had noted that 'parties are not classes. Between the position of a party and the interests of the social stratum upon which it rests, there may be a certain lack of harmony, which later on may become converted into a profound contradiction' (Trotsky 1962, p. 250). That he was forced into exile and later murdered as part of the process of consolidation led by Stalin, in which substitution of party for working class was a key ideological element, is one of history's innumerable ironies. So – to look beyond this study's scope – is the longer-term fact of the key role which the contradiction perceived already in 1915 was to play in the collapse of state socialism in 1989–91.

For the moment, as a corrective to the possible exaggeration of the importance of the contradiction in the interwar period outside the Soviet Union, it is necessary to remember how small almost every communist party in the peripheral formations – where they existed at all – was in the interwar period. In 1924 the claimed strength of Comintern member organizations outside Europe was 29 200 (the Americas 19 500; Asia 6350; Oceania 2250; Africa 1100). Moreover, from 1921 there was a continual overall decline (excluding the Soviet Union): 1921 887 745; 1922 779 102; 1924 648 090; 1928 445 300. In 1939 Asia, not including China, counted some 22 000 Communists, Latin America 90 000 and Africa 5000, mostly whites in North Africa and South Africa (Kriegel 1964, pp. 112–13; Claudin 1975, p. 244). Looked at in this way, the 'vanguard' often assumes minuscule proportions; it was down to 20 in India in 1934, as we have seen, in a population of some 340 million, around 0.000006 per cent. This seriously questioned the parties' claim to lead, while on the other hand the difficulty or impossibility of conducting revolutionary struggles in most 'colonies and semi-colonies' are clearly revealed. Nevertheless, this does not diminish the political importance of each and every communist party's *claim* to lead the revolutionary struggle in the name of the working class.

An analysis of Latin American experience, published just before the Comintern Seventh Congress in 1935, made a critique of communist parties there which could have been applied more generally and will have validity on into the next century.

On the question of national reformism, the inability of these parties to correctly distinguish and differentiate the role of the various bourgeois and petty bourgeois parties in the growing anti-imperialist and agrarian revolution led occasionally to the revolutionary perspectives being toned down and to an overestimation of the forces of the counter-revolution. The bourgeois and petty bourgeois parties, which differed in the political role they played, in their class character and social composition, were regarded as a simple reactionary front which would inevitably take action against the anti-imperialist revolution. The Communist parties underestimated the special importance of bourgeois national reformism, which has great influence over the petty bourgeoisie, peasantry and even over the working class in Latin America. As a result of this, they frequently adopted a 'neutral' position when big mass struggle took place, fell into a passive attitude, and isolated themselves from the masses of the toilers at times when big political events took place (Comintern 1935, pp. 122–3).

These comments were made in the particular context of a shift to the broadest possible united front, but out of the mouths of comrades and cadres they made the key general point, that the role of communist parties on the periphery was highly complex, and establishing a clear leadership position a very rare occurence, one which even the CCP had not managed by 1939.

What *had* happened by 1939 was the establishment of a clear leadership position in the world communist movement by the Communist Party of the Soviet Union, the writ of which ran from Moscow to all centres of communist organization except the caves of Yenan. That in turn was the organizational expression of the emergence in the Soviet Union of the phenomenon labelled Stalinism. Let us now consolidate the account of its linkages with the international struggle.

## THE STALINIST SHIFT

Writing already in 1922, Lukács in effect challenged the 'classical' Marxist view that a communist revolution would directly inherit and benefit from the developed industrial base of capitalism. He dismissed as 'utopian fantasy' the idea that

> anything tending towards socialism could arise within capitalism apart from, on the one hand, the *objective economic premises that make it a possibility* which, however, can only be *transformed* into the true elements of a socialist system of production after and in consequence

of the collapse of capitalism; and, on the other hand, the development of the proletariat as a class (Lukács 1971, p. 283, original emphasis).

In March 1923 Lenin attempted to face the 'utopian fantasy' of building socialism in Soviet Russia. Significantly for the argument that Marxism was situated in the Enlightenment tradition which impacted above all through capitalism on the periphery, he argued in 'Better Fewer, But Better' that while 'the Orientally backward countries', including his own, represented a global majority, in order to win – indeed, to survive – the revolutionary forces they 'must become civilized'. In contradiction to Lukács, he stated that '[w]e ... lack sufficient civilization to enable us to pass straight on to socialism', although he also argued 'we have the political requisites for this' (Lenin 1953(j), p. 750).

Stalin may therefore be seen, from 1928 onwards, as using the 'political requisites' to pass very rapidly to his version of socialism while simultaneously imposing his idea of 'civilization'. Contrary to Lenin, in his *Problems of Leninism* Stalin wrote of the building of socialism in the Soviet Union 'with the sympathy and the support of the proletariat of other countries, but without the preliminary victory of the proletarian revolution in other countries'.[14] This was, of course, the doctrine of 'socialism in one country'. The general secretary could in fact claim to be following Lenin's 1923 formula when he stated that the domestic conditions were working-class power and its ability to build socialism and 'solving the contradictions between the proletariat and the peasantry with the aid of the internal forces of our country'.

> Without such a possibility, the building of socialism is building without prospects, building without being sure that socialism will be built. It is no use building socialism without being sure that we can build it, without being sure that the technical backwardness of our country is not an *insuperable* obstacle to the building of a complete Socialist society. To deny such a possibility is to display lack of faith in the cause of building socialism, to abandon Leninism.

In the situation of a failure of 'world revolution' to spread beyond the Soviet Union, Stalinism was inseparable from Leninism, since one was the domestic side and the other the international side of the ideological aspect of the same phenomenon, the emergence of a new ruling elite in the Soviet Union. A major problem for the theorization of struggle on the periphery, therefore, was that task's insertion in a particular Soviet political struggle. One part of this was the pressure upon

Stalin, in consolidating the new Soviet elite which he represented, rapidly to formulate a discourse which could be interpellated as the only orthodoxy. This was projected onto the international level through the Comintern and its problems with various dissidents, notably Trotsky after his deportation in January 1929. Stalin had to establish himself as Lenin's successor inside the Soviet Union and in doing so turned theory into dogma, and in bringing the Comintern and its member parties under control he did the same.

With practical politics pushing theory into dogma, argument about the theoretical issues of world revolution, including the debate between Trotsky and Stalin, largely became dispute about the doctrine of 'socialism in one country'. In 1930 the exiled Trotsky conceded that the 'interval' between the Russian Revolution and one in the capitalist centre 'has turned out to be considerably longer than we had expected', but he still held to the 'permanent revolution' view that the 'workers' state can be preserved from mortal dangers, not only military but also economic, only by the victorious development of the proletarian revolution in the West'. Moreover, at the same time he put his dialectical finger on the implications of the view that socialism could, and must, be built first of all in one country as a base for the world revolution. 'By making a fetish of the law of uneven development', the exile said, 'Stalin proclaims it a sufficient basis for national socialism, not as a type common to all countries, but exceptional, Messianic, purely Russian.' The concrete result of this theoretical position was that then 'the task of the Comintern, along with the notorious "Friends of the Soviet Union," would be to protect the construction of socialism from intervention, that is, in essence, to play the role of frontier patrols' (Trotsky 1962, pp. 25, 27, 30–1 and 140).

Of course, the issue of the relationship between the foreign policy of the new socialist country and international revolution had arisen before Lenin died. A Dutch delegate to the Third Comintern Congress in mid-1922 plaintively remarked, for example, that it looked 'as if Russia was rather putting the brakes on the revolutionary process' (quoted, Carr 1966, vol. III, p. 393). With Stalin in the saddle in his isolated rapidly socializing country there was in fact a shift in the terms of the debate, which was now displaced not only from 'West' to 'East' but, partially at least, from the level of revolution as class struggle to that of 'world revolution' as a contest among states. This was ultimately to prove extremely damaging for the development of Marxism; more immediately in our present analysis, from 1928 it implied increasing subordination of world revolution to Soviet foreign policy, already begun under Lenin, and, even more fundamentally, to internal developments in the Soviet Union. After 1928 these became a basic point of reference for the Comintern's appeals, as in the ECCI 1934 May Day manifesto. 'Look at the Soviet Union. Look how the proletariat and working people of the Soviet Union, who know neither unemployment in the towns nor impoverishment in the village, who are free of the capitalist yoke, are building a new classless socialist society' (Degras (ed.) 1965, p. 328). In this sense, the Soviet 'national' level swallowed the international revolutionary one and then regurgitated it as a projection of itself.

Trotsky in fact saw the implication of this for internationalism already in 1930, when he wrote that

[t]he example of a backward country, which in the course of several Five-Year Plans was able to construct a mighty socialist society with its own forces, would mean a death blow to world capitalism, and would reduce to a minimum, if not to zero, the costs of the world proletarian revolution. This is why the whole Stalinist conception actually leads to the liquidation of the Communist International (Trotsky 1962, pp. 26–7).

Here the Comintern in fact really means the concept of world revolution, and it was to prove to be the case that world capitalism was able to accommodate the existence of a new socialist industrial power up to the point when it collapsed. When the Comintern was indeed dissolved by Stalin in June 1943, it was as a diplomatic move to please his new wartime capitalist allies, and we may take this as a further important step in subordinating world revolution to Soviet state needs as he perceived them.[15]

Nevertheless, the concern with world revolution and a continuing struggle for liberation, which remained in however a distorted form part of Leninism as a reaction to peripheral conditions, prevent us treating it as totally *identical* with Stalinism. The residually progressive side of Stalinism secured support for the Soviet Union even from those outside any Marxist orbit, as when in April 1936 Jawaharlal Nehru described the Soviet Union as 'stumbling occasionally' but representing a 'new order and a new civilisation' and 'the most promising feature of our dismal age' (quoted, Chandra 1975, pp. 1307 and 1309).

The basic weakness of the Leninist strategy was the failure of the prognostication of world revolution on a global scale. Here we may raise once more the concept of uneven and combined development. As noted in Chapter 3, Stalin's concept of 'socialism in one country' may be seen as emphasizing the uneven side, and in fact the concrete reality of capitalism's global structure supported him rather than Trotsky. Capital's uniformities were – and remain – heavily qualified by all the historical circumstances of its penetration of the world elsewhere and by what existed before that process; the Comintern's formula of 'colonial', 'semi-colonial' and 'dependent' countries was an attempt to deal with this. Any hope of orchestrating a series of revolutions in practice fell away rapidly and completely in face of this unevenness; that is borne out, almost caricatured, by the fact that in the period covered by this study only Mongolia, even then carried along in Russia's wake, witnessed a communist revolution at all.

Leninism thus became necessarily locked into the concrete reality of separate formations and in these circumstances ran into a profound contradiction. On one side, its Mr Hyde, Stalinism, prevailed in the isolated Soviet Union, where the Marxist privileging of the working class and 'its' vanguard party provided a cloak for Stalin's usurpation of power. In that sense – and, indeed, in the deeper one of social base which cannot be dealt with here – it cannot be denied that Marxism was 'responsible' for Stalinism.

The other moment of the contradiction was international – Leninism as a logical, better dialectical, result of Marxism's displacement to the periphery and its subsequent 'colonization' by Stalinism. This projected the dark side of Marxism, its implicit authoritarianism which had already existed in contradiction to Enlightenment liberationism in its pre-1917 phase of concentration on the European centre, out into a periphery which imperialism and colonialism had fully prepared by degrading the indigenous peoples and cultures. Sticking to the level of theory, we see that this contradiction produced a dogmatic and uninflected response to the complex and generally very inhospitable conditions of the periphery.

The question of dogmatic theory at an international level raises the issue of the nature of the Leninist discourse, the form given to theory and strategy in order to propagate them as doctrine. Given the focus of this study on the spread of Marxism to a new world, the recapitulation of the Leninism/Stalinism syndrome should be concluded on that level.

## LENINISM/STALINISM AS DISCOURSE

Initially, the core idea which acted as Leninism's organizing principle and criterion for assessment of new information – its explanatory capacity – was that of 'world revolution'. Around this revolved the initial debate over preserving the revolutionary regime and the building of socialism in Soviet Russia, 'uneven and combined development', 'permanent revolution' and the more practical assessment of opportunities in any given country.

However, from 1925 onwards, and increasingly with the dominance of Stalin in the Soviet Union and therefore the Comintern after 1927, the profoundly important elision from 'world revolution' to 'socialism in one country' occurred, with the latter in effect becoming the discourse's core idea. The effect of this was to make evaluation of revolutionary prospects increasingly subordinate to an estimation of how any given strategy or specific national tactics would affect the position of the Soviet Union's power bloc, which only finally consolidated its control in the late 1930s. The trend towards establishing the Soviet Union as one of a series of great powers, which was to culminate in the prewar period with the August 1939 pact with Hitler's Germany, also meant the final subordination of world revolution to the interests of Soviet foreign policy, a tendency which we have seen already emerging under Lenin's leadership.

It was suggested in Chapter 1 that a fully developed discourse would contain an ontology, a cosmology and an epistemology. The first of these is covered above, by the concept of world revolution (even when elided into 'socialism in one country'), which postulated a very particular 'being' for humans, of historical development in stages producing the contradictory hegemony of capital and the revolutionary role of the proletariat. Cosmology enters the picture less when we consider a specifically political discourse, but it might be suggested that the tendency towards an innate conceptual idealism took Leninism almost into the realm of transcending earthly realities. As for its epistemological capacities, the discourse as a dialectical interplay between action and thought finding and incorporating new ideas has been seen to have had the opposite tendency, towards pragmatism.

Idealism and pragmatism contradictorily combined created very serious tensions when the discourse was put into practice in any given concrete situation, the result of which was in fact a leaning to the idealist side in the face of stubborn realities. This meant that the solution increasingly came to be dogmatic assertion from Moscow, capital of the world's only 'socialist' country, which applied what the Stalinist leadership saw as universal historical truths. This dogmatism and the consequent ossification of thought were strongly supported by the new discourse's organizational model, the vanguard party, which in effect came to be identified with its own leadership and bureaucracy. As to the discourse's specification of appropriate action, this revolved around the concepts of stages and alliances, the theoretical and concrete problems of which have been explored at length in this study.

This question of a political discourse's action content takes us into the realm of interpellation, which means above all the finding of appropriate agents and subjects. Sociologically, in whatever country the former proved to be overwhelmingly members of the middle strata. The key question in terms of the latter was of course the selection of relevant identities for the revolutionary subject and giving of cohesion to collectivities. Leninism/Stalinism, perpetuating the original privileging, saw this emphatically in terms of the mandated two key classes, the bourgeoisie and the workers. The prescribed subjects for a revolutionary discourse were wage-workers, the privileged identity, of course, that of 'proletarian'. However, as we see in the 'stages' formula and positive historical role allocated to the 'national bourgeoisie', this privilege was in theory (and very dubious practice) extended. Leninism/Stalinism in effect created a second privileged class subject in history.

This move, and the efforts already in Lenin's lifetime to come to grips with the role of 'the East', brought the question of subjects also to the issue of national identity. The class content of this was never fully explored, and in effect abandoned when the Comintern shifted to the 'national salvation' line in 1935. The theorists floundered even more when it came to religious, racial and gender identities. Leninism/Stalinism proved to be not very apt at grappling with the issue of multiple identities and postulating new subjects.

Clearly, the invocation of individual and collective identities was closely related to the communicative competence of local party agents, their ability to establish a general world-view through recognition of their authenticity and sincerity.[16] Astounding acts of self-sacrifice and general dedication clearly demonstrated the latter quality, but, contradictorily, authenticity increasingly became, not a matter of involvement in local realities, but appeal to a Moscow-based legitimacy. Mao's ability to break out of this contradiction was an exception which was to prove very significant after 1949.

Above all with the imposition of Stalinist control in the 1930s, therefore, even the most local agents' authority was heavily derived from outside, given their claim to represent the centre of world revolution, the Soviet Union. The action prescriptions of the discourse could really only be validated – hence validating the discourse's agents – in practice, but in fact their validity (urban uprising in China, for example) was also basically set externally, by the Comintern leadership which was increasingly controlled by that of the Soviet Union. Moreover, the same authority was usually mobilized to assert the validity of Leninist/Stalinist ideas, even in the face of concrete experience. This brings us back again to the issue of the combination of dogmatism and pragmatism, the Marxist-Leninist oil and water which did not mix to form a viable revolutionary discourse.

## GENERAL CONCLUSIONS

The analysis presented in this book has hopefully shown how the basic Marxist political doctrine of revolution was reshaped after the Russian Revolution to try to meet the situation of a world which had been reshaped by capital. The Russian Revolution itself raised the whole issue of the 'displacement' of Marxist theory and action to the periphery, the shift which underlaid its transmutation into Leninism and then Stalinism. Above all, this was because the decisive action took the form of a revolution occurring where it should not have done in 'classical' terms, that is, on the periphery, and leading to a shift of struggle against capitalism above all to that constellation of formations. After 1917 the problem became the placing of the key issues there, national liberation and agrarian reform, within a new context of class struggle and revolutionary socialist goals. A very similar problem, albeit with a reshaping of key issues to include such as the globalization of capital's movements, the collapse of natural environments and the permanent immiseration of large parts of the periphery's population while a minority enjoys comfort, even affluence, arises again after 1991 in a world being reshaped by a triumphalist capital. It seems reasonable to assume that such a situation will provide a base for future revolutionary movements, so the question arises of what may be learned from the earlier period.

We have seen that Marxist theory on revolution became concretely located for some 70 years in a different historical conjunction from that originally envisaged, a relocation which may in fact have become permanent. As the Comintern groped for appropriate strategies, it was burdened by theoretical baggage carried out to the periphery as part of the process of displacement. This inevitably extended the privileging of capital as the historically decisive shaping force, and of its creation, the working class. The inevitability was in a sense correct: of course capital had inexorably shaped the world into centre and periphery, as it is now 'globalizing' it, including creating the conditions which led to the Russian Revolution and the Soviet Union, and eventually to the latter's collapse. Of course the working class has to be an important factor once capital has done its work. However, the radically different conditions on the periphery from those which had originally shaped Marx's and Engels's ideas raised two basic questions: could the liberatory doctrine of Marxism be carried directly over to the peripheral formations and were the class situations in capital's – hence, Marxism's – 'world elsewhere' compatible with the latter's revolutionary premises? Those questions remain key ones today.

The Bolshevik success in November 1917 located the theory's practice in that part of the globe where the ideas of the Enlightenment had only been a part of capital's self-justification for global expansion. Imperialism and colonialism gave the Enlightenment tradition a different meaning on the periphery, breaking with its critical and potentially liberating content and condemning majorities to new, and often more intensive forms of exploitation and destroying, or at least severely damaging, indigenous cultures. Bourgeois ideas of human emancipation never took root in the fragmented ground of peripheral material and psychic damage, or at least only among the small Western-educated minorities. Even then, at their most radical the ideas were usually only 'Jacobin', refracted away from the materiality of class exploitation and gender-blind. In the end, as in India, 'national liberation' remained the doctrine of a bourgeoisie seeking to follow the example of its centre prototypes by consolidating as a full capitalist class.

Hypothetically, after 1917 Marxism, in transferring its main activities in effect to the capitalist periphery, might itself have sustained such originally European principles as 'progress', human rights and popular sovereignty in contradiction to the destructive effects of untrammelled capitalism. Again hypothetically, it might have done so by creative symbiosis with cultures of the periphery to develop a strong content of mass liberation. Rather, Marxism shifted towards post-1945 Marxism-Leninism through the otiose and oppressive medium of Stalinism. Apart from uncritical deference to the 'first socialist country', this basically came through willingness, finally confirmed in 1935, to work with supposedly progressive 'national bourgeois' forces. After the Second World War, the two came together in the eventually deadening combination of the Soviet superpower's foreign policy and its willingness to work with any grubby dictatorship that termed itself 'revolutionary'.

In terms of strategy, from around 1920 Marxist theorists and practitioners were faced with a decisive displacement of major activities to the capitalist periphery, involving the development and interpellation of a new discourse to support them, and our case studies have shown how complex and difficult such an interpellation was. Given the theoretical problems after 1917 of analysing the relations between party organization and class, which raised the issue of forms of class politics, involving alliances and the relationship of class identity with others in constituting the subject, and seeing all these in terms of the even broader theoretical issues of the 'weak link' and 'stages' concepts then dominant, we can on one level readily understand why the Comintern's successes were so limited in the period 1920–39. On another level, now also adding in the dogmatism/pragmatism schizophrenia, we can see that the development of Leninism beyond the original body of theory was an incomplete and even distorted enterprise.

It is indeed arguable that the new discourse evolved after 1920 never adequately met the needs of struggle, as it tried to represent strategy as above all a class alliance issue and played with various tactical permutations of that formulation. We saw in Chapter 2 how Lukács spoke of 'movements which do not themselves proceed in the direction of socialism but which through the violence of the impact they make do hasten the realisation of the preconditions of socialism'. This did not occur in the period 1920–39, nor afterwards. Indeed, in most cases those forces came to dominate newly sovereign countries and provide contemporary ruling capitalist classes. That was also the fate of Trotsky's idea, noted in Chapter 3, of the 'privilege of historic backwardness', which would permit the 'skipping' of stages. In the end, capital has insisted on having a full historical run for its money.

In terms of issues and social forces not directly focused on socialism, we have seen that in China in the period dealt with here (as happened also in Viet Nam), Leninism/Stalinism was able to build class links to nationalism other than those of a supposedly 'national' bourgeoisie. However, *understanding* that complex and historically contingent process on the whole eluded the Comintern theorists. Major implications of this have become apparent in this study, in which concepts of discourse, agents and subjects led, as I sought to ground the development of the key discourse in the 1920s and 1930s in concrete analysis, to a plethora of the human elements, defined in class, national, gender and other terms.

Obviously, the shift of basic activity to the periphery called into question all of the theoretical 'privileges' assigned by Marxism, above all those of the working class as modern history's prime mover, of class consciousness over all other identities, and of men's activities over women's. Marxism's dubious experience as an implemented doctrine remained not merely symbolically but symbiotically attached to the historical class force which had determined its content as a critical theory from birth, but which had developed only very partially and unevenly on the periphery. This becomes a major issue as we move into the next century, because well-founded predictions are of an increasing erosion of the peasantry, Maos's and in a way Lenin's other basic class, and a migration into urban areas. The point is that the repressed and impoverished ex-peasant masses there will not be turned into a fully fledged stable working class. Capital prefers to have a more fluid workforce (often young females) which it can shift in composition and location at will, and, more fundamentally, it cannot in any case create stable waged work at the necessary pace.[17]

Nevertheless, if we make a distinction which follows from Marx's own treatment, between the working class and proletarianization, we get a clue to better understanding. As we have seen in our case studies, the latter *process* of producing the class worked in a quite different way in peripheral formations and was situated within complex pre-capitalist class systems which did not dissolve as they tendentially did at the centre. (Nor is that pattern being reproduced now.) This made/makes the working class in marked ways different from the one privileged by Marxism, and a similar observation can be made about capital's agent-class, what Leninism/Stalinism saw as the national bourgeoisie. With both their theoretical historical agents and subjects thus concretely differentiated from the 'norm', Marxists between the wars, despite all the postulation of uneven and combined development, stages, class alliances or whatever, basically retained the old shibboleths, even Trotsky, who, with Gramsci, was undoubtedly the most independent mind then at work.

This continuity forced the aspirant world revolutionaries into a mixture of idealism and pragmatism, which, combined with the dogmatism which the Stalinist bloc deployed, proved both theoretically stultifying and politically deadening on the periphery, except in China, where the conditions of systemic collapse and, by 1935, loss of Comintern ideological control had matured enough to support independent action by Mao and his supporters. Even then, at the time of the Japanese invasion in 1937, which in effect opened the Second World War for China, the CCP had been pushed out to the margins of the formation and into relative insignificance. Moreover, the fact that the now dominant Maoist faction was pushing a nationalist line in the face of Japanese aggression, as the Comintern had done since 1935, raises the issue, very marked in peripheral formations, of what this study has termed the polyvalent historical subject. That one is still very much with us in these days of women's liberation, destruction of cultures, gay rights, struggles of minority peoples and the overall issue of human existence as part of a natural environment. Will future revolutionaries be able to combine all of these liberatory struggles with that of material immiseration into a single revolutionary thrust, and can this be done in the scope of a single country?

The other main element in the shaping of Leninism was its inseparability from the power struggle within the new Soviet Union, as Stalin and the social forces he represented consolidated their power in the name of 'socialism in one country'. This slogan covered many necessary concrete activities designed to secure defence against a hostile capitalist system, but in serving as the revised core of the discourse masked the Stalinist power bloc's determination to preserve itself at all costs, even those of allied parties. This gravely affected the workings of the Comintern, which expressed those alliances but also served Moscow's domination of the other parties. Fortunately, this element is now gone, and future revolutionaries will not have to carry the huge burden of a deformed Soviet Union on their backs, as even the Trotskyists have done in their own way all these years.

However, they and the rest have not yet escaped from a fateful legacy. With particular Russian conditions determining the ideological and organizational conjunction, the success of the Bolsheviks and then the state socialist form which the dominant Stalinist faction developed made a universal model out of the doctrine of the supreme authority of the party as the expression of the will of the proletariat. That is still with us, with all its innate tendencies to authoritarianism.

The immediate object of this study has been to show the theoretical difficulties which arose in the attempted strategic and tactical reshaping of Marxist revolutionary doctrine from 1920 until the Second World War. Its overall conclusion must be that many of these arose from basic issues in Marxist theory which had existed since its initial formulation, or from reasoning which could defensibly be said to follow from early basic positions and assumptions. Some egregious errors were committed, such as the almost complete sacrifice of CCP autonomy in the period up to 1927 or the commitment of the revolution in Brazil to military adventurism in 1935. Nevertheless, the fact that even so fine a critical mind as Trotsky's could not fully transcend such questionable basics as the stages view of history and its political consequences indicates that to a large extent the Comintern theorists did the best they could with what they had. Moreover, even though Stalinism was a product of very specific conditions in Russia/the Soviet Union, it has to be recognized that its theoretical basis could be derived without total strain from basic privileges and assumptions present in Marxism from the beginning.

These may seem remarkable admissions from one whose basic message is that only Marxism contains the elements necessary for the formulation of a doctrine of liberation for the next century. The answer is that we are in that shadowy realm of the necessary but not yet sufficient. This study's basic thesis is that in its progress along the axis of twentieth-century history, Marxism came to be in effect centred in a distinctive group of social formations, directly created by capital's expansion from its original centre. By once more in effect following its parent, the prospective patricide was forced to adapt to unfamiliar climes. In the end it took the effects of the Second World War, as a global crisis of capitalism, to bring some success for an 'international' movement now almost totally under the hegemony of the Soviet leadership and make it feel more at home on the periphery than in its original birthplace.

This study's basic conclusion, therefore, must be that Leninism/Stalinism failed to, and probably could not have, come to grips with the true complexities of human liberation during the interwar period, on the periphery and, for that matter, at the centre, and failed to grasp the full nature of the historical human subject. Left only with possible permutations of supposed class roles and relations, in most cases it failed really to get off the ground as the doctrinal basis for revolutionary movements. In other cases these movements grew at first and then suffered a series of defeats, some of them conjunctural and temporary, such as in China in 1927, others in effect permanent, as in Brazil in 1935. This meant that when, after 1945, Leninism, now taken over by its monstrous alter-ego, Stalinism, expanded its international grip enormously, it did so without any real basis for serving as a liberation doctrine but rather as the justification for rule by a bureaucratic elite. The consequences of this – and of the continuing capacity of capitalism to expand on a global basis contrary to his followers' reading of Marx's original prognosis – led to Marxism's crisis, which we are now witnessing.

Stubbornly, however, I still insist that Marxism remains the bridge of rational understanding between the seminal shifts in Western European social structure, thought and politics in the period 1789–1850 and the present world, which at the most fundamental levels remains the capitalist one created by those shifts and for which Marxism therefore remains the seedbed for a theory of resistance. This opens up again the issue of Marxism's direct relationship to the Enlightenment and French Revolution via the transition into Modernism, which has been taken as one (assumed) basis of this study. It will need to feature again in other theoretical labours if those of us now exiled, like Coriolanus, from the political mainstream are to maintain the argument that Marxism is the only potentially viable executor of the testament of human liberation which was written in the late eighteenth century. In terms of this issue, therefore, and of the others raised during the weary pilgrimage through the desert of Marxism-Leninism-Stalinism's failures undertaken in this study, disaster must be turned into a learning experience.

# Notes

## 1 THE PROBLEMATIC

1. Certain comrades will note that I take Soviet (and Chinese) state socialism as being a deformed form of socialism, not a variant of capitalism; the latter view would of course lead to a different 'reading' of the collapse. My position on this topic and the basic nature of state socialism may be found argued in Post and Wright 1989.
2. Prior to 1939, capital's hegemony was virtually global; apart from Russia, the only other loss was Mongolia in 1921, where it had scarcely existed anyway.
3. The reasons for failure in Europe are examined in my companion study, Post 1997.
4. The expansion of capitalism to form the double global structure of centre and periphery cannot be dealt with here. However, two points need to be established. Firstly, the 'logic' of capital's dynamics, centred on surplus value creation and accumulation, was the same in both, but structured in quite different ways, which basically retained pre-capitalist labour and surplus extraction forms on the periphery. Secondly, the 'periphery' was not marginal, as the term implies, economically, but essential to capital's workings at the centre. The marginality found expression in terms of political power, openly in the colonial form, less directly in the case of formally sovereign states. For more on these issues see Post 1996, especially pp. 207–18.
5. Engels to Kautsky, 12 November 1882, in Feuer (ed.) 1959, p. 452. I owe the point on the original assumption of individual working-class struggles and revolutions to Denise Avenas; see Avenas 1976, p. 26.
6. These assertions are explored on the theoretical level in Post 1996.
7. For more extended discussion see Post 1996, pp. 270–6.
8. I would, however, like to make it clear that my interpretation runs counter to the Wallersteinian 'world system' view. For the necessary arguments see Post 1996, pp. 200–2 and 206–7.
9. Quotations here and in the next paragraph from Avineri (ed.) 1969, pp. 137, 138–9 and 234.
10. See Shanin (ed.) 1983 and the discussion in Post 1997, Chapter 2.
11. See the classic account of the movement led by Emiliano Zapata in Womack, Jr. 1968. A good recent general survey is Knight 1986.
12. See Esherick 1976, Shimkichi and Schiffrin (eds) 1995 and Wright (ed.) 1968.
13. Throughout this study I prefer to speak of 'working class' rather than 'proletariat', to signify a less cohesive entity than Marx and Engels, and even more their followers, tended to assume. I thus mean all wage-earners who produce, maintain, transport and retail commodities.
14. For detailed argumentation see Post 1997, Chapters 2 and 3.
15. See Löwy 1981, pp. 1–21. This author makes a valiant effort to defend Marx and Engels against any charges of a mechanistic reading of history,

making socialist revolution dependent on industrialization and emergence of the proletariat, but has himself to admit that they are often ambiguous in their qualifications of the thesis. I am indebted to his analysis in general, although my reading of the material may have different emphases. Moreover, it is significant of his own ultimate perspective that he speaks without qualification of twentieth-century *workers'* revolutions. The problem, of course, is largely that the founders' texts upon which all of us have to base arguments were political pieces of a highly conjunctural nature, not fully worked out theorizations.

16. The concept of a revolutionary terrain which has to be consciously created by a 'war of position' and then used in a 'war of manoeuvre' runs through my entire analysis of the Vietnamese Revolution; see Post 1989, 1990 and 1994 *passim*, and for a general statement, Post and Wright 1989, pp. 49–64. As detailed there, it derives from Gramsci. It will be picked up further in Chapter 3 below.
17. As we have done until recently in terms of the feminist movement and gender.
18. Marx and Engels 1973, pp. 84 and 85. It is noteworthy that the founders here spoke of exploitative relations among nations as a unit of analysis, anticipating the later view of whole 'proletarian nations' and the even later dependency theory.
19. A further problem I have with Löwy is that he fails to see clearly the problems of transposing historical stages into revolutionary class tasks by eliding too quickly from one to the other.
20. I recognize that middle-strata employees might be said by Marxists to produce no surplus value from their surplus labour, i.e. their labour is 'unproductive', which differentiates them clearly from workers and in itself would be enough to explain their lesser revolutionary propensity. However, this whole theoretical issue is very complex; do not engineers, for example, contribute to surplus value? My rather bland textual formulation is deliberately intended to dodge the issue. It should also be noted that I term these 'middle' elements a set of strata rather than a class, precisely because their ambiguous position in terms of sale of labour power leaves them with no clear material class basis of their own.
21. 'Regime' is used here to mean the overall distribution of power in a given social formation, anchored by the state. The latter has a variety of aspects often masked in discussion, but key ones here are that it is: a governing apparatus; a concentration of resources; a source of authority; and an arena in which various groups seek access to policy-making. Particularly in terms of the last, we may also conceptualize a 'power bloc' of elements drawn from the dominant class(es), or at least acting as their agents, which have direct access to/control over policy decisions. For an extended discussion of these concepts see the seventh essay in Post 1996.

## 2 EXPANDING TO THE EAST

1. I derive this point from a critique of Lenin's earlier analysis of capitalism in Russia in Avenas 1976, p. 27.

2. For a useful discussion see Larrain 1989, pp. 62–72. We must also remember that Lenin in particular acknowledged a debt to the work of J.A. Hobson, a non-Marxist critic of imperialism.
3. Suny 1972, p. 13, with calculation; Bennigsen and Wimbush 1979, p. 151. The latter source speaks of 100 000 Muslims in the Baku area alone (p. 10); much may depend on how 'Baku' is defined. It should also be noted that Azerbaijanis were categorized as 'Tatars' by the Russians at that time (Suny 1972, p. 16).
4. Bennigsen and Wimbush 1979, p. 10. I have drawn heavily on this study for data and quotations, but it should be noted that it is an anti-socialist work. Moreover, it very curiously makes no attempt to situate 'national communism' in relation to the evolution of Comintern policy, with which, I shall argue, it was less at variance than the authors suggest in their general comments (see, for example, their reference to 'Leninism' on p. 54).
5. For a discussion of these categories and the process of incorporation into the USSR, see Carr 1966, vol. I, Chapter 13.
6. Quoted, Bennigsen and Wimbush 1979, p. 209. I have slightly adapted this quotation, since one braids rather than weaves ropes.
7. Lenin 1953(c), pp. 322–3 and 329, original emphasis. For Luxemburg's views on the national question see Nettl 1966, *passim* and especially Appendix 2.
8. Sultan Galiyev 1919, pp. 131–2. Next two paragraphs based on ibid., pp. 132–5.
9. Ibid., p. 136. As is shown by the inclusion of the economically unimportant Afghanistan, he was obviously influenced by his origin as a Muslim in the tsarist empire, but the generalization here admits China at a later point in the article, as well as Black Africa. The latter was viewed by Sultan Galiyev along with North and South America as forming the original base for imperialism after which it shifted to Asia; this gives us the leeway to bring in Latin America as part of the periphery envisaged as the key to world socialist struggle by him as by the present author.
10. Quotations in the previous paragraph and this one cited by Bennigsen and Wimbush 1979, pp. 169, 170, 171 and 172. In the third quotation I have replaced 'unique' with 'single' as a clearer translation, although I have not seen the original. Bennigsen and Wimbush reproduce the 1921 programme in Appendix E; here see p. 168. The complaint, for example, was that cotton cultivation was still made compulsory at the expense of grain and rice, leading to famine when central Russia could not ensure supplies, as in 1917–18 (pp. 168–9).
11. For discussion on the period prior to this see Persits 1981.
12. Lenin 1953(f), p. 423, original emphasis, also following quotations.
13. I have tried in summarizing the views of Lenin and Roy to reconstruct their *original* formulations before coming to the final results, based on Carrère d'Encausse and Schram 1969, Section III, documents 2–4, especially the notes to these. I have omitted detailed references to save space; interested readers are urged to go back to these documents. The cited editors seem to have done a careful job in putting together various sources, and also to have observed E.H. Carr's warnings about these in Carr 1966, vol. III, nn. 3 and 4, p. 254. I have benefited from the discussion in

Claudin 1975, pp. 260–6, although my emphases and interpretations are not always his, and Datta Gupta 1980, pp. 15–44, is also valuable. For a critique of simplistic attempts to contrast a radical Roy and a moderate Lenin see Reznikov 1981, especially pp. 79–83.
14. On this formulation, which has caused some confusion in subsequent discussion, see Reznikov 1981, p. 88.
15. A number of points are in order here. First, it is not clear whether the 'victorious proletariat' means that of the 'backward' country or in a developed one where the revolution has already been successful. Given the general tenor of the analysis, I tend to think the latter, although that makes the further reference to 'the most advanced countries' superfluous unless it is to advanced countries *before* their revolutions. Again, 'Soviet governments' could mean the various constituent ones of the existing Russian federation or future ones in advanced countries; since the passage speaks of 'all the assistance they possibly can', I tend to think it means the former. Lastly, the formulation on stages does not make it clear whether the 'definite stage of development' is coterminous with the socialist stage which was by 1920 reckoned to precede the full communist consummation. Since the 'soviet' stage in the Russian case *preceded* socialism, the 'definite stage' must presumably be identified with the latter; later cases certainly saw it that way (for North Viet Nam see Post 1989(b), pp. 4–10).
16. Lukács 1971, pp. 274–5, original emphasis. Next two paragraphs based on ibid., pp. 289, 304 and 310–13 *passim*.
17. Quotations here from Degras (ed.) 1956, pp. 388, 390 and 418.
18. Claudin 1975, p. 258; Lenin 1971(a), pp. 606 and 608. Trotsky was asked by Lenin to push the issue of Stalin's character, but allowed himself to be persuaded that Stalin, since April 1922 general secretary of the Party, would mend his ways (on this see Deutscher 1959, pp. 90–3, and, for a more hostile interpretation of Trotsky's inaction, Ulam 1969, pp. 753–8).
19. Claudin 1975, pp. 250–1; Carr 1966, vol. III, pp. 288–9 and 301–4. The Turkish comrades were strangled and thrown into the sea, the traditional Ottoman method. Kemal later promised the Soviet government to liberate the rest and punish the men responsible for the murders and in March 1922 lifted the ban on the Communist Party (Carr 1966, vol. III, pp. 303–4 and 470).
20. This and next paragraph from Lenin 1953(j), pp. 748–9 and 750.

## 3 COMINTERN AND OTHER PERSPECTIVES

1. On the latter point see Post 1996, pp. 292–3.
2. The text may be found in Degras (ed.) 1960. Ironically, the movement for 'bolshevization' began shortly before as an attempt to restore/reinforce base-level democracy in the German party which got turned on its head: see Claudin 1975, pp. 141–2.
3. Deutscher 1959, p. 290. For a further critical assessment of this part of the debate see ibid., pp. 281–93.
4. The extensive use of Trotsky's analysis in the coming pages is thus not meant to serve as pure endorsement. The point is that he was the most

important critic of what was becoming Stalinist orthodoxy who came out of the same tradition and experience, and therefore his comments form a useful ground – if not a full terrain for struggle – upon which we may stand in order to get a longer-term view.
5. Bettelheim 1978, p. 366; Löwy 1981, p. 71. The two key articles by Stalin are 'October and Comrade Trotsky's Theory of Permanent Revolution' and 'The October Revolution and the Tactics of the Russian Communists'.
6. Important expositions without the proliferation of quotations may be found in the November 1929 and especially the March 1930 introduction to Trotsky 1962, which was basically completed in October 1928 and then had two more chapters added to it as well as the introductions. I have leaned heavily on this text here, but further important pieces are his 'The Draft Programme of the Communist International: A Criticism of Fundamentals' (1928), and the new material in *The Third International After Lenin* (1929), which reprints this.
7. They did not, however, play down its violence in the short term; Stalin in fact had later to promote the *exacerbation* of the struggle against such class enemies as 'kulaks' (rich peasants) and 'Trotskyites' as part of the new elite's consolidation of power. (Younger readers should note the variations in labels, 'ist' and 'ite', which in my youth could lead to verbal abuse and even fisticuffs.)
8. It also bears on the underlying approach of the present study to the centre–periphery relationship. Löwy 1981 is a valuable discussion of Trotsky, and I have also benefited from Avenas 1976 and Robens n.d., which is partly based on Vallier 1977.
9. Trotsky 1967, p. 22; next paragraph based on p. 23.
10. Quoted, Sobolev *et al.* 1971, p. 256. This source is valuable because, among other reasons, it is the only general history of the Comintern so far which is partially based on access to Communist Party archives in Moscow. As here, I have often used material from it which cites that source.
11. Poulantzas 1974, p. 41, original emphasis. The tendency is to the falling rate of capitalists' profits, which has to be compensated for by a rising rate of surplus value and therefore a rising rate of exploitation. For a critical discussion of this view see Post 1997, Chapter 1.
12. See Poulantzas 1974, pp. 78–82. The same author also correctly pointed out that Trotsky's ideas remained within the crisis-offence-stabilization-defence paradigm and were therefore also economist (ibid., p. 81, especially nn. 10 and 11).
13. Basic histories from different points of view may be found in Claudin 1975 and Sobolev *et al.* 1971.
14. The Congress also expelled Trotsky from the ECCI, a move authorized at the Executive's 8th plenum in June 1927 if he continued his 'factional activity' (Sobolev *et al.* 1971, p. 265).
15. Borkenau 1962, p. 338. We must note that this picture of a complex cumulative shift to 'left' militancy clearly – and correctly – runs against the prevalent concept of the Comintern as a well-oiled machine which swung rapidly, easily (and arbitrarily) from one strategic and tactical pole to another.

16. This and the next two paragraphs based on Reiman 1987, pp. 75–7, and Appendices, Document 3, pp. 131 and 132, and Document 5, pp. 138, 139, 140 and 142.
17. Ibid., p. 508. Much later, in the mid-1960s, the Maoist leadership in China was to pick up this theme in an extreme statement of 'third-worldism'.
18. This and the next four paragraphs based on Degras (ed.) 1960, pp. 506–7, 538–9, 540 and 542.
19. For a detailed analysis of this stabilization see Post 1997, Chapter 8.
20. It is worth noting that, at the beginning of 1928, total membership of Comintern organizations was 1 707 769, 70.9 per cent in the Soviet Union, while total Socialist International membership was 6 637 622, 51 per cent in Britain (Braunthal 1967, table, p. 319, with calculations).
21. Gramsci's writings were smuggled out of prison but not published until after 1945. He began to gain major attention in the late 1960s; for a sample of discussions see Clark 1977, Hoare and Nowell Smith 1971, Sassoon 1980 and Williams 1975.
22. Gramsci 1971, p. 238. It is interesting to note that in 1938 Mao, who of course had no knowledge of Gramsci's work, also believed that in 'capitalist countries', where legal struggle was possible, the revolutionaries' efforts would be protracted. In 'semi-colonial and semi-feudal' China 'insurrection and war' would be necessary in conditions of illegality (1965, p. 117), and the Chinese leader also suggested – incorrectly as it happened – that the struggle would be less protracted there.
23. Gramsci 1971, pp. 333–4. It should be understood that I am glossing, going beyond and adding to Gramsci's work here and in what follows.
24. At this point Gramsci's use of language again gets in the way, since 'traditional' has resonances which are not necessary here. These external intellectuals might well, in fact probably would, have 'modern' educations.
25. Gramsci 1971, p. 181. There is a danger of confusion here, because Gramsci used the term 'corporate' for both occupational and class common interests; clearly in the third 'moment' he is referring to class consciousness. It should also be noted that his 'moments' are not the same as mine, which are the unified but opposing parts of a contradiction.
26. Ibid., pp. 181–2.

## 4 SEMI-COLONIAL COMPLICATIONS

1. In what follows, it should be kept in mind that a more than 40-year habit holds me still to the old Western transcription of Chinese names. The basic account of the origins of the CCP is Meisner 1967; for a more recent analysis see Luk 1990 and for a broader perspective on socialist influences see van de Ven 1991, Chapter 2. It should be noted that access to new sources in the past 15 years has made study of the Chinese revolutionary movement markedly fluid at the moment. For a brief review of debates see Shum 1988, 'Introduction', and Esherick 1995 for a longer discussion of current issues which provides valuable points of focus. Van de Ven 1996 is a very useful literature review. Key works of the older generation are Brandt 1958, Isaacs 1961 (originally published in 1938)

and Schwartz 1979 (originally published in 1951). The 'second generation' produced Ch'ên 1965, Hsiao 1961, Rue 1966 and Chang 1972, and for the new one see Saich 1994 and Wou 1994. Much new work is directed towards a reassessment of communist penetration of rural areas: see for example Bernhardt 1992, Hartford and Goldstein (eds) 1989, Perry 1980 and Thaxton 1983. Saich and van de Ven (eds) 1994 gathers together a useful range of pieces. Closer to my own concerns with overall strategy, Dirlik 1989 is a reassertion of the importance of Comintern intervention and 'a Bolshevik-style political movement' (p. 9). For Trotskyist perspectives see Benton 1992 and Rousset 1987.
2. For treatments of the 1911 revolution and the Kuomintang in the whole of my period see Duara 1988, Eastman et al. 1991, Esherick 1976, Fairbank and Feuerwerker (eds) 1986, Shimkichi and Schriffin (eds) 1995 and Wright (ed.) 1968.
3. The extent and nature of this decline is a major matter of controversy. For different approaches and views see Bin 1992, Brandt 1989, Faure 1989, Huang 1985 and 1990, Martin 1991 and Rawski 1989. What seems to emerge is a broad difference in commercialization of agriculture and landlordism between the north and central region and the south, with controversy over which peasants were worst hit but the indications being those in the former areas (on this see Pomeranz 1993). Further research will have to establish definitively how these patterns affected communist penetration.
4. Carrère d'Encausse and Schram 1969, p. 194; Ch'ên 1965, p. 100; Chesneaux 1968, p. 266; van de Ven 1991, pp. 155–9. Apart from Chesneaux 1968, the basic study on the Chinese labour movement and the CCP is Thomas 1983. See also the second part of Perry 1993.
5. Quoted, Schram 1963, p. 24; Lenin 1953(f), p. 359; Sobolev *et al.* 1971, pp. 187–9. For a detailed treatment of the period 1920–27 with emphasis on Soviet participation see Wilbur and How 1989, which also reprints nearly 400 pages of documents. For the view that the CCP–KMT alliance was basically an indigenous development and not fostered by the Comintern see Glunin 1981, especially pp. 258–62. I am in sympathy with his rejection of the latter view as a product of 'Cold War' Western scholarship, and clearly there was a more complex process involved than simply orders issued by the ECCI. Soviet Communist Party archives reveal that the KMT itself applied unsuccessfully to join the Comintern as 'the general staff of the world revolution' (Sobolev *et al.* 1971, note, p. 252).
6. Rue 1966, p. 38, argues that the reason was factional struggle and related to Mao's alignment with the Comintern's now replaced representative, 'Maring', actually the remarkable Dutchman Henk Sneevliet, whose career included a major part in founding the Indonesian, Dutch and Chinese communist parties, and then as a Trotskyist in his native land, where he was shot by the German occupiers during the Second World War for his resistance activities. On Sneevliet's role see Saich and Tichelman 1985 and the documents and introduction in Saich (ed.) 1991, which give detailed insight into Comintern operations. For the memoirs of a later Comintern agent see Braun 1982.
7. Quoted, Rue 1966, p. 75; Mao 1963(d), p. 147. It should be noted that key phrases were deleted or changed as Mao's works began to be offi-

cially published in 1951. Wherever possible, therefore, I have followed the texts in Schram 1963 rather than the official ones.
8. On the other hand, in many areas the party cadres found the task of penetrating and organizing the peasantry to be complex and difficult. For studies of this process in addition to citations in n. 1 above see Averill 1987 and 1990 and Hofheinz, Jr. 1977.
9. This and following two paragraphs, Rue 1966, p. 54; Mao 1963(c), pp. 183 and 187; Mao 1963(a), p. 176.
10. In this emphasis Mao was not a dissident. In July 1926 the Central Committee devoted a whole resolution to the need to enlist the Red Spears organization in Chihli, Shantung and Honan provinces, where they were both 'bandits' and protectors of poor peasants (Wilbur and How 1989, pp. 750–1).
11. Mao 1963(b), p. 177. The necessary orthodox emendation was one of those made in 1951.
12. Here and next paragraph based on Mao 1964(a), pp. 117–18, 120–1.
13. Quoted, Ch'ên 1965, p. 156. An alternative translation reads '[e]vents are moving in such a way that the revolutionary situation will shortly encompass, if not the whole of Chinese territory, then at least the territory of a number of key provinces' (Carrère d'Encausse and Schram 1969, pp. 244–5). Further for this paragraph, Degras (ed.) 1965, pp. 115–18 *passim*.
14. Carrère d'Encausse and Schram 1969, p. 245. See also the extracts in Degras (ed.) 1965, pp. 137–41, which do not include the kulak point. The date is given there as November 1930 (p. 135 and note). It is interesting to note that one of the charges against Li was that he had risked involving the Soviet Union in a war with the imperialist powers by his adventurism, which threatened their interests in China (Rue 1966, p. 241).
15. Carrère d'Encausse and Schram 1969, pp. 246–7. See also the extracts in Degras (ed.) 1965, pp. 169–76, and a useful survey of other documents on pp. 167–8.
16. Rue 1966, p. 263, actually says that from July 1934 Mao himself was held under house-arrest by the Politburo, possibly under direct orders from Moscow, and released to take part in the October evacuation of the Kiangsi base. This does not seem to be true; see the account of events between July and October in Ch'ên 1965, pp. 182–4, where the detention story is not even repeated.
17. The population figure is Mao's own estimate, reported in Snow 1961, p. 73. The other five soviet base areas totalled, according to the same source, another 6 million people. The sexual discrepancy in numbers escaping is because only wives of top cadres were allowed to leave, and even they had to leave their children behind if too young to march. None of these was ever found again, including two of Mao's (Rue 1966, p. 266). Some 20 000 wounded and 6000 rearguard troops were left behind with the remaining women and children; most of them were murdered by the KMT troops and returning landlords, the younger women being sold as prostitutes at five Chinese dollars a head (Smedley 1956, p. 309).
18. Figures on the number of survivors differ; I follow Salisbury 1986, p. 31 and p. 353, n. 7. For a detailed account of the Long March see Salisbury 1986, and for the mythopoeic qualities it attained Apter and Saich 1994 *passim*.

19. For Mao's further struggles against other leaders, notably Wang Ming, see Apter and Saich 1994, Chapter 2.
20. In this context, it should be remembered that peasant-based resistance continued in the south: see Benton 1992.
21. Sobolev *et al.* 1971, p. 367. This source describes the appeal as coming from the CCP central committee and the 'provisional workers' and peasants' government'. It could be that the drafting was done by Wang Ming, who had now come round to the Dimitrov line, in Moscow.
22. Schram 1963, p. 138. My reading of this document is different from Schram's; he sees it as 'confirming the position attributed to Mao' except for 'a few nuances' (1963, p. 138). However, Schram does not go into the internal power situation in the CCP, but treats Mao as completely in control. Moreover, he takes the December 1935 speech as an alignment by Mao with the Comintern, which is quite untrue, as the data presented here show.
23. However, 'a thoroughly democratic system based on universal suffrage', in other words soviets, was to be retained in the 'special region' and the Red Army was only to 'accept guidance' from Chiang's high command (Ch'ên 1965, p. 231). The main study of policies implemented in the Shensi-Kansu area, which were important for post-1949 developments, is Selden 1971, but it should be noted that Selden 1995, which is basically a reissue of that one, contains important additions substantially modifying pro-Mao enthusiasm. A major treatment of the ideological importance of this Yenan period is to be found in Apter and Saich 1994, Part II.
24. Quoted, Rue 1966, p. 283. He points out that this major 'deviation' by Mao did not appear in the English-language *Selected Works*. Further on Mao's emergence as an independent Marxist theorist see Lew 1984, Ristaino 1987 and Rousset 1987, Chapter 6.
25. On this and capitalist control over economic policies in general in our period see Topik 1987. For a study of a local power structure see Chilcote 1990.
26. Dulles 1973, pp. 271, 273 and Table 7, p. 278 (with calculations). On the formation of the working class see Stolcke 1988 (plantation labour) and Wolfe 1993.
27. On the growth of the anarchist movement see Pinto de Góes 1988.
28. My account leans very heavily on Dulles 1973, which is in the best tradition of empiricist history, i.e. zealous in digging out obscure data and not overly concerned to slant them. There is one important account of the period from 1930 by a participant, Basbaum 1976. Apart from this work there are some recent Brazilian works on the communist movement in the interwar period: Pacheco 1984, Reis 1984, Sodré 1984, and Zaidan Filho 1985 and 1988. It is notable that, presumably for nationalistic reasons, they do not draw on Dulles. A specially important work from my point of view is Pinheiro 1991. For historical studies of Latin American communism and the Comintern in general see Alexander 1957, McKenzie 1964 and Poppino 1964, and for documents Clissold (ed.) 1970. Frankly, the quality of this literature is not high, being mostly of a 'Cold War' nature and under-documented; Goldenberg 1973 is superior. A more recent work, Caballero 1986, is also quite thinly spread. In terms of documentation,

Clissold's collection is weak for the pre-1945 period and Löwy (ed.) 1992 (actually a translation of a 1980 work) is also not strong. I have found the collection of texts in Aguilar (ed.) 1968 more useful.
29. See texts in Löwy (ed.) 1992, pp. 8–16.
30. An extra dimension to electoral politics in particular was added by the fact that a significant part of Brazil's population was of African (slave) descent, a key popular cultural influence in Bahia and elsewhere. The party seems to have made a 'serious effort' to gain support in this especially disadvantaged group, but it was eventually largely won over by President Vargas's pro-labour measures (see below). See Andrews 1991, p. 304, n. 53, Carona 1979, pp. 333–6 and 1982, pp. 167 and 178, and for the general historical background Scott *et al.* 1988.
31. There was some degree of urban social struggle; into which the party had difficulty in inserting itself: see Conniff 1981.
32. Although the myth became that of the 'Prestes Column', it is necessary to record that Major Miguel Costa ranked equally with Prestes as an original leader and that the latter and his men were able to escape because part of a second, 'Paulista' column sacrificed themselves in a rearguard action to cover them (Dulles 1973, pp. 245–6).
33. Ibid., p. 273, next citation p. 344. It should be noted that Dulles, not being a Marxist, consistently renders 'petty' as 'small'. In my terms the small bourgeoisie are a different phenomenon, a stratum of the capitalist class, so I have changed the word throughout.
34. This view was to take on some apparent validity with the 1932–36 'Chaco' war between Bolivia and Paraguay. It will be generally relevant again in twenty-first-century peripheral conditions.
35 Ibid., pp. 412, with calculation, and 413. For the background to Vargas's move to a pro-labour position see Gomes 1988.
36. Dulles 1973, pp. 393–4, 396, 398–9. Next paragraph pp. 416–18. Further on Prestes, the Comintern and the PCB at this time see Pinheiro 1991, Chapter 13 and 14.
37. Dulles 1973, p. 418. Further data here from Zaidan Filho 1985, p. 98 and Dulles 1973, pp. 418–19. The Comintern's South American Secretariat, based in Argentina, began to function in 1925, probably at the end of the year, under the direction of the Latin Secretariat in Moscow. In June–July 1928 it was reorganized under the direction of the Uruguayan Vittorio Codovilla. Until the end of 1931 the Moscow direction was headed by Humbert-Droz, a former Protestant pastor, who left under pressure from Stalin because he supported Bukharin in the struggle to control the Soviet party. He avoided the usual fate of losers in the Soviet Union because he had returned to alpine peace (Caballero 1986, pp. 26–9 and 158). After this the main Comintern figure in Latin American affairs, based in Argentina, was August Guralskii (real name Abraham Heifetz), a Lithuanian who had been a Bolshevik before 1917 and served in the Red Army and then as an agent in Germany during the 1921 rising; he headed an underground successor to the South American Secretariat, which was dissolved in May 1930. Guralskii was less lucky than Humbert-Droz, becoming a victim of the later purges, although he survived the labour camps (Caballero 1986, p. 158; Dulles 1973, n. 3, p. 418).

38. For further discussion see Pinheiro 1991, pp. 227–30 and 241–2.
39. Dulles 1973, pp. 515–16. Bonfim had only joined in 1932, and Leôncio Basbaum had originally suspected him of being a police spy, a story which did not disappear (Dulles 1973, p. 501; Aguilar 1968, pp. 28–9).
40. Dulles 1973, pp. 469–70. By associating the 'saviour' phenomenon with the petty bourgeoisie (middle strata) the PCB leaders thus undervalued, as they always had, the strong 'millennarian' resistance tradition among peasants and rural workers. In this, of course, they were firmly in the general Marxist tradition. Such Brazilian movements were typified by the rising of Antonio Conselheiro in Bahia in 1896–97 or the 'holy war' waged by the followers of José Maria, last of a line of prophets taking that name since 1844, in Santa Catarina in 1912–15 (on this phenomenon see da Cunha 1944, Diacon 1991, Levine 1992 and Monteiro 1974). It seems probable that Prestes's wandering in the backlands had tapped this tradition and put him for many rural people into the category of 'saviour'.
41. On these episodes see Cerdas-Cruz 1993, especially Chapters 3, 5 and 6.
42. Dulles 1973, pp. 518 and 520, I have retranslated his 'conscience'.
43. Dulles 1973, p. 524. Dulles gives the Chinese theorist's name as 'Wan Min'. He is also quite wrong, as can be seen from the earlier analysis, in describing this as the voice of 'agrarian China' (p. 531).
44. Aguilar 1968, n. 8, pp. 28–9. Further on the rising see Silva 1970.
45. For a detailed account of this see Dulles 1983 and especially Morais 1991, Chapters 8–15, which focuses on Prestes's remarkable partner Olga Benario, who, as a German citizen, was handed over to the Gestapo and gassed at a special extermination facility in February 1942. Prestes served 10 years in gaol. Ewert went insane under torture but survived to become a pensioner in the German Democratic Republic.

## 5 CONFRONTING COLONIALISM: REVOLUTION AND THE RAJ

1. Figure from Kumar (ed.) 1983, Table 5.7, p. 448.
2. Alavi 1964, p. 118; Chandra 1966, pp. 124–7. Since the 1960s Indian historians have developed the concept of a 'colonial mode of production', which characterized a 'colonial' economy which was neither a developed capitalist nor a 'traditional' pre-capitalist formation. See in particular Alavi 1975 and further references there.
3. For various aspects of Congress's development see the contributions to Sisson and Wolpert (eds) 1988.
4. Banaji 1977, p. 26. At this point I should acknowledge a debt to Banaji's article, which put me on to the importance of India as a test case. This does not mean that I would agree with all his interpretations. His belief in the importance of a combination of the tradition of 'terrorist' action with 'an early independent development of the working class movement on a political basis', for example, seems to be misplaced on two major grounds. Firstly, he gives the usual Marxist privilege to the working class in a basically peasant country; secondly, he seems to mistake the limited actions described by the British as terrorism for armed struggle. China and Viet Nam are of course the basic reference points here for both

issues. For an important study of working-class formation see Chakrabarty 1989.
5. Paragraphs based on Chandra *et al.* 1989, Chapter 15. Quotation from Banaji 1977, p. 29.
6. It must be borne in mind that, within the scope of this generalization, conditions varied. For data and analysis see Ali, 1988, Bose 1987, Cooper 1988, Das Gupta 1992 and Patnaik (ed.) 1990.
7. On peasant movements in the interwar period see Das 1982, Dhangare 1983 and Sen 1982.
8. For these early efforts see Persits 1981, which makes some use of Soviet archives.
9. Data here and next two paragraphs, Adhikari (ed.) 1974, p. 97; Degras (ed.) 1956, p. 385; Overstreet and Windmiller 1959, pp. 43, 44–6, 50–2 and 54.
10. Data in this and next paragraph from: Carrère d'Encausse and Schram 1969, pp. 202–3; Degras (ed.) 1960, p. 12; Overstreet and Windmiller 1959, p. 70.
11. Here and next two paragraphs: Adhikari (ed.) 1974, pp. 592 and 671–2; Chandra *et al.* 1989, pp. 235–6, 240–1 and 248; Degras (ed.) 1960, p. 558; Haithcox 1971, pp. 44–6; Overstreet and Windmiller 1959, p. 127.
12. Overstreet and Windmiller 1959, pp. 71 and 75–6. They suggest that Roy's departure for China was probably an ECCI move to clear the way for the CPGB (1959, p. 94), but I am inclined to accept Haithcox's counter-arguments (1971, pp. 51–2 and 63).
13. Banaji 1977, pp. 30–1; Chandra *et al.* 1989, p. 219; Degras (ed.) 1960, p. 557. For details of communist involvement in the Bombay and other labour movements at this time see Haithcox 1971, pp. 97–107, and for Congress's role Bhattacharya 1988.
14. The source here is Haithcox 1971, p. 111, but it seems possible that this incident occurred at the 8th ECCI plenum in June.
15. Haithcox 1971, pp. 113–14. On this very important debate, which had general implications, see Datta Gupta 1980, pp. 73–90, 124–5 and 137–9.
16. Banaji 1977, p. 33. Further on the Sixth Congress discussion see Haithcox 1971, pp. 114–21, Overstreet and Windmiller 1959, pp. 118–19, and above all Datta Gupta 1980, pp. 115–59.
17. Further on artisan production between the wars see Roy 1993 and 1996.
18. Here and next two paragraphs, Degras (ed.) 1960, pp. 506, 535, 538–9 and 540.
19. Ibid., p. 35. It should be noted that in a postscript to this piece Banaji stated that it had been written in 1972–73 and that on subsequent reflection he felt that he had overrated the strength of the Indian working class and also that 'the critique of Indian Stalinism proposed in the article remains, *to some extent*, "subjectivist" and ahistorical' (1977, p. 41, original emphasis).
20. Haithcox's argument that Roy was basically pushed out because of his associations with Bukharin is convincing, including the criticism of Overstreet and Windmiller on this point: see Haithcox 1971, pp. 135–8. Paradoxically, Roy retained his admiration for Stalin (ibid., pp. 141–2). For an extended 'Leninist' assessment of Roy see Martyshin 1981.

21. Degras (ed.) 1965, p. 20; Chandra *et al.* 1989, p. 220. Dange and Spratt eventually got a 12-year sentence, Bradley 10, although these were reduced on appeal (Overstreet and Windmiller 1959, p. 136).
22. Chatterjee 1986, p. 98. However, I disagree with the view here on Gandhi's 'formal' ideas, which seem to me a more coherent part of his overall discourse than they may appear to 'rational' Marxist or liberal critics. That they contained internal contradictions is another matter.
23. For a detailed discussion, which brought me to this example in the first place, see Bayly 1986, pp. 286–302, and on Gandhi pp. 309–15. See also Chatterjee 1986, pp. 117–24, for later developments. Further data in this paragraph from Bayly 1986, pp. 309–10, 312–13 and quoted, p. 320.
24. For useful details on this see Chandra *et al.* 1989, pp. 290–5.
25. In this respect, it is extremely interesting that, in a manifesto published in July 1930 as part of an abortive effort to create an independent Marxist movement, Roy called for an initial 'Jacobin' programme, drawing a direct parallel with the French Revolution and arguing that overt materialism be suppressed in favour of nationalism (Haithcox 1971, pp. 171–2).
26. Overstreet and Windmiller stated that there are 'no indications where it originated' (1959, p. 145), but it presumably had been worked out laboriously in the absence of those sentenced at the Meerut trial after the CPI central committee accepted the Sixth Congress Colonial Theses a year earlier (Adhikari 1982, p. 454). It is significant that it took 15 months for the party leaders to assimilate the Comintern's new line and then another year to draft the programme.
27. This and the next paragraph based on Chandra *et al.* 1989, pp. 287–8 and 314–16.
28. Chandra *et al.* 1989, pp. 306 and 308. I have taken the liberty of correcting a grammatical error in the quotation.
29. Datta Gupta 1980, pp. 199–200 and 201–2. Generally on the shift between 1928 and 1935, in both India and the Comintern, see pp. 208–13.
30. In his diary for May 1934 he asked, '[h]ow can one work with Bapu [Gandhi] if he functions in this way and leaves people in the lurch?' (Chandra 1975, p. 1313). Further quotations here as cited in Chandra 1966, n. 78, p. 159; Chandra 1975, p. 1307, and n. 73, p. 1323.

## 6  LENINISM/STALINISM AS THEORY AND DISCOURSE

1. In a letter written in September 1890 Engels himself recognized this problem: see Feuer (ed.) 1959, pp. 399–400.
2. For the basic discussion see Poulantzas 1974, pp. 38–47. One of his main concerns was to defend Lenin from an accusation of economism in the context of Lenin's proposition that imperialism was the last stage of capitalism, an ambition which I do not necessarily share. Nor, clearly, was Lenin's phenomenon capitalism's final fling.
3. A theoretical working out of future possibilities must be left to another work, but the answer may be telegraphed here: yes, a truly democratic socialism is possible and will be more than ever necessary in the twenty-first century.

4. It is worth remembering here that the key difference between Bolsheviks and Mensheviks was that the latter held that only the bourgeoisie could carry out the tasks of capital, and that therefore the November 1917 seizure was in a sense premature and the basis for going on to build socialism very, if not impossibly, weak.
5. See Post 1996, pp. 239–46, for theoretical background.
6. Trotsky 1962, pp. 130–1. Following references pp. 129, 130, original emphasis, and 155.
7. In this context, it is significant that after his break with the Comintern M.N. Roy moved to the position of a need to 'raise the banner, not of Communism, but of Jacobinism' and for a 'Jacobinism of the 20th century' (Haithcox 1971, pp. 171–2; see also Martyshin 1981, pp. 206–8).
8. Quoted in 'Minh Khai', *Vietnam Courier*, no. 35, April 1975, p. 14.
9. It should be made clear that the material for this story comes via Dulles 1973 (pp. 490–2 and 502) from Basbaum, hardly an objective source (although on the whole a devoted and self-sacrificing comrade, later pushed out of the party by the Stalinists). However, I think it is clear that I have turned his own evidence against him.
10. Methodological issues are of course intimately bound up with power and control over knowledge and are therefore political.
11. Attentive readers may note an apparent contradiction here, since I have already spoken of three great revolutions in the twentieth century, the Russian, Vietnamese and Chinese. While counting the second of these as a major event in the post-1945 period, I do not regard it, for reasons which it would be out of place to enter here, as one of the all-time greats, beginning of course with the French Revolution of 1789.
12. For a detailed argument along these lines see Post 1989(a), *passim*.
13. Trotsky 1962, p. 80, original emphasis, and quoted, ibid., pp. 90–1. Radek, described by Trotsky as 'one of my closest political friends' (ibid., p. 38), had tried to reconcile him with Stalin before his exile but had now joined the victor and published a major critique of Trotsky's theoretical capacities.
14. Quoted, Deutscher 1960, n. 1, p. 287; also next quotation, original emphasis.
15. A qualification is necessary here. I accept that the building of an industrial base for state socialism in the Soviet Union in the name of 'socialism in one country', at appalling human cost, made it later possible to defeat Nazi invasion and turn the whole tide of the war against the Hitler regime. The point is that this could have been done without erecting the process theoretically into a whole new approach to world revolution; as Trotsky (again) put it, this meant that 'the fate of socialism is ... decided by the highest possible authority – the State Planning Commission of the U.S.S.R.' (1962, p. 27).
16. I derive the concept of communicative competence from Jürgen Habermas, although with considerable reworking. See Habermas 1979 *passim* and Post 1996, pp. 282–3.
17. I fully realize that these are assertions rather than proven points, but anyone familiar with the literature will recognize their validity. I am working on a study which develops this more 'futurist' argumentation.

# Bibliography

Note: Where an edited collection contains at least two cited items it is listed separately. Lenin references are unfortunately scattered, as the exigencies of using various holdings prevented me making uniform reference to the English version of the *Collected Works*.

Adhikari, G. (ed.), 1971, *Documents of the History of the Communist Party of India*, vol. I, 1917–1922, People's Publishing House, New Delhi.
Adhikari, G. (ed.), 1974, *Documents of the History of the Communist Party of India*, vol. II, 1923–1925, People's Publishing House, New Delhi.
Adhikari, G. (ed.), 1978, *Documents of the History of the Communist Party of India*, vol. IIIA, 1926, People's Publishing House, New Delhi.
Adhikari, G. (ed.), 1979, *Documents of the History of the Communist Party of India*, vol. IIIB, 1927, People's Publishing House, New Delhi.
Adhikari, G. (ed.), 1982, *Documents of the History of the Communist Party of India*, vol. IIIC, 1928, People's Publishing House, New Delhi.
Aguilar, Luis E., 1968, 'Introduction', in Aguilar (ed.) 1968.
Aguilar, Luis E. (ed.), 1968, *Marxism in Latin America*, Knopf, New York.
Alavi, Hamza, 1964, 'Imperialism Old and New', in Ralph Miliband and John Saville (eds), *The Socialist Register 1964*, Monthly Review Press, New York.
Alavi, Hamza, 1975, 'India and the Colonial Mode of Production', *Economic and Political Weekly*, vol. 10, nos 33–5, August.
Alexander, Robert J., 1957, *Communism in Latin America*, Rutgers University Press, New Brunswick, N.J.
Ali, Imran, 1988, *The Punjab under Irrigation 1885–1947*, Princeton University Press, Princeton.
Ali, Tariq (ed.), 1984, *The Stalinist Legacy*, Penguin Books, Harmondsworth.
Andrews, George Reid, 1991, *Blacks and Whites in São Paulo, Brazil, 1888–1988*, University of Wisconsin Press, Madison.
Apter, David E., and Saich, Tony, 1994, *Revolutionary Discourse in Mao's Republic*, Harvard University Press, Cambridge, Mass.
Aricó, José (ed.), 1978, *Mariátegui y los orígenes del marxismo latinamerico*, Ediciones Pasado y Presente, Mexico City.
Avenas, Denise, 1976, 'Trotsky's Marxism', Part 1, *International*, vol. 3, no. 2, Winter.
Averill, Stephen C., 1987, 'Party, Society and Local Elite in the Jiangxi Communist Movement', *Journal of Asian Studies*, vol. 46, no. 2, May.
Averill, Stephen C., 1990, 'Social Elites and Communist Revolution in the Jiangxi Hill Country', in Joseph W. Esherick and Mary Backus Rankin (eds), *Chinese Local Elites and Patterns of Dominance*, University of California Press, Berkeley.
Avineri, Shlomo (ed.), 1969, *Karl Marx on Colonialism and Modernization*, Anchor Books, Garden City.
Banaji, Jairus, 1977, 'The Comintern and Indian Nationalism', *International*, vol. 3, no. 4, Summer.

# Bibliography

Basbaum, Leoncio, 1976 (5th edn), *Historia sincera da República de 1930–1960*, Alfa-Omega, São Paulo.
Bayly, C.A., 1986, 'The Origins of Swadeshi (Home Industry): Cloth and Indian Society 1700–1930', in Arjun Appadurai (ed.), *The Social Life of Things*, Cambridge University Press, Cambridge.
Bennigsen, Alexandre A., and Wimbush, S. Enders, 1979, *Muslim National Communism in the Soviet Union*, University of Chicago Press, Chicago.
Benton, Gregor, 1986, 'The South Anhui Incident', *Journal of Asian Studies*, vol. 45, no. 4, August.
Benton, Gregor, 1992, *Mountain Fires*, University of California Press, Berkeley.
Bernhardt, Kathryn, 1992, *Rents, Taxes, and Peasant Resistance*, Stanford University Press, Stanford.
Bettelheim, Charles, 1978, *Class Struggles in the USSR: Second Period: 1923–1930*, The Harvester Press, Hassocks.
Bhattacharya, S., 1988, 'Swaraj and the Kamgar: The Indian National Congress and the Bombay Working Class, 1919–31', in Sisson and Wolpert (eds) 1988.
Bin Wong, 1992, 'Chinese Economic History and Development: A Note on the Myers-Huang Exchange', *Journal of Asian History*, vol. 51, no. 3.
Borkenau, Franz, 1962, *World Communism*, Univerity of Michigan Press, Ann Arbor.
Bose, Sugata, 1987, *Agrarian Bengal, Economy, Social Structure and Politics, 1919–1947*, Cambridge University Press, Cambridge.
Brandt, Conrad, 1958, *Stalin's Failure in China, 1924–1927*, Harvard University Press, Cambridge, Mass.
Braun, Otto, 1982, *A Comintern Agent in China 1932–1939*, Stanford University Press, Stanford.
Braunthal, Julius, 1967, *History of the International*, vol. II, Nelson, London.
Broué, Pierre (ed.), 1976, *La Question chinoise dans l'Internationale communiste*, EDI, Paris.
Caballero, Manuel, 1986, *Latin America and the Comintern 1919–1943*, Cambridge University Press, Cambridge.
Carona, Edgar, 1979, *Movimiento operaio no Brasil, 1877–1944*, DIFEL, São Paulo.
Carona, Edgar, 1982, *O PCB (1922–1943)*, vol. I, DIFEL, São Paulo.
Carr, E.H., 1966, *The Bolshevik Revolution 1917–1923*, 3 vols, Penguin Books, Harmondsworth.
Carr, E.H., 1969, *The Interregnum 1923–24*, Penguin Books, Harmondsworth.
Carrère d'Encausse, Hélène, and Schram, Stuart R., 1969, *Marxism and Asia*, Allen Lane, The Penguin Press, London.
Cerdas-Cruz, Rodolfo, 1993, *The Communist International in Central America, 1920–36*, Macmillan, Basingstoke.
Chakrabarty, Dipesh, 1989, *Rethinking Working Class History*, Princeton University Press, Princeton.
Chandra, Bipan, 1966, *Rise and Growth of Economic Nationalism in India*, People's Publishing House, New Delhi.
Chandra, Bipan, 1975, 'Jawaharlal Nehru and the Capitalist Class, 1936', *Economic and Political Weekly*, vol. 10, nos 33–5, August.
Chandra, Bipan et al., 1989, *India's Struggle for Independence*, Penguin Books, Harmondsworth.

Chang Kuo-tao, 1972, *The Rise to Power of the Chinese Communist Party, 1928–1938*, 2 vols, University of Kansas Press, Lawrence.
Chatterjee, Partha, 1986, *Nationalist Thought and the Colonial World*, Zed Books for the United Nations University, London.
Ch'ên, Jerome, 1965, *Mao and the Chinese Revolution*, Oxford University Press, London.
Chen Yung-fa, 1986, *Making Revolution: The Communist Movement in Eastern and Central China, 1937–45*, University of California Press, Berkeley.
Chen Yung-fa and Benton, Gregor, 1986, *Moral Economy and the Chinese Revolution*, Antropologisch-Sociologisch Centrum, University of Amsterdam, Amsterdam.
Chesneaux, Jean, 1968, *The Chinese Labor Movement, 1919–1927*, Stanford University Press, Stanford.
Chesneaux, Jean, 1973, *Peasant Revolts in China 1840–1949*, W.W. Norton, New York.
Chilcote, Ronald, 1990, *Power and the Ruling Classes in Northeast Brazil*, Cambridge University Press, Cambridge.
Clark, Martin, 1977, *Antonio Gramsci and the Revolution that Failed*, Yale University Press, New Haven.
Claudin, Fernando, 1975, *The Communist Movement from Comintern to Cominform*, Penguin Books, Harmondsworth.
Clissold, Stephen (ed.), 1970, *Soviet Relations with Latin America, 1918–1968*, Oxford University Press, London.
Comintern, 1935, 'Struggles of the Communist Parties of South and Caribbean America', *Communist International*, vol. 12, no. 10, 20 May, reprinted in Aguilar (ed.) 1968.
Conniff, Michael L., 1981, *Urban Politics in Brazil*, University of Pittsburgh Press, Pittsburgh.
Cooper, Adrienne, 1988, *Sharecropping and Sharecroppers' Struggles in Bengal, 1930–1950*, K.P. Bagchi, Calcutta.
Cunha, Euclides da, 1944, *Rebellion in the Backlands*, Phoenix Books, Chicago.
Damodaran, K., 1984, 'The Tragedy of Indian Communism', in Ali (ed.) 1984.
Das, Arvind N., 1982, 'Peasants and Peasant Organizations: The Kisan Sabha in Bihar', *Journal of Peasant Studies*, vol. 9, no. 3, April.
Das Gupta, Ranajit, 1992, 'Plantation Labour in Colonial India', *Journal of Peasant Studies*, vol. 19, nos 3 and 4, April–July.
Datta Gupta, Sobhanlal, 1980, *Comintern, India and the Colonial Question, 1920–37*, K.P. Bagchi and Co., Calcutta.
Davidson, Alastair, 1974, 'Gramsci and Lenin 1917–1922', in Ralph Miliband and John Saville (eds), *The Socialist Register 1974*, Merlin Press, London.
Degras, Jane (ed.), 1956, 1960 and 1965, *The Communist International 1919–1943: Documents*, 3 vols, Oxford University Press, London.
Deutscher, Isaac, 1954, *The Prophet Armed*, Oxford University Press, London.
Deutscher, Isaac, 1959, *The Prophet Unarmed*, Oxford University Press, London.
Deutscher, Isaac, 1960, *Stalin: A Political Biography*, Vintage Books, New York.
Dhanagare, D.N., 1983, *Peasant Movements in India: 1920–1950*, Oxford University Press, Oxford.
Diacon, Todd A., 1991, *Millenarian Vision, Capitalist Reality*, Duke University Press, Durham.

## Bibliography

Dimitrov, Georgii, 1935(a), *The United Front Against Fascism*, New Century, New York.
Dimitrov, Georgii, 1935(b), *The Working Class Against Fascism*, Modern Books, London.
Dirlik, Arif, 1989, *The Origins of Chinese Communism*, Oxford University Press, New York.
Dornhorst, Robert, 1977, 'The Communist Parties of Western Europe: The Origin of the National Roads to Socialism', *Revolutionary Communist*, no. 6, April.
Duara, Prasenjit, 1988, *Culture, Power and the State*, Stanford University Press, Stanford.
Dulles, John W.F., 1973, *Anarchists and Communists in Brazil, 1900– 1935*, University of Texas Press, Austin.
Dulles, John W.F., 1983, *Brazilian Communism 1935–1945*, University of Texas Press, Austin.
Eastman, Lloyd E., et al., 1991, *The Nationalist Era in China, 1927–1937*, Cambridge University Press, Cambridge.
Esherick, Joseph W., 1976, *Reform and Revolution in China*, University of California Press, Berkeley.
Esherick, Joseph W., 1995, 'Ten Theses on the Chinese Revolution', *Modern China*, vol. 21, no. 1, January.
Fairbank, John K., and Feuerwerker, Albert (eds), 1986, *The Cambridge History of India*, vol. XIII, part II, Cambridge University Press, Cambridge.
Faure, David, 1989, *The Rural Economy of Pre-Liberation China*, Oxford University Press, Oxford.
Feuer, Lewis S. (ed.), 1959, *Basic Writings on Politics and Philosophy, Karl Marx and Friedrich Engels*, Anchor Books, Garden City, N.Y.
Fitzgerald, C.P., 1964, *The Birth of Communist China*, Penguin, Harmondsworth.
Frank, Pierre, 1979, *Histoire de l'Internationale Communiste*, 2 vols, La Bréche, Paris.
Glunin, V.I., 1981, 'Comintern Policy for China (1921–1927)', in Ulyanovsky (ed.) 1981.
Goldenberg, Boris, 1973, *Kommunismus in Lateinamerika*, Verlag Kohlhammer, Stuttgart.
Gomes, Angela de Castro, 1988, *A Invencão do Trabalhismo*, Instituto Universitario de Pesquisa do Rio de Janeiro, Rio de Janeiro.
Gramsci, Antonio, 1971, *Selections from the Prison Notebooks of Antonio Gramsci*, edited by Quintin Hoare and Geoffrey Nowell Smith, Lawrence and Wishart, London.
Habermas, Jürgen, 1979, *Communications and the Evolution of Society*, Heinemann, London.
Haithcox, John Patrick, 1971, *Communism and Nationalism in India*, Princeton University Press, Princeton.
Hartford, Kathleen, and Goldstein, Stephen M. (eds), 1989, *Single Sparks*, M.E. Sharpe, Armonk, N.J.
Henderson, W.O. (ed.), 1967, *Engels: Selected Writings*, Penguin, Harmondsworth.
Hoare, Quintin, and Nowell Smith, Geoffrey, 1971, 'Introduction', in Gramsci 1971.

Hofheinz, Jr, Roy, 1977, *The Broken Wave*, Harvard University Press, Cambridge, Mass.
Hsiao Tso-liang, 1961, *Power Relations within the Chinese Communist Movement*, University of Washington Press, Seattle.
Huang, Philip C.C., 1985, *The Peasant Economy and Social Change in North China*, Stanford University Press, Stanford.
Huang, Philip C.C., 1990, *The Peasant Family and Rural Development in the Yangtzi Delta, 1350–1988*, Stanford University Press, Stanford.
Ianni, Octavio, 1964, 'Political Process and Economic Development in Brazil', *New Left Review*, no. 25, June and no. 26, August.
Isaacs, Harold R., 1961 (revised), *The Tragedy of the Chinese Revolution*, Stanford University Press, Stanford.
Johnson, Chalmers, 1962, *Peasant Nationalism and Communist Power*, Hoover Institution for War, Revolution and Peace, Stanford.
Johnson, Chalmers, 1977, 'Peasant Nationalism Revisited: The Biography of a Book', *China Quarterly*, no. 72, December.
Knight, Alan, 1986, *The Mexican Revolution*, University of Nebraska Press, Lincoln.
Kriegel, Annie, 1964, *Les Internationales ouvrières*, Presses universitaires de France, Paris.
Krishnamurty, J., 1983, 'The Occupational Structure', Chapter VI in Kumar (ed.) 1983.
Kumar, Dharma (ed.), 1983, *The Cambridge Economic History of India*, vol. II, Cambridge University Press, Cambridge.
Laclau, Ernesto, 1977, *Politics and Ideology in Marxist Theory*, New Left Books, London.
Landau, Bruce, 1977, 'Lenin and the Bolshevik Party', *Revolutionary Communist*, no. 6, April.
Larrain, Jorge, 1989, *Theories of Development*, Polity Press, Cambridge.
Lee Feigon, *Chen Duxiu, Founder of the Chinese Communist Party*, Princeton University Press, Princeton.
Lenin, V.I., 1953, *Selected Works in Two Volumes*, vol. I, part 2, vol. II, parts 1 and 2, Lawrence and Wishart, London.
Lenin, V.I., 1953(a), 'One Step Forward, Two Steps Back', in Lenin 1953, vol. I, part 1.
Lenin, V.I. 1953(b), 'Two Tactics of Social Democracy in the Democratic Revolution', in Lenin 1953, vol. I, part 2.
Lenin, V.I., 1953(c), 'The Right of Nations to Self-Determination', in Lenin 1953, vol. I, part 2.
Lenin, V.I., 1953(d), 'Imperialism, the Highest Stage of Capitalism', in Lenin 1953, vol. I, part 2.
Lenin, V.I., 1953(e), 'The Proletarian Revolution and the Renegade Kautsky', in Lenin 1953, vol. II, part 2.
Lenin, V.I., 1953(f), '"Left-Wing" Communism, An Infantile Disorder', in Lenin 1953, vol. II, part 2.
Lenin, V.I., 1953(g), 'Preliminary Draft of Theses on the National and Colonial Questions', in Lenin 1953, vol. II, part 2.
Lenin, V.I., 1953(h), 'Theses of Report on the Tactics of the Russian Communist Party to the Third Congress of the Communist International (Preliminary Draft)', in Lenin 1953, vol. II, part 2.

Lenin, V.I., 1953(i), 'On Cooperation', in Lenin 1953, vol. II, part 2.
Lenin, V.I., 1953(j), 'Better Fewer, But Better', in Lenin 1953, vol. II, part 2.
Lenin, V.I., 1971(a), 'The Question of Nationalities or "Autonomisation"', *Collected Works*, vol. XXXVI, Lawrence and Wishart, London.
Lenin, V.I., 1971(b), 'Remarks on the Report of A. Sultan-Zade Concerning the Prospects of a Social Revolution in the East', *Collected Works*, vol. XLII, Progress Publishers, Moscow.
Lerner, Elinor, 1974, 'The Chinese Peasantry and Imperialism: A Critique of Chalmers Johnson's Peasant Nationalism and Communist Power', *Bulletin of Concerned Asian Scholars*, vol. 6, no. 2, April–August.
Levine, Robert M., 1970, *The Vargas Regime*, Columbia University Press, New York.
Levine, Robert M., 1992, *Vale of Tears*, University of California Press, Berkeley.
Lew, Roland, 1984, 'Maoism, Stalinism and the Chinese Revolution', in Ali (ed.) 1984.
Lindsey, Charles W., 1982, 'Lenin's Theory of Imperialism', *Review of Radical Political Economics*, vol. 14, no. 1, Spring.
Lowe, Donald M., 1966, *The Function of 'China' in Marx, Lenin, and Mao*, University of California Press, Berkeley.
Löwy, Michael, 1976, 'Marxists and the National Question', *New Left Review*, no. 96, March–April.
Löwy, Michael, 1981, *The Politics of Combined and Uneven Development*, Verso, London.
Löwy, Michael, 1992, *Marxism in Latin America from 1909 to the Present*, Humanities Press, Atlantic Highlands.
Luk, Michael, 1990, *The Origins of Chinese Bolshevism*, Oxford University Press, Oxford.
Lukács, Georg, 1971, *History and Class Consciousness*, Merlin Press, London.
McKenzie, Kermit E., 1964, *Comintern and World Revolution, 1928–1943*, Columbia University Press, New York.
Mao Tse-tung, 1963(a), 'An Analysis of the Various Classes of the Chinese Peasantry and Their Attitudes Toward Revolution', in Schram 1963.
Mao Tse-tung, 1963(b), 'Analysis of All the Classes in Chinese Society', in Schram 1963.
Mao Tse-tung, 1963(c), 'Report of an Investigation into the Peasant Movement in Hunan', in Schram 1963.
Mao Tse-tung, 1963(d), 'The Hegemony of the Proletariat in the Bourgeois-Democratic Revolution', in Schram 1963.
Mao Tse-tung, 1964, *Selected Works of Mao Tse-tung*, vol. I, Foreign Languages Press, Peking.
Mao Tse-tung, 1964(a), 'A Single Spark Can Start a Prairie Fire', in Mao 1964.
Mao Tse-tung, 1964(b), 'On Tactics Against Japanese Imperialism', in Mao 1964.
Mao Tse-tung, 1964(c), 'Problems of Strategy in China's Revolutionary War', in Mao 1964.
Mao Tse-tung, 1965, 'Problems of War and Strategy', *Selected Works of Mao Tse-tung*, vol. II, Foreign Languages Press, Peking.
Mariátegui, José Carlos, 1927, 'Yankilandia y el marxismo', reprinted in Aguilar (ed.) 1968.

Mariátegui, José Carlos, 1971, *Seven Interpretative Essays on Peruvian Reality*, University of Texas Press, Austin.

Martin, Michael F., 1991, 'Rural Living Conditions in Pre-Liberation China: A Survey of Three Recent Studies', *Journal of Peasant Studies*, vol. 19, no. 1, October.

Martyshin, O.V., 1981, 'Some Problems of the Strategy and Tactics of the Indian National Liberation and Communist Movement', in Ulyanovsky (ed.) 1981.

Marx, Karl, 1971, *Capital*, vol. III, Progress Publishers, Moscow.

Marx, Karl, 1973, *The Revolutions of 1848*, Penguin Books, Harmondsworth.

Marx, Karl, and Friedrich Engels, 1973, 'Manifesto of the Communist Party', in Marx 1973.

Meisner, Maurice, 1967, *Li Ta-chao and the Origins of Chinese Marxism*, Harvard University Press, Cambridge, Mass.

Monteiro, Duglas Teixeira, 1974, *Os Errantes de Novo Seculo*, Livraria Duas Cidades, São Paulo.

Morais, Fernando, 1991, *Olga*, Cardinal, London.

Morris, Morris D., 1983, 'The Growth of Large-Scale Industry to 1947', Chapter VII in Kumar (ed.) 1983.

Nettl. J.P., 1966, *Rosa Luxemburg*, 2 vols, Oxford University Press, London.

North, Robert C., 1963, *M.N. Roy's Mission to China*, University of California Press, Berkeley.

Overstreet, Gene D., and Windmiller, Marshall, 1959, *Communism in India*, University of California Press, Berkeley.

Pacheco, Eliezer, 1984, *O Partido Comunista Brasileiro (1922–1964)*, Editora Alfa-Omega, São Paulo.

Patnaik, Utsa (ed.), 1990, *Agrarian Relations and Accumulation*, Oxford University Press, Bombay.

Perry, Elizabeth J., 1980, *Rebels and Revolutionaries in North China, 1845–1945*, Stanford University Press, Stanford.

Perry, Elizabeth J., 1993, *Shanghai on Strike*, Stanford University Press, Stanford.

Persits, M.A., 1981, 'The Origin of the Indian Communist Movement and the Comintern's Oriental Policy (1918–1921)', in Ulyanovsky (ed.) 1981.

Pinheiro, Paulo Sérgio, 1991, *Estrategias da Ilusão*, Companhia das Letras, São Paulo.

Pinto de Góes, Maria Conceiçao, 1988, *A Formaçao de Classe Trabalhadora*, Jorge Zahar, Rio de Janeiro.

Pomeranz, Kenneth, 1993, *The Making of a Hinterland*, University of California Press, Berkeley.

Poppino, Rollie E., 1964, *International Communism in Latin America*, Free Press of Glencoe, London.

Post, Ken, 1989(a), (b) and (c), *Revolution, Socialism and Nationalism in Viet Nam*, vol. I *Viet Nam, An Interrupted Revolution*, vol. II *Viet Nam Divided*, vol. III, *Socialism in Half a Country*, Dartmouth, Aldershot.

Post, Ken, 1990, *Revolution, Socialism and Nationalism in Viet Nam*, vol. IV, *The Failure of Counter-Insurgency in the South*, Dartmouth, Aldershot.

Post, Ken, 1994, *Revolution, Socialism and Nationalism in Viet Nam*, vol. V, *Winning the War and Losing the Peace*, Dartmouth, Aldershot.

Post, Ken, 1996, *Regaining Marxism*, Macmillan, London.

Post, Ken, 1997, *Communists and National Socialists*, Macmillan, London.
Post, Ken, and Wright, Phil, 1989, *Socialism and Underdevelopment*, Routledge, London.
Poulantzas, Nicos, 1974, *Fascism and Dictatorship*, New Left Review Editions, London.
Prestes, Luís Carlos, 1945, 'Os comunistas na luta pela democracia', translated extract in Aguilar (ed.) 1968.
Rawski, Thomas, 1989, *Economic Growth in Pre-war China*, University of California Press, Berkeley.
Reiman, Michal, 1987, *The Birth of Stalinism*, I.B. Tauris, London.
Reis, Dinarco, 1984, *A Luta de Classes no Brasil e o PCB*, vol. I, Editora Novos Runos, São Paulo.
Reznikov, A.B., 1981, 'The Comintern's Oriental Policy', in Ulyanovsky (ed.) 1981.
Ristaino, Marcia R., 1987, *China's Art of Revolution*, Duke University Press, Durham.
Robens, John, n.d., *Imperialism, Stalinism and Permanent Revolution*, I.M.G. Publications, London.
Rosdolsky, Roman, 1965, 'Worker and Fatherland: A Note on a Passage in the *Communist Manifesto*', *Science and Society*, vol. 29, no. 20.
Rousset, Pierre, 1987, *The Chinese Revolution*, 2 parts, *Notebooks for Study and Research*, Nos 2 and 3, January and May, International Institute for Research and Education, Amsterdam.
Roy, Thirthankar, 1993, *Artisans and Industrialization*, Delhi.
Roy, Thirthankar, 1996, 'Home Market and the Artisans in Colonial India: A Study of Brassware', *Modern Asian Studies*, vol. 30, part 2, May.
Rue, John E., 1966, *Mao Tse-tung in Opposition 1927–1935*, Stanford University Press, Stanford.
Saich, Tony, 1994, *The Rise to Power of the Chinese Communist Party*, M.E. Sharpe, Armonk, N.J.
Saich, Tony, and Tichelman, Fritjof, 1985, 'Henk Sneevliet: A Dutch Revolutionary on the World Stage', *Journal of Communist Studies*, vol. 1, no. 2, June.
Saich, Tony (ed.), 1991, *The Origins of the First United Front*, Brill, Leiden.
Saich, Tony, and van den Ven, Hans (eds), 1994, *New Perspectives on the Chinese Revolution*, M.E. Sharpe, Armonk, N.J.
Salisbury, Harrison, 1986, *The Long March*, Pan Books, London.
Salvadori, Massimo, 1979, *Karl Kautsky and the Socialist Revolution 1880–1938*, New Left Books, London.
Sassoon, Ann Showstack, 1980, *Gramsci's Politics*, Croom Helm, London.
Schram, Stuart R., 1963, *The Political Thought of Mao Tse-tung*, Praeger, New York.
Schwartz, Benjamin, 1979, *Chinese Communism and the Rise of Mao*, Harvard University Press, Cambridge, Mass.
Scott, Rebecca, *et al.*, 1988, *The Abolition of Slavery and the Aftermath of Emancipation in Brazil*, Duke University Press, Durham.
Selden, Mark, 1971, *The Yenan Way in Revolutionary China*, Harvard University Press, Cambridge, Mass.
Selden, Mark, 1995, *China in Revolution*, M.E. Sharpe, Armonk, N.J.

Sen, Sunil, 1982, *Peasant Movements in India*, K.P. Bagchi and Co., Calcutta.
Shanin, Teodor, (ed.), 1983, *Late Marx and the Russian Road*, Routledge and Kegan Paul, London.
Shimkichi, Eto, and Schiffrin, Harold Z. (eds), 1995, *China's Republican Revolution*, University of Tokyo Press, Tokyo.
Shum Kui-kwong, 1988, *The Chinese Communists' Road to Power*, Oxford University Press, Hong Kong.
Silva, Hélio, 1970, *1935 A revolta vermelha*, Editôra Civilaçao Brasileira, Rio de Janeiro.
Sisson, Richard, and Wolpert, Stanley (eds), 1988, *Congress and Indian Nationalism*, University of California Press, Berkeley.
Smedley, Agnes, 1956, *The Great Road*, Monthly Review Press, New York.
Snow, Edgar, 1961, *Red Star Over China*, Grove Press, New York.
Sobolev, A.I., et al., 1971, *Outline History of the Communist International*, Progress Publishers, Moscow.
Sodré, Nelson Warmeck, 1984, *Contribuçao a História do PCB*, Global Editora, São Paolo.
Stalin, Iosif, 1936, *Marxism and the National and Colonial Question*, Lawrence and Wishart, London.
Stolcke, Verena, 1988, *Coffee Planters, Workers and Wives*, St Martin's Press, New York.
Sultan Galiyev, Mir-Said, 1919, 'The Social Revolution and the East', in Bennigsen and Wimbush 1979.
Sultan Galiyev, Mir-Said, 1921(a), 'The Tatars and the October Revolution', in Bennigsen and Wimbush 1979.
Sultan Galiyev, Mir-Said, 1921(b), 'The Methods of Antireligious Propaganda among the Muslims', in Bennigsen and Wimbush 1979.
Suny, Ronald Grigor, 1972, *The Baku Commune 1917–1918*, Princeton University Press, Princeton.
Tetsuya, Kataoka, 1974, *Resistance and Revolution in China*, University of California Press, Berkeley.
Thaxton, Ralph, 1983, *China Turned Rightside Up*, Yale University Press, New Haven.
Thomas, S.B., 1983, *Labor and the Chinese Revolution*, University of Michigan Center for Chinese Studies, Ann Arbor.
Topik, Stephen, 1987, *The Political Economy of the Brazilian State 1889–1930*, University of Texas Press, Austin.
Trotsky, Leon, 1953, *The First Five Years of the Communist International*, 2 vols, Pioneer Publishers, New York.
Trotsky, Leon, 1957, *The Third International After Lenin*, Pioneer Publishers, New York.
Trotsky, Leon, 1962, *The Permanent Revolution* and *Results and Prospects* (in 1 vol.), New Park Publications, London.
Trotsky, Leon, 1967, *The History of the Russian Revolution*, 3 vols, Sphere Books, London.
Ulam, Adam B., 1969, *Lenin and the Bolsheviks*, Collins Fontana Library, London.

# Bibliography

Ulyanovsky, Rostislav A. (ed.), 1981, *The Comintern and the East*, Progress Publishers, Moscow.
Vallier, Jacques, 1977, '40 Theses on Imperialism and Permanent Revolution', *International*, vol. 3, no. 4, Summer.
van de Ven, Hans J., 1991, *From Friend to Comrade*, University of California Press, Berkeley.
van de Ven, Hans J., 1996, 'Recent Studies of Modern Chinese History', *Modern Asian Studies*, vol. 30, part 2, May.
van Slyke, Lyman P., 1967, *Enemies and Friends*, Stanford University Press, Stanford.
Wang Ming, 1979, *Mao's Betrayal*, Progress Publishers, Moscow.
Wilbur, C. Martin, and How, Julie Lien-ying, 1989, *Missionaries of Revolution*, Harvard University Press, Cambridge, Mass.
Williams, Gwyn A., 1975, *Proletarian Order*, Pluto Press, London.
Wolfe, Joel, 1993, *Working Women, Working Men*, Duke University Press, Durham.
Womack, Jr., John, 1968, *Zapata and the Mexican Revolution*, Thames and Hudson, London.
Wou, Odoric Y.K., 1994, *Mobilizing the Masses*, Stanford University Press, Stanford.
Wright, Mary C. (ed.), 1968, *China in Revolution*, Yale University Press, New Haven.
Yang, Benjamin, 1986, 'The Zunyi Conference as One Step in Mao's Rise to Power: A Survey of Historical Studies of the Chinese Communist Party', *China Quarterly*, no. 106, June.
Zaidan Filho, Michel, 1985, *PCB (1922-1929)*, Global universitária, Rio de Janeiro.
Zaidan Filho, Michel, 1988, *O PCB e a Internacional Communista, 1922-1929*, Vértica, São Paulo.

# Index

agents, historical/revolutionary 4, 6–9 *passim*, 27, 46, 69, 168, 180, 183
Africa 31, 32, 190
Algeria 3, 135
All-India Muslim League 116
All-India Trades Union Congress (AITUC) 117, 122, 123, 145
Amritsar Massacre 117
anarchists (Brazilian) 99–100, 104
Argentina 60, 97, 99
artisans 3, 5
 in India 125, 126, 131–3
Ataturk, Kemal 43, 44, 191
Attenborough, Richard 136
Austria-Hungary 23
Azerbaijanis 26, 29, 190

Banaji, Jairus 114, 118, 127, 138, 148, 168–9, 198, 199
Basbaum, Leôncio 100, 165, 198, 201
Benario, Olga v, 198
Bengal 121
Bernstein, Eduard 8
Besant, Annie 116
Bigev, Musa 26–7
Birla firm 116, 146, 147
Birla, G.D. 147, 148
Bolshevik/October Revolution 7, 8, 23, 25, 27, 30, 31, 46, 53, 67, 68, 80, 96, 151, 152, 161, 181, 182
Bolsheviks 21, 27, 28–31 *passim*, 34, 35, 41, 54, 99, 170, 182, 185, 201
Bolshevization 49, 55, 191
 *see also* vanguard party
Bombay 117, 118, 121, 123, 134, 141
Bonfim, Antônio Maciel 109–12 *passim*, 198
Borkenau, Franz 58, 62

Bose, Subhas Chandra 128, 130, 145
bourgeois democracy 3, 13, 15, 113, 135, 153, 158, 172
bourgeois-democratic revolution 36–9 *passim*, 42, 60, 80, 82, 85, 103
 *see also* national bourgeoisie
Bradley, Ben 122, 128, 129, 144, 200
Brandão, Otavio 99, 100, 105
Brazil 56, 60, 97–113, 143, 149, 159, 167, 169, 185, 186, 197
 dependence on coffee 98, 102, 103, 107
 *see also* capitalists; Comintern; ECCI; landlords; Partido Comunista do Brasil; peasants; Vargas, Getulio; working class
Britain/United Kingdom 23, 44, 58, 62, 114, 125, 166
 colonial rule in India 114–16, 120, 121, 125, 126, 129, 134, 135, 138, 141, 148, 149, 149–50
 *see also* Simon Commission
Bukharin, Nikolai 23, 52, 58, 124, 197

Calcutta 123
Canton 76, 77, 79, 81
capitalism 3, 13, 22, 192
 crisis of 3, 5, 23, 42, 56, 57–8, 62, 63, 146, 151, 152–3, 155, 156, 169, 174–5, 182, 186
 weak link in 12, 53, 56, 91, 152–3, 183
 world 10, 22–3, 31–3, 53, 151–2, 157, 177, 178, 181, 184, 186–7, 188
 *see also* bourgeois democracy; capitalists; centre, capitalist

212

# Index

capitalists/bourgeoisie 3, 5, 7, 9, 13, 16, 17, 21, 30–3, 53–4, 61, 114, 124, 126, 157–8, 163, 183, 201
  in Brazil 98, 102, 103, 105, 113, 149
  in China 61, 81, 149
  in India 61, 115, 116, 127, 132–3, 138, 139, 146–8, 149
  see also Birla firm; bourgeois-democratic revolution; capitalism; national bourgeoisie
Cardenas, Lazaro 12
Cawnpore conspiracy case 120
Central Provinces 121
centre, capitalist 2–3, 4, 7, 9, 10, 11, 20, 23, 39, 44, 48, 67, 70, 143, 153, 188
  see also Britain; France; uneven and combined development; USA; Western Europe
Chaco War 197
Ch'en Tu-hsiu 75
Chiang Kai-shek 77–9, 81, 92, 93, 95, 167
China 1, 11–12, 15, 17, 25, 30, 51, 55, 56, 59, 60, 68, 74–97, 113, 126, 127, 130, 135, 166–7, 169, 172, 180, 183, 184–5, 186
  see also capitalists; Chinese Communist Party; Comintern; ECCI; Kuomintang; landlords; Mao Tse-tung; peasants; working class
Chinese Communist Party (CCP) 74–5, 77–81 passim, 84, 86, 87–96 passim, 103, 149, 150, 174, 184, 185
  see also Comintern; ECCI; Li Li-san; Long March; Mao Tse-tung; Red Army; '28 Bolsheviks'; Wang Ming
civil disobedience 117, 133, 134, 135, 138, 141
  see also Gandhi, Mohandas; swadeshi movement
class 4–6, 18, 24, 55–6
  consciousness 5, 18, 19, 68–71,
72, 135, 136, 137–8, 159, 171, 193
  see also artisans; capitalists; identity; landlords; middle strata; peasants; petty bourgeoisie; subjects; working class
class alliances 14, 19, 24, 25, 33–7 passim, 40–3 passim, 62, 65, 86, 97, 110, 123, 156, 180
  see also revolutionary bloc; revolutionary stages; united front
*The Class Struggles in France* 3
Claudin, Fernando 43, 49, 62, 152
colonial mode of production 199
  see also periphery
Comintern 18, 25, 35, 36, 42, 46, 55, 66, 83, 87, 97, 102, 108, 109, 113, 114, 122, 126, 127, 128, 135, 150, 152, 162–3, 165–70 passim, 171–4 passim, 176, 177, 179, 180, 181–6 passim, 190, 192, 193, 197
  on Brazil 105, 106, 112
  on China 78, 93–4, 159
  on India 119, 124–7, 128, 135–6, 138–9, 143–4, 145, 148
  on Latin America 103–4, 104, 105–6, 109, 173–4
  Commission on the National and Colonial Question 36–40
  Second Congress 36–40, 118, 158, 164
  Third Congress 172, 176
  Fourth Congress 42–3, 76, 83–4, 86, 100, 123
  Fifth Congress 120, 122
  Sixth Congress 56–8, 59–62, 65, 97, 101, 102–3, 123, 124–7, 128, 167, 168
  Seventh Congress 56, 63–5, 93, 95–6, 110, 113, 143, 164
Communist International *see* Comintern
*Communist Manifesto* 3–4, 14, 16
Communist Party of India (CPI) 121–3, 128, 130, 130–1, 135, 136, 139–45, 149–50

*see also* Comintern; ECCI
Communist Party of Great Britain (CPGB)   122, 124, 125, 126, 128, 134, 140
Congress Socialist Party (CSP)   142–5 *passim*, 147, 169
Costa, Miguel   108, 197
Coriolanus   2, 187
Cuba   1, 109

Dange, S.A.   118, 119, 120, 129, 145, 200
Das, C.R.   121
decolonization debate (on India)   124–7
discourse   6–7, 8, 14, 18, 25, 46, 50, 56, 65, 150, 183
   Gandhian   131–3, 134, 135–8 *passim*, 140, 161
   Leninism/Stalinism as   178–81
   *see also* agents; class consciousness; identity; interpellation; subjects
Dimitrov, Georgii   63, 64, 93, 110–11, 143
dogmatism   53, 55, 59, 66, 120, 156, 168, 169, 170, 176, 178, 179, 181, 183, 184
   *see also* Stalinism
Dutt, R.P.   140, 144

ECCI   18, 24, 50, 54, 55, 57, 58–9, 62–3, 110–11, 124, 169, 172, 177
   and Brazil   104, 105, 110, 111
   and China   77, 79, 81, 86, 88–96 *passim*
   and India   119, 119–20, 120, 122, 128, 130, 134, 139–40
   on Latin America   100, 103, 109–10, 111
   *see also* Comintern
economism   55, 56, 69, 84, 153, 200
Egypt   3, 9, 61, 122, 127, 130, 161
El Salvador   110
Engels, Friedrich   1, 3, 9, 11, 12, 13, 45, 66, 151, 152, 153, 188
   *see also* Marx, Karl

Enlightenment   4, 10, 31, 52, 153, 175, 178, 182, 187
Ethiopia   65
Ewert, Arthur   112, 198
Executive Committee of the Communist International *see* ECCI

Fascism   63, 65, 94, 107, 108–9, 109
French Revolution   4, 8, 12, 13, 18, 153, 187, 201
feudalism   13, 16, 28, 33–4, 53, 102
   *see also* landlords
First World War   2, 11, 23, 44–5, 116, 152
France   23, 62, 64, 113

Gandhi, Mohandas   116–17, 119, 121, 130, 131–8 *passim*, 140, 141, 145, 146, 147, 150, 200
   *see also* discourse, Gandhian
gender   6, 7–8, 85, 153, 164–5, 189
   *see also* identity; women
George, Henry   12
Georgia   30
Germany   2, 5, 14, 15, 23, 30–1, 44, 59, 62, 64, 109, 125, 154, 162, 168–9, 179, 201
globalism   22, 46, 181, 182
   *see also* capitalism
golpism/*golpismo*   103, 112, 113, 149
Gompers, Samuel   97
Gramsci, Antonio   65–73, 160–1, 169–70, 184, 193
Great Crash   58, 62, 156
Guralski, August   197
Guralski, Ines   108

hegemony   68–9, 71–2, 81, 92, 103–6 *passim*, 127, 157, 160
   *see also* class alliances
Hilferding, Rudolf   23
Hinduism   116, 131–2
Hindustan Republican Association (Army)   121, 133–4

# Index

Hobson, J.A. 190
Hong Kong 77, 79
Hsiang Chung-fa 88, 91
Humbert-Droz, Jules 103, 105, 197
Hunan 74, 77–81 *passim*, 84, 86
Hungary 20, 31

idealism/universalist theory 165–70 *passim*, 179–80, 184
 *see also* dogmatism; Leninism/Stalinism; pragmatism; Stalinism
identity 6, 7, 24, 28, 71, 85, 136, 153, 180
 *see also* class consciousness; discourse; gender; nation/nationality; race; religion
*Imperialism, the Highest Stage of Capitalism*, 22
India 3, 15, 17, 25, 56, 114–50 *passim*, 161, 166, 167, 168–9, 169, 171, 182, 198
 *see also* capitalists; Comintern; Communist Party of India; decolonization debate; ECCI; Indian National Congress; landlords; national bourgeoisie; peasants; working class
Indian Communist Party 118
 *see also* Communist Party of India
Indian National Congress 37, 115–21 *passim*, 123, 127, 128, 130, 131, 133, 135–48 *passim*, 150, 169
Indonesia 9, 113, 130, 135, 161
industrialization 7, 124
 Brazilian 98
 Indian 115, 116
 Russian/Soviet 26, 59
intellectuals/intelligentsia 18, 26, 69–71
interpellation 14, 25, 40, 46, 56, 65, 131, 134, 170, 171, 180
 *see also* agents; discourse; subjects
Ireland 31, 163–4
Islam 26–7, 28, 29, 33, 34, 43, 161
 *see also* Muslims
Italy 62, 65, 107

Jacobinism 9, 12, 13, 15, 27, 62, 153, 160–2, 182, 201
 in Brazil 111, 167
 in China 77, 81, 82–3
 in India 131, 137–8, 167, 200
Japan 62, 63, 93
Jekyll and Hyde 20, 178

Kautsky, Karl 3, 27, 30
Kiangsi 87, 92, 93
Kuomintang (KMT) 75, 77–8, 81–3 *passim*, 87, 92–6 *passim*, 103, 114, 127, 139, 149
 *see also* Chiang Kai-shek
Kuusinen, Otto 63, 125, 127

Lacerda, Ericina de 164–5
Lacerda, Fernando de 108
Laclau, Ernesto 15, 161–2
Lajpat Rai, Lala 117, 130, 134, 136–7
landlords 17
 in Brazil 98, 102, 103, 104, 105, 113, 149
 in China 75–6, 84
 in India 118, 135
Latin America 3, 97, 102, 113, 114, 190
League Against Imperialism 122–3, 137, 142
Lenin, V.I. 2, 12, 16, 19, 21, 22, 23, 27, 46, 48, 50, 51, 61, 66, 69, 70, 77, 78, 99, 129, 152, 154, 158, 160, 163–4, 166, 171, 172, 175, 179, 191, 200
 on international struggle 30–1, 35–7, 38–40, 44–5
Leninism 2, 19, 20, 47, 80, 113, 151–2, 154–6, 162, 163, 177, 178, 179, 183, 187
 *see also* Leninism/Stalinism; Marxism; Marxism-Leninism; Stalinism; vanguard party
Leninism/Stalinism 6, 7, 8, 18, 20, 24, 46, 49–50, 56, 65, 73, 97,

Leninism/Stalinism – *continued*
  99, 123, 136, 139, 150, 152,
  168, 170, 171, 175, 178–81,
  183, 184, 186
  *see also* Leninism; Marxism;
    Marxism-Leninism; Stalinism
Leuenroth, Edgard 99
Li Li-san 87, 90, 91, 139, 159, 195
Lima, Heitor Ferreira 107, 108
Li Ta-chao 75, 79
Long March 92, 94, 101
Löwy, Michael 13, 188–9, 189
Luhani, G.A.K. 129
Lukács, Georg, 41–2, 171, 174, 183
Luxemburg, Rosa 23, 30, 40, 41, 67, 68

MacDonald, Ramsay 141
Madras 121, 141
Manchuria 63, 93
Manuilskii, Dmitrii 57, 93, 105, 111, 120, 139
Mao Tse-tung 74, 77, 78, 87, 88–9, 91–6 *passim*, 111, 113, 139, 149, 159, 167, 180, 184, 193, 195
  analysis of Chinese Revolution 80, 84–6, 89–90, 96
Mariátegui, José 155, 157
Marx, Karl 1, 9–11, 12, 13–16, 17, 45, 66, 74, 124, 151, 152, 153, 188
  *see also* Engels, Friedrich
Marxism ix, 2–4, 5–7, 8, 13–18 *passim*, 20, 23–4, 27, 45, 49, 60, 65–6, 73, 80, 86, 113, 114, 115, 123–4, 131, 136, 151, 159, 162, 164, 165, 178, 181–7
  as discourse 170
  *see also* economism; idealism/ universalist theory
Marxism-Leninism 2, 30, 47, 49, 57, 96, 139, 142, 153, 164, 170, 170–1, 182
  *see also* Leninism; Leninism/ Stalinism; Marxism; Stalinism
Meerut trial 129, 137, 142, 200

Mensheviks 30, 54, 201
Mexico 11–12, 35
middle strata/class 13, 17, 27, 61, 82, 109, 116, 138, 139, 158, 161, 189
  *see also* petty bourgeoisie
Mif, Pavel 91, 93
Minas Gerais 98
Mongolia 178, 188
Monroe Doctrine 97
Muslims 28–9, 116, 118, 190
  *see also* Islam
Muzaffar, Hanafi, 29

Nanking massacre 95
Naoroji, Dadabhai 115–16, 117, 124
Narayan, Jayaprakash 142
nation/nationality 6, 7–8, 25, 64, 153, 161–2, 163–4, 170
  *see also* nationalism
national bourgeoisie 33–4, 60–1, 62, 94, 114, 116, 119, 127, 138, 143, 149, 167, 171, 180, 182, 183, 184
  *see also* united front
national communism/socialism 25, 43, 162, 176, 190
nationalism 16, 36–7, 40–1, 44, 55, 71–2, 124, 160, 162–4
  Central Asian 27–34 *passim*, 43, 163
  CPP and 77, 78, 79, 81, 82–3, 85, 86, 94, 95, 96, 183
  Indian 11, 116, 117, 119, 128, 135, 137–8, 150, 163
  *see also* national bourgeoisie; nation/nationality
National Liberation Alliance (Brazil) 111, 112
Nazis 63, 109, 201
Nehru, Jawaharlal 117, 119, 128, 129, 130, 133, 134, 136, 137, 138, 140, 142, 146–8, 177
Nehru, Motilal 116, 117, 119, 121, 130, 136, 138
Netherlands 64
Nguyen Thi Minh Khai 164
Nicaragua 110

## Index

Ottoman Empire 23, 26, 101

Partido Comunista do Brasil (PCB) 99–113 *passim*, 149, 164–5, 172, 198
  *see also* Comintern; ECCI
peasants 3, 5, 11–12, 126, 184
  role in revolution 16, 17, 36–9 *passim*, 42, 54, 61, 85, 158–9
  in Brazil 98, 111, 198
  in China 75–6, 78, 84, 85–6, 88–9, 194, 195, 196
  in India 74, 118, 123, 127, 131–3, 134, 135, 137, 139, 140, 141
Pereira, Astrogildo 99, 104, 107
periphery 1–5 *passim*, 7, 8–12 *passim*, 17, 20, 23, 24, 27, 39, 46, 47, 60–1, 67, 69, 80, 85, 113, 115, 118, 123–4, 124, 143, 153, 156, 160, 166, 167, 169, 178, 181–7 *passim*, 188
  *see also* capitalism; colonial mode of production; uneven and combined development
permanent revolution 12, 13–15, 19, 50–5, 61, 80, 82, 102, 103
  *see also* revolution, stages of
Persia 26, 30, 43
Peru 157
petty bourgeoisie 13–17 *passim*, 21, 61, 62, 109, 132, 135–6, 158, 161, 164, 167
  in Brazil 102, 103, 104, 106, 109
  in China 82–3
  in India 128, 135–6, 138, 143
  *see also* artisans; middle strata
philosophical anthropology 5, 6
Po Ku 92
Poland 16, 60
Popular Front 65, 110
Portugal 60
Poulantzas, Nicos 55, 56, 152
power bloc 26, 27, 74, 98, 113, 124, 149, 158, 179, 185, 189
  *see also* regime
pragmatism 55, 160, 165–70, 171, 179, 181, 183, 184

  *see also* dogmatism; idealism/universalist theory
*Preface to a Critique of Political Economy* 14
Prestes, Luis Carlos 101, 102, 104–7 *passim*, 109, 111, 111–12, 197, 198
Punjab 121, 141

race 6, 7–8, 15, 153
  *see also* identity
Radek, Karl 52, 76, 117, 134, 172, 201
Red Army 88, 90, 91, 92, 95
Red International of Labour Unions 122, 129
Recife 109, 112
regime 19, 65, 67, 74, 157, 189
religion 6, 16, 153, 164
  *see also* identity; Hinduism; Islam; Muslims
revolution 1, 2, 3, 5, 8–19 *passim*
  stages of 12, 13–17, 27, 50–5, 60, 78, 97, 155–7, 169, 180, 183, 191
  in China 80–1, 82
  in India 120
  world 10, 22–5, 45, 48, 123, 155, 163, 177, 179
  *see also* capitalism; Comintern; ECCI; Lenin; Mao Tse-tung; 'socialism in one country'; Stalin; Trotsky
revolutionary bloc 14, 17–18, 41, 50, 113
  *see also* class alliances
revolutionary space 19, 65, 66–7, 72
revolutionary terrain 14, 19, 23, 24, 46–7, 56, 66–7, 93, 113, 119, 149, 154, 189
  *see also* class alliances; revolutionary bloc; war of manoeuvre; war of position
Rio de Janeiro 99, 101, 107, 112
Rio Grande do Sul 101, 104
Roy, M.N., 35, 37–40, 44, 118, 119, 120, 122, 125, 128, 129, 191, 199, 200, 201

Rue, John E., 87
Russia 2, 3, 7, 11, 12, 18, 20, 21, 23, 30, 46–7, 154, 155, 166, 178, 188
  minorities in 25–35 *passim*, 190
  1905–6 revolution 11, 12, 18, 26, 50, 67, 80
Russian Social Democratic Labour Party (RSDLP) 16, 19, 30, 54

Salgado, Plinio 108–9
Sandino, Augusto César 110
Santos 101
São Paulo 98, 99, 104, 108, 109
Sarekat Islam 135, 161
Second International 155
Second World War 1, 33, 68, 126, 182, 184, 186
Sen, Surya 121, 134, 135
Shakespeare, William 2
Shanghai 76, 79, 87, 95
Simon Commission 123, 130
Singh, Bhagat v, 121, 134
Sneevliet, Henk 194
Sobolev, A.I. 58
Social Democratic Party (German) 8
'socialism in one country' 47–9, 51–2, 53, 80, 175, 176–8, 179, 185
  *see also* Stalinism
Socialist International 63, 193
Socialist Party of Turkestan ('Will') 34, 44
South Africa 6
sovereign/national states 22, 156, 176–7, 183, 189
Soviet Union 1, 2, 25, 36, 48–50, 55, 57, 63, 64, 107, 136, 150, 152, 153, 155, 172, 174, 175–81 *passim*, 182, 184, 201
  minorities in 25–35 *passim*, 43, 48
  *see also* 'socialism in one country'; Stalinism
soviets 38, 84, 104, 129, 130, 134, 144, 196
  *see also* workers' and peasants' dictatorship
Spain 60
Spartacists 21

Spratt, Philip 122, 128, 129, 200
Stalin, Iosif 2, 21, 22, 28, 43, 44, 47–57 *passim*, 58–9, 63, 110, 114, 129, 154, 155, 156, 158, 160, 169, 172, 175–8 *passim*, 179, 184, 191, 197, 201
  and China 79, 81–2, 103, 120
  on world revolution 51–5, 61
Stalinism 6, 7, 8, 18, 20, 24, 47, 48, 70, 89, 145, 154, 171, 174–8, 180–1, 182, 186, 187
  *see also* dogmatism; idealism/universalist theory; Leninism; Leninism/Stalinism; Marxism; Marxism-Leninism; vanguard party
subjects, historical/revolutionary 4–9 *passim*, 12, 18, 27, 46, 64, 71, 85, 90, 131, 149, 153, 156–7, 163–5, 166, 171, 172, 180, 183, 185, 186
  *see also* agents; discourse; interpellation; working class
Sultan Galiyev, Mir-Said v, 28–9, 31–4, 35, 39, 190
Sun Yat-sen 12, 75, 77
*swadeshi* movement 116, 117
Swaraj party 120–1, 139

Taiping Rebellion 75
*tenentes* 101–2, 102, 108, 111–12
Third Worldism 33, 193
Togliatti, Palmiro 64
Trotsky, Leon 21, 22, 43, 50–5 *passim*, 57, 58, 70, 99, 129, 151, 154, 160, 162, 163, 166, 168, 172, 173, 176, 177, 184, 185, 191, 191–2, 192, 201
  on China 82–3, 85–6, 158
  on India 114, 157
  on world revolution 51–5, 155–60 *passim*, 183
Trotskyism/ists 89, 103, 108, 113, 185, 192
Turkey 30, 44, 191
'28 Bolsheviks' 91, 92, 93

Ukraine 27, 30, 31
unequal exchange 115

uneven and combined
   development   27, 51, 53, 57,
   65, 155, 159, 162, 166, 169,
   176, 177–8
Union of Soviet Socialist Republics
   *see* Soviet Union
united front   17, 43, 100, 157, 169
   in Brazil   109
   in China   77–8, 87, 95
   in India   119, 139, 143–4
   *see also* class alliances
United Provinces   118, 134
Untouchables (*Harijan*)   135
Uruguay   99
USA   23, 59, 62, 97, 113, 125, 157
   Lenin on 'Negroes'   164

vanguard party   6, 12, 19, 24,
   37–8, 62, 65, 68, 72, 80, 155,
   170–4, 178, 179–80, 185
Varga, Eugen   124
Vargas, Getulio   104, 106, 107,
   108, 109, 149, 159, 167
Viet Nam   1, 38, 68, 87, 97, 135,
   168, 183

Wafd   161
Wang Ming   63, 91, 92, 93, 95,
   112, 143–4, 196
war of manoeuvre   14, 24, 27,
   66–8, 73, 149, 150, 153
   in Brazil   97
   in China   86–7, 88–9, 96, 97
   in India   119
war of position   14, 27, 66–8, 71,
   73, 149
   in Brazil   97–8
   in China   80–6, 96, 97
   in India   119
   *see also* class alliances;
      revolutionary bloc; terrain;
      vanguard party
Western Europe   12, 63, 182, 186
   in Communist analyses   29, 31,
      32, 34, 39, 45, 48, 52, 90,
      154, 159, 163–4
*What Is To Be Done?*   69

women   27, 85, 92, 108, 125, 131,
   134, 137, 184, 185, 195
   *see also* gender *and make a
      'gendered reading' of*
      artisans, peasants, workers
Worker and Peasant Bloc
   (Brazil)   101, 103, 105
workers' and peasants'
   dictatorship   54, 168
   in China   82, 88,
   in Brazil   101
   in India   128, 129, 143
   *see also* working class/proletarian
      dictatorship
workers' and peasants' parties   38
   in Brazil
   in India   114, 119, 121, 122,
      128–9, 130, 141
working class/proletariat   3, 5, 6, 7,
   9, 184, 188
   Brazilian   98–9, 100, 104, 107–8,
      108
   Chinese   76–7, 87–8
   Indian   117–18, 123, 125–6, 129,
      134, 137, 139, 140, 141–2
   revolutionary role   11–12, 13, 16,
      17, 19, 24, 36–9 *passim*,
      41–2, 53–4, 61, 62–3, 64,
      110, 151, 152, 154–5,
      159–60, 162, 163, 164, 166,
      170, 171, 173, 178, 180,
      183–4
   Russian   26
working class/proletarian
   dictatorship   3, 29, 40, 53, 61,
      62, 158, 159, 160, 168
   in China   79, 85, 92
   in Brazil   100, 105
   *see also* workers' and peasants'
      dictatorship
Wuhan   79, 81, 87, 88, 95

Yenan/Shensi-Kansu   92, 93, 94, 96
Young Turks   26, 101

Zapata, Emiliano   188
Zinoviev, Grigorii   58, 79, 117